PRAISE FOR *ENGINEERING SECUR*

"Dominik Merli finally wrote the textbook that everyone teaching on embedded system security was waiting for. The focus on the practical aspects of real-world embedded systems with the relevant theoretical background makes it an excellent base for education and practitioners. I am really excited to use it in my courses."

—DR. STEFAN WALLENTOWITZ, PROFESSOR OF
EMBEDDED SYSTEM SECURITY, HOCHSCHULE
MÜNCHEN UNIVERSITY OF APPLIED SCIENCES

"This book is exactly what you need to read as an engineer working in the automotive, industrial, or IoT domain to level up with comprehensive security know-how—from secure design processes to comprehensive security concepts and their secure implementations. The scope clearly covers what is needed in practice."

—DR. JOHANN HEYSZL, SECURITY
ENGINEERING MANAGER, GOOGLE

"This book has so much valuable and practical information on engineering secure devices with lessons learned by the author and comprehensible case studies. . . . Whether you are a developer for an embedded system, responsible for product security, or just interested in the topic, this book is an excellent read!"

—DR. MATTHIAS NIEDERMAIER, OT SECURITY
EXPERT, AIRBUS

"This book is an indispensable technical guide for the design, implementation, and maintenance of embedded systems in security-sensitive applications. It presents fundamental elements and illustrates how they are utilized in practice, providing seasoned insight into the construction of a secure embedded system."

—DR. MARC STÖTTINGER, PROFESSOR OF
COMPUTER ENGINEERING AND SECURITY,
RHEINMAIN UNIVERSITY OF APPLIED
SCIENCES

"The book provides a well understandable introduction on how to design and implement secure embedded devices."

—DR. RAINER FALK, PRINCIPAL KEY EXPERT
FOR EMBEDDED SECURITY, SIEMENS AG

ENGINEERING SECURE DEVICES

A Practical Guide for Embedded System Architects and Developers

by Dominik Merli

no starch press®

San Francisco

Printed in the United States of America

First printing

28 27 26 25 24   1 2 3 4 5

ISBN-13: 978-1-7185-0348-9 (print)
ISBN-13: 978-1-7185-0349-6 (ebook)

Published by No Starch Press®, Inc.
245 8th Street, San Francisco, CA 94103
phone: +1.415.863.9900
www.nostarch.com; info@nostarch.com

Publisher: William Pollock
Managing Editor: Jill Franklin
Production Manager: Sabrina Plomitallo-González
Production Editor: Miles Bond
Developmental Editor: Jill Franklin
Cover Illustrator: Josh Kemble
Interior Design: Octopod Studios
Technical Reviewer: Colin O'Flynn
Copyeditor: Sharon Wilkey
Proofreader: Katrina Horlbeck Olsen

Library of Congress Control Number: 2023056779

For customer service inquiries, please contact info@nostarch.com. For information on distribution, bulk sales, corporate sales, or translations: sales@nostarch.com. For permission to translate this work: rights@nostarch.com. To report counterfeit copies or piracy: counterfeit@nostarch.com.

[S]

To Sebastian,
who taught me so many practical things
one doesn't learn at university

About the Author

Dominik Merli is a professor of IT security at the Augsburg Technical University of Applied Sciences, with 15 years of experience in security engineering research and the implementation of practical protection measures. His research on embedded systems security for industrial, automotive, and semiconductor companies led to his PhD at the Technical University of Munich; he then worked on security innovations for industrial products at Siemens before entering the education field.

About the Technical Reviewer

Colin O'Flynn is an embedded engineer who started the ChipWhisperer project, which is a wide-ranging project designed to help academics and engineers understand side-channel and fault injection attacks. O'Flynn is currently an assistant professor at Dalhousie University in Halifax, Canada, and he also remains involved with the company he founded based on the ChipWhisperer project (NewAE Technology, Inc.) that offers commercial hardware tools for embedded security work.

BRIEF CONTENTS

CONTENTS IN DETAIL

PART I
FUNDAMENTALS

1
SECURE DEVELOPMENT PROCESS   3

2
CRYPTOGRAPHY

PART II
DEVICE SECURITY BUILDING BLOCKS

3
RANDOM NUMBER GENERATORS

4
CRYPTOGRAPHIC IMPLEMENTATIONS   69

5
CONFIDENTIAL DATA STORAGE AND SECURE MEMORY   85

6
SECURE DEVICE IDENTITY

7
SECURE COMMUNICATION

PART III
ADVANCED DEVICE SECURITY CONCEPTS

8
SECURE BOOT AND SYSTEM INTEGRITY   141

9
SECURE FIRMWARE UPDATE   159

10
ROBUST DEVICE ARCHITECTURE
181

11
ACCESS CONTROL AND MANAGEMENT
199

12
SYSTEM MONITORING
223

FOREWORD

The connotations of a book titled *Engineering Secure Devices* explains a lot about the state of many embedded systems and why the topic of this book is of such importance. There is no cutting-edge book titled *Engineering Bridges That Don't Fall Down* (I checked), because it's clear the point of a bridge is to not fall down. Engineers learn about how forces work on a bridge, how materials behave under compression and tension, and use all that knowledge to build a bridge that doesn't fall down. But it's inherently known that the goal of a bridge should be to not fall down. Is the goal of embedded systems to be secure? Or is it something that gets thought about after?

The complications of embedded systems arise once you realize the wide-ranging and often conflicting goals that designers are given. Security may not be the prime goal of a system because the system must also be easy to use, robust, low cost, high performance, reliable, safe, and secure. And of course, the same sort of requirements may be applied to a system using a small 8-bit microcontroller as one using a 32-bit or 64-bit system-on-a-chip (SoC) running Linux or Android.

With so many conflicting asks and such a wide range of systems, it's almost impossible for a single engineer to address these requirements. The embedded system that is running your coffee maker might be the same sort as the one running your airbag controller in your car, but you probably care a little more about one of them (I'm convinced for some people it's still the coffee controller). One important consideration in the embedded field is there's simply no way to cover every possible combination of controller complexity and security requirement, yet alone cover it within one book. So while you may not be running embedded Linux, understanding the fundamental ideas of what it means to securely store data is relevant across all systems.

I encourage you to take the lessons to heart even if at first glance you think they aren't relevant for your system. For example, when working on a microcontroller, you might wonder why learning about Linux access control systems (Chapter 11) is relevant. But your small real-time operating system (RTOS) is still likely to have tasks that have differing amounts of user interaction, and you wouldn't want a task exposed to an insecure interface to have access to the same memory as a task dealing with secure data. So while you might not use the Linux access control system in your device, understanding the goals will guide you toward a secure design.

This book makes very concrete the idea that building secure systems is not a simple challenge, but you can take many simple steps toward that goal. Deciding that security is an important engineering goal is the first step, and you'll find many of the subsequent steps within the pages of this book. I hope you picked up this book because you've decided to take that first step, and I can then hope that one of you, dear readers, will design the next connected device I buy, and I'll be a little more confident of its security thanks to the work Dominik Merli has made to guide you on your journey.

Throughout many of the steps you will take, learning that there is an existing body of work or ready-made tools will save you time and effort while also improving the security of your system. As part of my research, which involves reverse engineering devices, I look at how vendors have implemented firmware updates, often by well-known companies. For most of these devices, they would have been better off following the example from Chapter 9 of this book, using the SWUpdate tool. Even as a user of devices with embedded computers, I always wince when the manual describes how the firmware update cannot be interrupted or else I have to return the device to the manufacturer. These are not fundamental problems that devices need to have, and that is one of many examples where following existing best practices will almost always work better than trying to reinvent the wheel (even if the engineer in me loves reinventing the wheel).

If you're taking some of your first steps into the field of embedded security, you may realize that entire subfields of research exist for you to follow. I sincerely hope you follow those paths, as you may find that this is a very multidisciplinary world where new perspectives lead to important results. While my own work concentrates on attacks such as power analysis and fault injection, the field includes everything from high-performance cryptographic implementations in software and hardware, to post-quantum and future-proof implementations, to reverse engineering of software or hardware, and everything in between.

So whether you are an undergraduate student interested in embedded systems or a hardened embedded engineer who still tries to save every byte of RAM, you'll find a lot of interesting and useful information in the pages to come. And, more important, you'll find a guide to help you build a secure embedded device—just like the title promises.

Colin O'Flynn
Instigator of the ChipWhisperer Project
Halifax, Canada

ACKNOWLEDGMENTS

I grew up in a little village in Germany and was the first in my whole family to go to university. During my youth, no one would've ever imagined that I would someday get a PhD, work as a professor, and even write an *English* book. Looking back, hundreds of people supported me on my way, starting with my parents, my siblings, all my friends, soccer coaches, and teachers, through to fellow students, professors, colleagues, and international contacts. Thank you so much!

Working on this book with No Starch Press was an amazing experience, and I've learned a myriad of things throughout the process. I'd like to thank Jill and the whole team for their patience with me and their excellent support. Also, it was an honor to have Colin O'Flynn as a technical reviewer. Our discussions about practical experiences led to several improvements and extensions for the book at hand.

Thanks to Florian Fischer and Peter Knauer, who supported me in creating the practical case studies contained in the book and in fixing all the toolchain issues I came across.

The eagle-eyed scrutiny by Fabian Bley, Florian Förster, Claudia Meitinger, and Elisabeth Schröppel discovered all sorts of mistakes and inaccuracies in early versions of this book. Thank you!

Finally, I would like to thank my wife and my children for their patience throughout this project and for cheering me up whenever I got stuck.

INTRODUCTION

Internet connectivity, digital business models and data-driven services, remote access, and data analytics—all contribute to a variety of needs and challenges across nearly every industry. To put it simply, most modern products need some kind of computer integrated into them. More specifically, they usually require an *embedded system*, which means an electronic system including a processing unit, memory, and input/output interfaces that are embedded within a larger mechanical or electronic system.

The application domains of embedded systems are extremely wide. They're used in controllers, sensors, and actuators in industrial automation, transportation, and critical infrastructure systems. Communication and network hardware like routers, switches, and base stations are based on them too. In the consumer market, typical products with embedded systems include smart washing machines, intelligent heating systems, and gaming consoles. Even the plastic cards we use for banking and building access control can be considered a type of embedded system.

Compared to personal computers (PCs) and server systems, these devices often face constraints, like the need to keep down manufacturing costs or run on hardware with low to moderate computational power, in addition to the rather limited options for input and output capabilities. Embedded systems are used in very specific, sometimes critical areas, and they usually operate with few user interactions, if any. Further, these devices are built from a wide range of hardware, firmware, and operating systems in use across different products, manufacturers, and industries.

On top of those limitations, adding security requirements to the equation doesn't make the life of an embedded systems engineer easier. The development of security measures for these devices, their specific application environments, and their constrained resources lead to challenging tasks for architects and developers. As if all these things weren't enough, in many cases, embedded systems also face physical attackers, which are a more powerful attack model in comparison to remote access on cloud or web services, for example.

The State of Embedded System Security

If we look at different application domains and industries, the state of security measures in embedded systems varies greatly. For example, smart card solutions for pay-TV were confronted with fraud cases as early as the 1990s. If people could circumvent the scrambling and shuffling algorithms, they were able to watch pay-TV for free. In addition, if attackers succeeded in cloning those smart cards, they could sell them at a lower price, leading to a loss in revenue for the original provider. Since the business model was under pressure, the security awareness of these companies was relatively high, and corresponding investments and developments in smart card security were prioritized.

Another field of embedded systems in entertainment exhibits a similar pattern: gaming consoles. The natural interest of console manufacturers is that only original game media can be played on their devices. If attackers succeed in running cloned discs, the business model suffers. After the reverse engineering community gained interest in analyzing game consoles, which, for example, led to the renowned book *Hacking the Xbox* by Andrew Huang (No Starch Press, 2003), the industry responded with increased security mechanisms. As a result, they reached a solid state of embedded system security that requires attackers to invest in a lot of resources, expertise, and sophisticated tools to successfully bypass protection measures.

However, in other application areas of embedded systems, the components don't have such mature security features. In 2016, this became quite obvious with the discovery of the *Mirai* malware that exploited hundreds of thousands of internet of things (IoT) devices, mainly IP cameras and home routers, turning them into botnets that performed enormous distributed denial-of-service (DDoS) attacks against websites. Further, the compilations of vulnerabilities dubbed *Ripple20* and *Amnesia:33* showed various weaknesses in TCP/IP stacks for embedded systems in 2020. According to estimates, more than 15 million devices were affected, from medical to building automation to industrial control systems (ICS).

Strangely enough, devices used in industrial automation and critical infrastructures, where robustness and reliability are crucial, also have long security to-do lists. Although the *Stuxnet* incident reports in 2010 were a wake-up call for industrial automation manufacturers, more than 10 years later, the market still has a significant lack of well-protected devices. In 2022, a collection of vulnerabilities in operational technology (OT) components was published under the name of *OT:ICEFALL*. The authors characterized the security engineering failings as *insecurity by design* because the analyzed products missed even the most basic security controls.

Emerging Requirements, Laws, and Standards

As strange as it sounds, without these incidents, vulnerabilities, and attacks, only marginal security awareness would probably exist. However, since we've seen many of these issues during the last 20 years while at the same time online connectivity, digital services, and data analytics grew increasingly relevant to companies, cybersecurity "suddenly" has become a requirement—for example, in the procurement process.

This doesn't mean customers immediately show deep and comprehensive security knowledge, but they increasingly demand risk analyses, protection measures, or a (random) collection of standards to be fulfilled by product manufacturers. From my experiences in the industrial context, this sometimes initiates communication between customers and manufacturers to find a compromise between the practical need for security and the associated costs, which can be a reasonable and fruitful discussion for both parties.

Governments, on the other hand, are increasingly concerned with developing national laws and signing international agreements pushing for basic security requirements that every product on the market should fulfill. In Europe, the Cybersecurity Act (CSA) of 2019 aims to establish a security certification framework for all products and services sold in the European Union, and the Cyber Resilience Act (CRA) of 2024 regulates cybersecurity requirements for products with digital elements. The European Standard ETSI EN 303 645 already defines baseline security requirements, especially for consumer IoT products. On the other side of the Atlantic Ocean, Biden's Executive Order 14028 from May 2021 takes a similar line and aims to improve cybersecurity in IoT devices and software solutions. The National Institute of Standards and Technology (NIST) already provides recommendations for cybersecurity labeling of these products.

In parallel, consortia in various industries try to agree on common security standards in their fields. A prominent example is International Electrotechnical Commission (IEC) standard 62443, targeting ICS security and the industrial IoT (IIoT). It combines security requirements for operators, system integrators, and component manufacturers, which allows for a unified and interrelated security view of industrial systems. Regarding secure device engineering, Parts 4-1 and 4-2 of IEC 62443 are the most relevant: Part 4-1 covers practices for a secure development process, and Part 4-2 is concerned with technical product security requirements.

Who Should Read This Book?

If you're an embedded systems architect who is involved in customer discussions like those described previously, this book provides you the necessary knowledge to debate with your partners at eye level.

If you're an embedded systems engineer or an IoT developer who is in charge of implementing security features and you want to know about the reasoning behind these features and typical obstacles, this book will prepare you for the journey ahead.

If you're part of a product's requirements engineering process or do embedded systems testing in your day-to-day work, this book will help you understand the value of certain security features and why your colleagues from the development team might be reluctant to implement them.

If you're a student and wonder why many protection measures can't be taken for granted in IoT products, this book will confirm that you have the right mindset, and you'll learn that embedded system security is an important but sometimes tedious task.

And if, some minutes ago, somebody yelled at you, "We need to implement this f****** device security! NOW!!!" take a deep breath, cancel all appointments, and read through this book carefully. Afterward, you'll be ready for a friendly, objective discussion about "security."

What Does This Book Cover?

This book's contents are based on my hands-on experiences and research insights from the last 15 years in the field of embedded system security.

In **Part I: Fundamentals**, you'll learn foundational knowledge related to providing a secure development life cycle and how cryptography is used.

Chapter 1: Secure Development Process Covers the basic elements necessary to follow the principle of security by design within a product development process.

Chapter 2: Cryptography Summarizes the cryptographic essentials relevant for practical security engineering.

Part II: Device Security Building Blocks details the basic physical and logical building blocks for embedded system security.

Chapter 3: Random Number Generators Dives into the magical field of randomness, highlights its importance for security, and gives practical hints on how to generate and assess random data.

Chapter 4: Cryptographic Implementations Discusses implementation options for cryptographic algorithms and the corresponding impacts on properties such as performance.

Chapter 5: Confidential Data Storage and Secure Memory Focuses on storing small and large portions of data in a secure, confidential way.

Chapter 6: Secure Device Identity Is concerned with the generation and management of unique identities for embedded systems.

Chapter 7: Secure Communication Presents state-of-the-art protection measures for communication channels, and answers common questions regarding their implementation on embedded systems.

Part III: Advanced Device Security Concepts focuses on comprehensive protection concepts relevant for secure IoT devices.

Chapter 8: Secure Boot and System Integrity Covers security considerations during the sensitive operation phase when an embedded system is booting up.

Chapter 9: Secure Firmware Update Describes the complexity of providing software updates for products with security in mind.

Chapter 10: Robust Device Architecture Discusses the question of how to continue the operation of critical processes while under attack.

Chapter 11: Access Control and Management Considers the restriction of users and processes on a device and its practical consequences.

Chapter 12: System Monitoring Completes the book by exploring measures that allow you to detect and analyze anomalies or attacks on embedded systems.

While reading this book, keep in mind that your goal should not only be to absorb as much technical knowledge as possible but also to understand *when* and *why* device security measures make sense.

A Note on the Case Studies in This Book

Several chapters in this book contain practical case studies. Their purpose is *not* to serve as copy-and-paste examples to be reproduced easily on your own device or even to be used for productive development. That would require a level of detail beyond the scope of this book, and the relevant security insights would vanish in a sea of implementation issues.

Some of the case studies illustrate gaps between the theory and the messy real world. Others demonstrate the advantages or disadvantages of different implementation options, and some of the case studies just provide a specific application context that should help you understand the preceding ideas and concepts.

As mentioned earlier, embedded systems are a diverse class of devices and so are their processors, memories, and interfaces. In order to provide a reasonable demonstration device—not too high end, not too tiny and constrained—I chose a hardware platform with medium performance that also includes hardware-based security measures that can be analyzed in practical case studies: the STM32MP157F-DK2 evaluation board from STMicroelectronics (ST). (For the record, I have no affiliation with ST.)

Whenever it comes to operating systems for medium- and high-performance embedded systems, Linux is the natural choice. It's used in cars, dishwashers, programmable logic controllers (PLCs), TVs, energy monitoring systems, and also in the case studies within this book. Specifically, I used ST's OpenSTLinux distribution with a Linux 5.15 kernel.

PART I

FUNDAMENTALS

I've known brilliant embedded system engineers in the industry who have a passion for the lowest-level hardware development, who know every script in their toolchains by heart, and who can squeeze the last bit of performance out of a microcontroller's firmware. However, when it comes to the security of embedded systems, I regularly discover a lack of knowledge in two fundamental areas.

First, many aren't familiar with the essential methods and organizational measures necessary to establish a secure development process. Second, even if they know some cryptographic algorithms by name, they may not fully understand their properties, parameters, and limits as well as the reasoning behind them. With that in mind, the first part of this book describes the foundational concepts required for developing secure products.

1

SECURE DEVELOPMENT PROCESS

When I was a student, I thought organizational processes were among the most boring topics in engineering. However, after working in security engineering for over a decade and helping organizations optimize their security efforts, I have to admit that processes are more interesting than I thought and not at all irrelevant when developing secure products.

Although a product's technical protection features can be fulfilled and marked as *done*, a secure development process is *never done*; it must be maintained and improved continuously, which is why the qualitative measure for security engineering processes is called *maturity*. It can rise and fall, depending on the regularity, quality, and organizational structures of activities supporting the development of a secure product within an organization.

This chapter's goal is to convince students, engineers, and developers that there is more to processes than creating documents nobody reads. A *secure development life cycle (SDL)* is about culture and day-to-day human behavior; it's about maintaining quality and security under changing conditions, and it clarifies how everybody involved in a product engineering process can continuously contribute to a secure end product.

On the Variety of Guidelines

Recommendations for secure development processes have been around for quite some time. However, depending on your industry, it's possible that nobody in your organization has considered pursuing such a systematic approach until now, or at least not explicitly.

Companies developing operating systems and web applications were confronted with security issues relatively early, so it's not surprising that Microsoft and the Open Web Application Security Project (OWASP) were some of the first to work on and talk about SDLs. Since the IEC's publication of IEC 62443 Part 4-1, more and more manufacturers of the industrial components used in production facilities, critical infrastructures, and a variety of automation applications have been aware of the necessity to implement a secure development process.

Microsoft's SDL follows 12 practices (*https://www.microsoft.com/en-us/ securityengineering/sdl/practices*) that describe the processes the company uses in order to develop secure (software) products. These processes range from training to requirements engineering and threat modeling to security testing. Also targeted at the software community, OWASP uses five categories to summarize its Software Assurance Maturity Model (SAMM, *https:// owaspsamm.org/model/*): governance, design, implementation, verification, and operations. Part 4-1 of IEC 62443 (*https://webstore.iec.ch/publication/ 33615*) aims at establishing a secure development process for industrial component manufacturers. It's structured into 8 practices, each containing 2 to 13 subpractices detailing recommended activities from security management to design and implementation to update management in the field.

All three of these guidelines use a different structure to explain the idea of a secure development process; however, you might notice that they overlap significantly. For example, the Microsoft SDL tells you to perform *threat modeling*, while OWASP uses the term *threat assessment* in its *design* category, and IEC 62443-4-1, requirement SR-2 (which is part of the *specification of security requirements* practice) explains the necessity to establish a process to create and maintain a *threat model* for a product.

In addition, the importance of security knowledge and abilities is present in all three: Microsoft lists *provide training* as its first practice, while OWASP considers *education* as part of *governance*, and IEC 62443-4-1 uses the term *security expertise* to summarize the identification and development of skills in requirement SM-4 of its *security management* practice. As a final example, *penetration testing* is an explicitly named practice at Microsoft; it's included by the same name in requirement SVV-4 in IEC 62443-4-1's practice of *security verification and validation testing*, and the SAMM refers to it in the *security testing* task under the *verification* item.

We could continue in this manner for topics like the use of state-of-the-art cryptography, clarification of third-party dependencies, and vulnerability management. The point is that content-wise, these guidelines have many similarities, so the answer to the question "Which of the many available resources is the best one?" is "It doesn't make a big difference."

Microsoft has more than 30 years of experience in secure software engineering. OWASP provides not only valuable recommendations but also open source tooling to support these processes. On the other hand, IEC 62443-4-1 targets the industrial domain and component manufacturers that are different from classic IT companies. Also, independent bodies can certify compliance with IEC 62443, but that's not possible for Microsoft's and OWASP's SDLs, which can be a further decisive factor.

These three documents are just common examples. The NIST *Special Publication 800-160* (*https://csrc.nist.gov/pubs/sp/800/160/v1/r1/final?*), the Building Security In Maturity Model (BSIMM, *https://www.bsimm.com*) initiative, and the European Union Agency for Cybersecurity (ENISA) *Good Practices for Security of IoT–Secure Software Development Lifecycle* (*https://www.enisa.europa.eu/publications/good-practices-for-security-of-iot-1*) are also helpful.

Responsibility for Product Security

Every product's security success starts with the clarification of responsibilities. It doesn't matter whether it's the founder of a startup, a product security officer (PSO) of a global company, or a member of the development team who takes the responsibility, but it's of great importance that *someone* does and that this someone has the necessary time and resources to do the job.

A secure development process consists of a heterogeneous set of activities, which also means the person responsible for security has to be involved in many product development phases. That person has to ensure that *security by design* is part of the development culture. Of course, that's not the most charming position, especially when security hasn't been a focus in your organization before. Although (product) management usually loves to talk about the potential of new technologies and device features, regularly stressing the involved risks doesn't make you everybody's darling.

However, in the long run, this someone will eliminate the sources of errors, vulnerabilities, and internal misunderstandings. They will not only increase device security but also contribute to transparency within the product development team and toward management.

IN PRACTICE: SECURITY ENGINEERING EXPERTS

I once worked as a consultant for a medium-sized company to introduce security into its product engineering processes. At the time, the company had a security expert working for the IT department, but nobody with security knowledge was available on the embedded system engineering team.

Luckily, the company was able to hire a motivated young professional with sound security expertise and even device engineering experience to fill that gap and take responsibility for product security. With several ideas in mind on how

(continued)

---

to establish a secure development process, he made himself comfortable with the organization's specific processes, people, and products.

From time to time, he was asked to support the development team in software and hardware engineering projects because of urgency. Sadly, the number of those tasks rose while management's interest in product security decreased significantly. After about two years, he quit. And this company lost twice: it lost committed security talent and the chance to establish a secure development process before its competitors did.

Awareness and Training

Some years ago, I attended a talk by a German security consultant about how European companies are prepared (or not prepared) for upcoming cyber threats and how much stress and frustration people working in the security area must experience every day. Aimed at management representatives, he concluded with this: "Neither tools nor technologies—*people* create security!"

From requirements engineering to software and hardware development to vulnerability handling, it's people who creatively identify ways to misuse a product feature, meticulously follow secure coding rules agreed upon within the team, and separate relevant from irrelevant security issues reported by third parties.

To put it another way, if your development team isn't able to imagine potential attack scenarios; regards security practices as hindrances; and counters vulnerability reports with anger, fear, or a complete lack of understanding, your product won't improve in security, even if you bought the most expensive licenses for top tools in order to "support" them. The obvious question to pose is, "Who has to have what security knowledge to follow the security-by-design principle each workday?"

For the majority of employees, general security awareness is a fundamental requirement. This requirement is also true for engineers, developers, and device architects. However, security awareness is not something you learn at school (at least until now). It's also not a mandatory part of university education or typical on-the-job training programs. Further, awareness often vanishes over time, which means it must be refreshed regularly. Within your teams, it's essential to address and discuss the perspectives of attackers, their intentions, and the possibilities for countering those strategies.

From my experience, web-based training is often a "click-and-forget" activity for employees, while social gatherings, workshops, and team-building events lead to interaction, discussions, and, most preferably, reflection, which enables people to link security knowledge with their day-to-day jobs.

Besides security basics, individuals on your product engineering teams might need specific capabilities. For example, developers can benefit from secure coding training, while testers can improve their skills by attending a penetration testing course. Often neglected, especially in medium-sized companies, participating in a security engineering community may be a worthwhile way to exchange ideas, challenges, and lessons learned with other organizations for both management-level and technical employees.

Again, training is not a one-shot activity. Continuously nudging people to reflect on the security of their work and daily processes is an integral part of a vivid security culture.

Assets and Protection Goals

Imagine a sunny Monday morning. The week ahead seems to get busy as usual, but then somebody from management asks if you can spare a minute:

> Manager: "Please turn our product into a secure product!"
> You: "What exactly do you mean?"
> Manager: "Hacking it should be impossible!"
> You: "Where does this requirement come from?"
> Manager: "Don't you read the news? Everything is being hacked these days!"
> You: "Okay. Well, which part of our product would be worth hacking?"
> Manager: "I have no idea; you tell me!"

This dialogue is fictional, but you may have had similar discussions. It makes one trivial point obvious: you can't secure a device if you don't know what to protect. Essentially everybody in your company should know what's worth protecting or what's fundamentally important to keep your business running. We usually call this an *asset*.

Valuable Product Parts

Assets can be of various kinds—for example, a cryptographic key necessary for a pay-per-use scenario, measurement data that is transferred from your device to a cloud application in order to enable predictive maintenance services, a configuration file that activates or disables product features, code in your firmware that issues an alert in case of an emergency, or a web service necessary for even basic device operation. In a nutshell, assets are everything that's somehow important and valuable.

Identifying these assets is the initial analysis to kick off a secure development process and the basis for all your protection efforts. Logically, you should determine what your assets are before implementing countermeasures or ordering a penetration test, because if you don't know what you want to protect, how can you implement effective countermeasures and specify worst-case attack scenarios? However, since most modern devices aren't standalone, this process also involves establishing a *common system understanding* within your organization, which includes the relevant objects, data flows, people, third-party components, and life-cycle processes, as well as the business model behind all that.

Reading that list, you might think it covers a whole lot of information, and you're right. The topics range from business insights to deep technical knowledge to processes and organizational structures. No matter how small or large your company is, one single person likely isn't responsible for all those tasks, especially not within a development team, so approaching this analysis in a multidimensional way is crucial.

I've had good experiences with setting up a workshop with a moderator, a security expert, and a diverse group of employees involved in the business operations around a specific device. Besides a developer, tester, and product manager, it makes sense to invite people from maintenance, customer support, digital services, device safety, sales, and whatever other departments might be relevant for your product.

The starting point for discussing cybersecurity with team members is a basic overview that collects the information available on the architecture. Figure 1-1 shows an example of such a representation for a fictional Wi-Fi-controlled industrial ventilator.

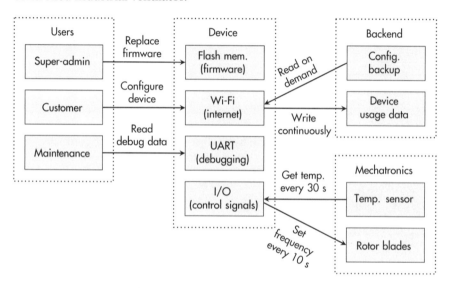

Figure 1-1: An example of a basic device context overview

This initial overview should be simple but as detailed as necessary. Later, in a sometimes chaotic process during a workshop or discussion, this overview will be enriched and refined with information, maybe with data flows not obvious from the original documents, relations to third parties not known before, or implicit process steps known only by those who perform them every day.

After everybody is satisfied with the detail and correctness of the overall system representation, the actual asset identification starts with this question: "Which parts of the system are critical for our business model and/or our organization?"

Relevant Protection Needs

Determining not only *what* is important to protect but also *why* it is important directly leads us to the definition of *protection goals*.

Every asset should have at least one protection goal; otherwise, the asset isn't likely relevant (from a security point of view). The following list, starting with the famous C-I-A triad (confidentiality, integrity, availability), indicates typical protection goals that define which property of an asset is worth protecting. However, if you identify a specific protection need that doesn't fit the standard goals in this list, there's nothing wrong with writing it down in your own words.

Confidentiality (C) This protection goal is probably the most widely known. We could say that a corresponding asset has to stay "secret" to be "secure." More formally, it means that read access on a specific asset should not be possible, except for authorized entities. Although this goal likely comes to every layperson's mind when talking about security, it's not always the correct one, and it's not necessary for all possible assets. Typical examples of assets requiring confidentiality are stored cryptographic keys or executables that contain intellectual property.

Integrity (I) Only authorized subjects should be able to alter a given object or data, and if others alter it, you should be able to detect the manipulation. Common use cases include a monotonic counter for billing purposes or control commands sent over a communication channel. Further, you can apply this goal to whole devices or machines in order to stress the importance of *system integrity*, for example, if it is possible to replace parts of the system. Be aware that the term *integrity* is used differently in the safety domain, where a cyclic redundancy check (CRC) is often regarded as "integrity protection." This doesn't hold for the security area, where an active attacker can easily forge a CRC.

Availability (A) While most parts of a device should be available to operate correctly, this protection goal is used for data or services (on the device or on the backend) if an attacker could possibly interrupt or delay access to them. Examples of corresponding assets are a web service that delivers live data to the device, a stream of random numbers within the device's main processing unit, or even backups on a server system. Especially in automotive and industrial use cases, a similar requirement exists in the context of *hard real-time communication*. There, current information (for example, from a safety sensor or a brake controller) has to be available *before a given deadline*.

Authenticity (Au) We can consider this protection goal an extension of integrity. In addition to ensuring that data is free from manipulation, this goal demands that we can clearly verify that the data originates from a specific identity. Authenticity is especially relevant if parts of your device have to be "original," such as spare parts, the firmware stored in flash memory, or a license file.

Nonrepudiation (Nr) Closely related to authenticity, nonrepudiation means that an entity can't plausibly deny having performed a given operation. In general, this requirement is useful for device and/or user activities that lead to a contract—for example, ordering refill ink for your printer on the device directly, but also if your product includes a pay-per-use functionality.

Privacy (Pr), pseudonymity (Ps), and anonymity (An)   At least since the introduction of the European General Data Protection Regulation (GDPR) in 2018, privacy and data protection have gained attention. If your device works with personal data (for example, medical equipment), you might want to specify protection goals for that data as well. Typical goals could be *pseudonymity*, which means that data can be tracked to an alias but not to a real person, or *anonymity*, which means that processed or collected data can be linked to neither a real person nor an alias.

Finally, you might end up with a table of assets and corresponding protection goals, as shown in Table 1-1. Note that the Comment column might be useful if you want to give the chosen protection goal more context.

Table 1-1: Example Assets and Corresponding Protection Goals

ID	Asset	Protection goal(s)	Comment
AS01	Firmware	I, Au	Only original firmware
AS02	Certificate private key	C	If leaked, device can be cloned
AS03	Temperature sensor data	I, Au, A	Essential to detect device misuse
AS04	Debug interface	C	Access only for internal technicians
AS05	. . .	. . .	. . .

After working through such a heap of information, people are often stunned about the entanglement of device security with various areas of product development and operation. However, they are usually satisfied that the first step toward a secure device is taken and that they learned something new about the product they thought they knew from A to Z.

IN PRACTICE: THREAT-MODELING WORKSHOPS

Several years ago, I was asked to perform a two-day risk analysis workshop at an industrial control system manufacturer. Following my suggestion, the company invited several people from various disciplines.

During the first hours of the workshop, a developer was explaining how the separation of the critical industrial network and the IT network was implemented in the device, when a guy from technical maintenance intervened: "This is not how we do it out there." He continued explaining that during maintenance, it's much more convenient to bridge these networks, and that this bridging connection sometimes remains even during operation.

This single moment initiated many discussions, contributed to one of the top identified risks and, in the end, led to the development of an additional network-monitoring feature of the device. Subsequently, the maintenance instructions manual was also updated with security in mind. This issue emerged only because

---

Attackers, Threats, and Risks

After establishing a common system for understanding and identifying your device's assets and environment, the road is paved to analyze the threats and risks for your specific use cases. The goal of this second phase is to develop a set of scenarios that represent your current threat landscape and rate them according to their probability of occurrence and their potential impact on your business and your organization.

A *threat scenario* usually consists of a *threat actor* (the person doing the attacking), a possible *vulnerability* (an exploitable weakness of your device), *attack vectors* (the path or method used to attack), and an effect on at least one of the assets you identified earlier. This phase tries to predict which threats your device might face in the future, even if it's neither developed nor produced yet.

Of course, you can't achieve this prediction comprehensively with 100 percent accuracy. It's a creative process demanding that participants slip into the roles of attackers and imagine ways to reach their malicious goals. Yes, developing threat scenarios might be a bit unstructured for technical staff, surprises could arise, and the results are not cast in stone. You'll also need to update your scenarios in the future if you discover new threats.

Potential Adversaries

A good starting point is usually imagining potential attackers who vary in motivation, opportunities, and resources. The following may serve as basic examples:

Script kiddies   These attackers don't necessarily have to be teenagers, but they're people who analyze devices and services out of curiosity and as a pastime. They usually have few resources (other than spare time), use standard tools available on the internet, and acquire their basic skills from watching videos.

Security researchers   These people have specialized knowledge and access to powerful equipment, typically at universities. Although they usually don't have a financial interest, they aim to publish their found vulnerabilities and the preparation of corresponding fixes. In contrast to other attacker types, they're usually willing to cooperate with companies to improve product security.

Cybercriminals   Driven by financial profit, organized crime attacks IT products on a daily basis. Whether they're focused on ransomware, denial-of-service (DoS) attacks, or sale of personal data, these attackers have at least a moderate amount of resources, are actively monitoring industries, and are able to adapt their tools to new scenarios.

Product pirates   Cloning devices is a major concern for embedded systems. These attackers are well equipped to copy hardware designs and software components for their own purposes. They take advantage of the development investments made by the original device manufacturers in order to offer fake products at lower prices.

Nation-state attackers   Sophisticated equipment, almost endless resources, and unique access to intelligence data are only a few properties of these attackers. They act out of political or military motivation, so they're usually rather beyond the scope of standard business solutions. However, especially for devices that operate in federal or critical infrastructures, considering such adversaries is important.

These broad and general attacker types are helpful for identifying common risks, but usually a device and its applications will have more specific adversaries that allow you to make the threat scenarios more concrete and help you identify individual risks for your organization. For example, in the automotive and motorcycle domain, engine tuning could be a goal of a specific group of attackers who aim to circumvent protection measures in order to apply their custom performance settings.

Maybe even the customers themselves could have an interest in manipulating their devices. Looking at farming IoT systems, environmental and animal protection activists might be quite realistic attackers with their own objectives, resources, and approaches.

Finally, don't forget *insiders as attackers*, because they have unique knowledge about and access to internal documents, data, and processes. Of course, most employees likely are trustworthy, but thinking about what colleagues could do if they had bad intentions can be worthwhile for this phase. Table 1-2 shows a sample list of attackers for the assets listed in Table 1-1 and their corresponding properties.

Table 1-2: Examples of Possible Attackers and Properties

ID	Attacker	Motivation	Resources
AT01	Cybercriminal	Financial	Medium, access to malware
AT02	Script kiddie	Fun	Low, internet tools, spare time
AT03	Environmental activist	Publicity	Medium, PR contacts
AT04	Maintenance insider	Financial/anger	Technical documents, device account, read access to source code
AT05	Customer	Financial	Daily device usage, time to experiment
AT06	. . .	. . .	. . .

While generating this list, people sometimes remember real-world stories about theft, sabotage, or piracy that occurred in the past. This information can be really helpful in optimizing your future protection efforts.

Potential Negative Impacts

On one side, we have assets that are of central importance for our business, and on the other side, we have suspects waiting for their chance to attack them. The logical next question is, "How could these potentially malicious actors have an impact on our assets?"

Constructing attack vectors and imagining possible vulnerabilities in your system may result in myriad threat scenarios that probably overlap, increase processing efforts, and still won't cover everything. One way to address this issue is to try the pragmatic approach of running through your list of assets and applying relevant threats suggested by the *STRIDE methodology* developed at Microsoft.

Table 1-3 explains this methodology by showing what the STRIDE acronym stands for—namely, five standard threats—and then referencing the targets they aim to break as well as sample questions the moderator can ask all participants. For AS01 in Table 1-1—a firmware image that carries the protection goals of integrity and authenticity—the task would be to think creatively about ways to tamper with it or spoof the identity of the image's original manufacturer.

Table 1-3: The STRIDE Checklist of Threats

Threat	Target	Question to pose
Spoofing	Authenticity	Is there a way to impersonate any entity?
Tampering	Integrity	Is there a way to manipulate any data?
Repudiation	Nonrepudiation	Is there a way to plausibly deny an action?
Information disclosure	Confidentiality	Is there a way to read/extract information?
Denial of service	Availability	Is there a way to interrupt/delay a service?
Elevation of privilege	Authorization	Is there a way to act without permission?

If any of the other STRIDE threats seem applicable, add them to your discussion. In the firmware case, for example, you might have confidential intellectual property that hasn't been considered before. Finally, match any additional threat to your list of attackers and discuss who would be a suitable actor for that threat.

In addition to threats that devices and software have in common, physical products face another issue that should be in the back of everyone's mind while brainstorming threats: *they can be attacked physically.* In some cases that might not be critical, because if people have physical access to a device, they can also destroy other parts of the machine or system that the device controls. However, physical accessibility makes a difference in at least two situations:

> **Pre-attack device analysis** In many cases, devices can be purchased and analyzed for vulnerabilities, cryptographic secrets, and relevant behavior in an attacker-controlled environment. Physical access allows attackers to extract the device's firmware and perform detailed reverse

engineering or to eavesdrop on communication on traces of the printed circuit board (PCB), which might reveal confidential data.

Invisible manipulation   Using a hammer to "manipulate" a machine usually involves noise and visible damage that humans can detect. However, any physical access or proximity that can be used to alter device or system parameters that aren't recognizable without deeper analysis of the attacked system might represent a rather strong attack vector that can cause long-lasting impact.

Repeating the process for all assets takes time. However, since this format often involves experts from several fields, it is usually restricted to one or a few days in practice. After putting your assets through the mill, you obtain a collection of threat scenarios for your product. Table 1-4 shows the first rows of a result from an example workshop.

Table 1-4: Example Threat Scenarios

ID	Asset	Attacker(s)	Threat(s)	Impact(s)
TS01	AS01	AT04	Currently no integrity and authenticity protection; maintenance staff has physical access to many devices; knows how to open device and tamper with firmware	Dysfunctional product and customer complaints
TS02	AS02	AT01, AT03	If purchased, attackers can extract the private key from device firmware; attackers can act as device	Injection of forged data into backend
TS03	AS02	AT01, AT03, AT04	Attackers might publish the private key online to damage company reputation; anyone in the world can impersonate our devices	Media attention; maybe even product recall
TS04	AS03	AT05	Physical manipulation of temperature sensor; secure communication channel does not protect against that; temperature is always measured to be cool while actually being continuously over the limit	Misuse can't be proven in damage case
TS05	. . .	. . .	. . .	. . .

The noted scenarios will help you illustrate the identified issues and communicate them within your company or to management.

No Risks, No Priorities

Up to this point, every potential attack vector and every potential vulnerability has been collected without discarding anything as being "not relevant."

However, the list might be long, and resources to handle the identified issues are typically limited. It's time to separate the wheat from the chaff by rating (at least) two properties of each threat scenario: its probability of occurrence and, if it occurs, its potential impact.

In the safety domain, you can describe almost every probability of occurrence with a number. If functional safety experts are part of your interdisciplinary workshop, they might offer this methodology and argue that probabilities have to be expressed in numbers. However, no one could ever distill an imagined human adversary into a percentage that has any meaning at all, so ranking probability by a qualitative scale of low, medium, or high is likely best.

For impact, I also prefer to use the same simple scale of low, medium, or high. However, defining what those terms stand for in each individual analysis is important and depends on the product, the size of your company, and your business cases. For example, your team could agree on relating your impact rating to damage values, as shown in Table 1-5.

Table 1-5: Example Impact Ratings

Impact	Damage
Low	$10,000
Medium	$100,000
High	$1,000,000

To get a final *risk score* per threat scenario, I have one last thing to explain: the probability and impact ratings of low, medium, and high take values of 1, 2, and 3. If you multiply them for a given scenario, you obtain a corresponding risk score.

After rating all threat scenarios, you end up with a list similar to the one shown in Table 1-6. Adding explanations to the ratings allows for better understanding and reasoning, especially weeks after everybody forgets the details of the workshop discussions.

Table 1-6: Example Threat Scenario Ratings

Threat scenario	Probability of occurrence	Impact	Risk score
TS01	Low (few opportunities)	Low (single device)	1
TS02	Medium (offline attack)	Medium (few cases)	4
TS03	Medium (know-how necessary)	High (product recall)	6
TS04	Medium (financial interest)	Medium (if several cases)	4
TS05	. . .	. . .	. . .

After you and your colleagues have compiled a list of rated threat scenarios, you can sort it by risk score or present it in a two-dimensional risk matrix with probability and impact as the axes. This approach enables device architects and product managers to better prioritize risks, as there are never enough resources to implement every mitigation and protect from all possible threats.

Security Requirements and Security Architecture

Threat modeling and risk analysis are essential for your own company to separate your device's necessary protection needs from the ones that are only nice to have. However, it's important to understand that your organization is not the only stakeholder. Customers, certification bodies, and governments all might impose additional security requirements on your product.

Some of those requirements might overlap with your own interests, and others might be opposed to them. Make sure to handle your identified top-priority risks, but also consider external requirements like legal obligations, customer needs, and industrial standards in your security requirement process.

If product certification is your goal, this is the point where you should take a look at the detailed requirements of your intended certificate. For example, industrial component manufacturers can align their device security requirements with the protection features demanded by IEC 62443 Part 4-2. But even without a clear certification perspective, documents like ARM's Platform Security Architecture (PSA) Level 1 questionnaire can serve as guidance and inspiration for creating solid security requirements for your specific product.

In addition, security requirements always compete with other requirements, such as device performance, backward compatibility, and lower prices for components without security features. Therefore, you need to consider any interference with other requirements at an early stage.

Considering the whole product life cycle—from development to production to usage in the field to decommissioning—is often neglected in the process of identifying security requirements. Each phase has its own requirements and dependencies. However, if a device's owner might change or if confidential data on the device has to be destroyed before its disposal has ever been discussed, there might be no corresponding requirement for such purposes, which can lead to headaches later.

Risk Treatment

When it comes to defining a security architecture, all previous work on threats, risks, and requirements has to be funneled into a selection of technologies, protection measures, and organizational arrangements that lead to a secure product in the end. You can address risks in multiple ways:

Reduce A common approach to handling risks is to reduce them. Integrating suitable protection measures can either reduce the probability of a successful attack or limit the damage that could be done. Both strategies lower the risk of a certain threat scenario.

Eliminate Sometimes the removal of software components, interfaces, or product features can completely eliminate a given risk. This strategy is perfect from a security point of view, but it's usually a hard decision to make from a business and marketing perspective.

Transfer You can transfer security risks from your company to a supplier or from the manufacturer to the product's users. Usually, this transfer requires appropriate documentation and/or legal agreements, but it might further contribute to transparency and awareness among your partners and customers.

Accept Responsible entities in your company can accept risks, which might be an option if mitigation would be more expensive than handling any security incident that occurs in practice.

Secure Development Principles

Although Parts II and III of this book are intended to support architects in deciding for or against certain technical security features, you should also keep conceptual principles in mind when developing a security architecture.

Perform Defense in Depth

Every protection measure might fail someday, either because of a sophisticated attacker or an exceptional circumstance. A security architecture should implement multiple layers of protection. If one layer breaks, one or more remaining layers might guarantee security or at least limit potential damage.

Use Proven Secure Technology or Components

Some companies refuse to use existing technology and components from external parties, even if they are of high quality. Of course, in some cases, developing a security component from scratch is reasonable. However, doing so might involve a steep learning curve with many failures. Use software and hardware that has proven to be robust and secure if you don't have good reasons not to.

Implement Least Privilege

For a solid security architecture, all involved roles and permissions must be documented. When it comes to granting or denying access rights to people and services, specific roles should be allowed access only to the resources necessary to fulfill their tasks. This practice also helps limit the threat potential of insider attacks.

Keep It Simple

Complexity and nontransparency are the natural enemies of security because they make it even harder to analyze risks, identify attack paths, and implement effective countermeasures. Maintaining simplicity in your device and security architecture leads to better chances that security efforts actually reach your defined protection goals.

Reduce the Attack Surface

You can add by subtracting! This idiom is very true when it comes to a product's attack surface. A wireless interface that doesn't exist can't be attacked, and a debug port that was removed from the PCB can't be the entrance point for a physical attacker. Remove all unnecessary features, interfaces, hardware, and software components from your device architecture or at least from the final product design that enters the market.

IN PRACTICE: DISCARDING FEATURES

I was once part of a security consulting team that was invited to participate in architecture discussions for a new industrial product at an early stage. Topics ranged from secure communication to secure storage of device secrets to location tracking of the device while it was moved from one customer's site to another. Back then, the latter topic was somehow critical, and we spent quite some time discussing it.

In the end, considerations about security and international laws led to the removal of that tracking mechanism from the list of product features. The risks of forged tracking data and similar attacks were completely eliminated, and product management had peace of mind again.

Secure Implementation and Security Testing

While the previous sections focused mainly on *doing the right things*, this section is concerned with *doing the things right*. Naturally, hardware and software developers want to implement a fully functional, working product. However, if security is not on everybody's mind (and maybe even on nobody's mind), you'll end up with a fully functional product that has several weaknesses and vulnerabilities that might be discovered by criminals, researchers, or customers sooner or later after market launch.

Shift Left

One strategy to avoid this situation is to *shift left*, which means that the detection of implementation errors doesn't happen after rollout, but as soon as possible (as far left as possible) in the development process. Besides enabling fast feedback loops, this also lowers the costs of error detection and correction.

These considerations are already relevant at the very beginning of the implementation phase as your team makes important decisions that may have crucial security implications, such as central hardware components, an operating system (OS), secure coding rules, and so on. Let's look at two examples.

Hardware Component Selection

The hardware development for a physical product usually starts earlier than the software development. At some point in time, a project deadline called a *hardware freeze* will occur, after which you can't change the components of the device's hardware anymore. Detecting hardware security issues after that deadline leads to dirty fixes, expensive redesigns, or bad device security.

Be sure to consider security requirements when selecting the basic hardware components for a device. If component costs aren't a key factor, choose components that have more security features rather than those that have fewer, which might save you a lot of trouble and money later in the development process.

Programming Language Selection

Ask 10 people for the best programming language for a specific task and you might get 11 answers. However, we've seen, especially in the area of embedded systems and IoT devices, that the C language laid the ground for a myriad of memory safety issues that resulted in security vulnerabilities. According to statistics from Android, Chromium, and Microsoft, 70 to 90 percent of their common vulnerabilities and exposures (CVEs) can be traced back to memory management issues. Just imagine how much money and effort you could save if code analysis tools, code reviews, and incident handling for memory management problems were no longer necessary.

It's not surprising that Rust is gaining more and more attention in development communities that work on embedded, system-level, and high-performance software, because it's one solution to overcome the security issues and all the consequential costs of using C or C++.

IN PRACTICE: PLANNING FOR SECURITY

I once had a conversation with a hidden champion at a company in the industrial automation industry. My team and I analyzed one of the company's products and were surprised to find a secure element (SE) on its PCB. When approached on the subject, the chief technical officer (CTO) explained that the costs of the chip weren't critical but that security would be one day, so they integrated the SE into their device, even though they didn't use it at product launch. They were able to activate it for secret storage and secure communication at a later time; preparation for future security challenges is key.

Continuous Testing and Analysis

Of course, initial design decisions can't anticipate all possible security issues. The second puzzle piece of secure implementations is robust automation of the building, testing, and review processes. Especially during software development, developers must get immediate feedback after weaknesses and potential problems are identified in their code. While security is not the primary target for automation and continuous integration (CI), they contribute to higher quality and reduce human errors, which are typically the origin of security vulnerabilities.

From a security point of view, be sure to cover the following areas when automating an SDL (some of these are software-specific, but most can also be applied to the hardware development process).

Third-Party Component Transparency

In hardware design, generating a bill of materials (BOM) is a daily routine, but the demand for a software bill of materials (SBOM) for certain products is growing. Both aren't primarily intended for security purposes but are important for tracking security vulnerabilities in third-party dependencies, including software libraries, microcontrollers, and OSs.

Static Security Testing

Using static application security testing (SAST) in software development is an important part of issue detection. These tools can help you identify insecure functions in the C language: they may detect hardcoded secrets that have to be removed before release and can highlight code sections that might be vulnerable to common security risks like the OWASP Top 10. These static code-analysis tools can be seamlessly integrated into CI pipelines and provide developers with timely feedback.

Dynamic Security Testing

Static analysis can't detect some vulnerabilities because the related issues result from *insecure behavior* of software or a device, which means dynamic security testing is necessary. You can automate this testing to a certain extent—for example, by deploying software built in a CI pipeline to a test device that can, in turn, be challenged with test cases. However, since the test space is huge, and dynamic application security testing (DAST) requires specific runtime environments, this discipline usually comes with a significantly higher effort than static analysis.

Implementation Review

While we often reserve the term *code review* for software processes, we might just as well apply reviews to device hardware design in order to discover implementation weaknesses, the use of forbidden components, or bad design patterns that facilitate physical attacks. Although this is a human task, automation may support you in scheduling reviews or triggering reviews upon changes to critical hardware or software parts.

Attackers as a Service

All the described techniques aim for verification and validation of explicit security requirements and protection features or for avoidance of implementation flaws that might undermine device security. However, while secure implementation and security testing continue to converge to form a secure, incremental, and agile development process, one security testing method is usually applied manually and outside a CI environment: penetration testing.

In a *penetration test*, internal or external security experts slip into the role of attackers. By simulating attacks on the device at hand, they try to trigger worst-case scenarios that demonstrate the feasibility of attacks, the involved efforts, and the possible attack paths. In turn, this type of test enables a manufacturer to rework relevant product parts and discover further related issues.

Since penetration testing is usually a time-limited service, it's important to use the available days efficiently. If you order a penetration test for your device, make sure to specify three important aspects: the scope; the worst case; and whether you expect black-, gray-, or white-box testing.

Scope

If you don't set a defined scope for a penetration test, the tester will just look for the easiest way into your device. However, that might include opening up the device, which might be far from the attack model you had in mind.

Clarify your expectations. Are physical attacks in scope? Which interfaces should be attacked, and which are out of scope? Is it okay to manipulate the device's firmware?

The focus isn't to narrow the scope to a minimum in order to get a positive test result. The aim of a clear scope is to yield results that support your protection efforts in the best possible way.

Worst Case

Usually, your device carries a few critical assets, the crown jewels that, if compromised, would lead to severe damage. Optimally, you've already identified them in your risk analysis earlier in the process, and you're probably most interested in attacks that have an effect on those assets. If you don't specify them, penetration testers might spend days trying to find fancy ways to manipulate a graphical user interface (GUI) that is relevant only for internal purposes.

Black-/Gray-/White-Box Testing

Black-box attacks assume that an attacker has no information about a device at all, which makes sense if you want to see what information an attacker can collect about a given product in a short amount of time. However, it doesn't make sense to do this for weeks and essentially pay a penetration tester for reverse engineering information you already know.

One way to improve efficiency for the manufacturer could be a phased approach. After a few days of black-box testing, the testers could present initial results and propose possible next (reverse-engineering) steps. However, instead of actually reversing the device afterward, the manufacturer could supply the testers with information about protocols, hardware, and/or software so they can continue their appreciated penetration-testing work. You can repeat this procedure multiple times, resulting in a time-saving process that's much more likely to identify valuable security insights.

IN PRACTICE: PENETRATION-TESTING GOALS

"Could you perform a penetration test for our product?" That was the question that started off my interesting journey with an industrial partner some years ago. I could have said, "Sure! Give me one or two of your devices, and I'll see what we can do for you!" Instead, I initiated a discussion about security testing, an SDL, and where the latter should actually start, namely, at the beginning.

Luckily, I encountered open-minded and motivated people willing to establish an SDL and to *really improve* their device's security. We ended up doing a solid threat and risk analysis and, based on the results, set priorities for mitigation development. The bottom line is that driving the security of a product solely by the results of a penetration test is not a reasonable strategy. It bears repeating.

Finally, don't forget that for a physical product like an IoT device, the last steps of implementation do not happen in the offices of the development team but during production in a factory. Selecting a secure production environment, protecting your device assets while being transferred to a production site, and performing post-production testing to validate the proper activation of protection features are essential for a securely implemented device.

Vulnerability Monitoring and Response

No matter how large your company is, how much effort you put into organizing your secure development process, or how smart your engineering team is, a chance always remains that vulnerabilities are hidden in your device. Some might result from human failure during development, others might originate in third-party components, and still others might emerge because of advancements in attacker tools and methodologies that you couldn't foresee. If you acknowledge that fact, the best thing you can do is be prepared and plan for the following phases to run in a structured way.

Reporting Vulnerabilities

Some customers, penetration testers, and security researchers honestly care about your product's security and will report found vulnerabilities to manufacturers in a responsible, coordinated disclosure process. However, if your website doesn't list a security contact, such as a simple *security@company.com*, those people might have trouble reporting their findings to somebody who cares. They might then use the *info@company.com* contact, but the message might drown in that inbox, and you'll never learn about the discovered issue.

In other cases, finders of vulnerabilities will turn to national or international security organizations or even to the media to cause attention, which is probably not what you want. Establish a simple, visible security contact on your web page. Second, some people report security issues to mailing lists or vulnerability databases instead of contacting the manufacturer. Monitoring relevant sources for your industry is essential for detecting and learning about vulnerabilities as early as possible.

Reviewing and Assessing Vulnerability Reports

A vulnerability report can range from a short email message to a comprehensive analysis document. After receiving a report, first review it to check whether it actually is a security issue or intended device behavior, or whether the researcher made some mistakes. If your product is prone to the described attack vector, the follow-up task is to clarify why. The result of this phase should be an internal understanding and rating of the vulnerability at hand.

Fixing or Addressing the Issue

If the cause of the problem lies within device software that can be updated, you can develop a patch with two goals in mind. On the one hand, it should eliminate the vulnerability as comprehensively as possible. On the other hand, it shouldn't impact any other device features or properties.

In addition, consider the possibility of mitigating the vulnerability by device reconfiguration that even the customer can perform. In some cases, hardware or non-updatable software is responsible for a security issue. These situations are hard to handle because they might require physical access to every single device or even a product recall.

Testing

Whether the solution is a software patch, a physical rework, or a configuration workaround, it must be tested before it's rolled out to all devices in the field. In some cases, updates might impair device performance; in others, changes to the software could transfer the issue to another part of the device and create a new vulnerability. Make sure your solution does exactly what it is supposed to do.

Disclosing the Solution

One day, your fix will be released to customers. Depending on industry standards, the severity of the found issue, and the efficiency of your vulnerability-response handling, one week or more than a year might have passed since the initial report. However, even at that point, the world doesn't know the details. Make sure your proposed solution is accompanied by a helpful explanation of the problem that clearly indicates actions for customers, administrators, or operators. Be prepared to answer media requests if your product is of public interest.

Avoiding Future Issues

A secure development process is a continuous improvement cycle. Every found vulnerability should lead to discussions about possible enhancements for your development process in order to avoid similar issues in the future.

Establishing Trust

It's in every manufacturer's best interest to establish a trusting relationship with the people who discover and report vulnerabilities. These people actually support your secure development process without being on your payroll. Clear and regular communication about the status of the vulnerability-handling process is essential.

Depending on the severity and extent of the found issue, you might consider rewards or security bounties to express your appreciation. But even if you feel like the reported issue is only a trifle, offering a little thank-you might be worthwhile to acknowledge the reporters' efforts and encourage them to find more critical weaknesses in the future.

IN PRACTICE: VULNERABILITY REPORTING

I once was part of a team that identified several vulnerabilities in a product of an international corporation. After a quick online search, we found a vulnerability-reporting form provided by its Asian headquarters and were confident that the company had a solid vulnerability-response process in place. We filled in all the details, attached our comprehensive 25-page analysis, and hoped for the best.

We soon received an email message that more or less read like this: "Thank you for your report, but we think there is not much for us to do." A bit stunned, we tried to stress again that we found critical issues, without success. Next, we reported the issues to a German security organization that forwarded them to the manufacturer's European contact and stressed their relevance. After several months, a team of experts concluded that the vulnerability-handling engineer in Asia just misjudged our report. They assigned multiple CVEs.

However, if we had been less forgiving, the issue could have gone public, cybercriminals could have been developing exploits within weeks, and the reputation of that corporation could have been severely damaged, merely because a single person in the vulnerability-handling process said, "I don't think that has much relevance."

If you still think, "Nah, nobody will look for or find vulnerabilities in our devices," consider the consequences if someone does. If you don't prepare for a vulnerability-handling process, one of two scenarios might result. A device vulnerability might get too little attention because nobody cares or feels responsible, which might lead to attacks in the field, real damages on the customer side, bad press, and loss of reputation for your product or company. Or, if a vulnerability report causes everybody in your team or even beyond to run around like frightened chickens, vulnerability response becomes a chaotic process that exhausts emotions and resources and will not deliver a reliable solution for the issue.

Summary

This chapter summarized important activities and processes that organizations should follow when aiming for secure products. In the beginning, I explained that you can choose from multiple guidelines that are similar in content. While the Microsoft and OWASP recommendations are targeted at software products, IEC 62443 Part 4 is clearly meant for industrial components that can be certified.

A basic requirement for all secure development processes is that people are aware of risks and receive the security training they need for their daily tasks. The key to creating a secure product is a solid analysis of assets, corresponding protection goals, possible attackers, threats, and involved risks. You can tackle this task with a structured approach that leads to transparency, explicit trust and risk decisions, and clear documentation.

Based on this preliminary work, you can subsequently implement product-specific security requirements and an individual security architecture. Cultivate secure implementation habits like secure coding among developers and engineers, and check implementation results with security testing regularly. Vulnerability monitoring together with efficient and effective vulnerability-response processes complete the security life cycle of a high-quality product.

If you want to dive deeper into the area of secure development processes and corresponding methodologies, take a look at *Designing Secure Software* by Loren Kohnfelder (No Starch Press, 2021) and Adam Shostack's *Threat Modeling: Designing for Security* (Wiley, 2014).

2

CRYPTOGRAPHY

The guarantees and powers of cryptographic algorithms often sound like magic. A layperson isn't able to verify any of these properties and neither are most engineers. In some cases, even cryptographers can't prove the security of a scheme, but they assume or believe that the underlying mathematical problem is hard to solve. Nevertheless, cryptographic algorithms are necessary tools that every developer and architect should know how to use.

The word *cryptography* comes from the combination of the Greek words *kryptós* and *gráphein*, which translate to *secret writing*. Nowadays, however, cryptography is much more than the protection of confidential messages. It's also used to protect the integrity of files, to derive reliable fingerprints of gigabytes of data, and to sign documents and code digitally.

This chapter provides a pragmatic overview of modern cryptographic algorithms and their practical properties while keeping mathematical formulas at a minimum. We'll start with some basic principles, then take a peek at typical symmetric algorithms and hash functions. A look at the intriguing field of asymmetric crypto concludes the chapter.

Kerckhoffs's Principle

Auguste Kerckhoffs was a Dutch cryptographer in the 19th century. In the security community, he's known for his proposals to improve practical cryptography in the French military. Among the six recommendations he published in 1883, one became famously known as *Kerckhoffs's principle*: "The system must not require secrecy and can be stolen by the enemy without causing trouble."

For cryptographic algorithms, this principle means that procedures like encryption, decryption, or signing should not be kept secret and that no one should rely on this secrecy to guarantee security. The only secret in the system should be a secret cryptographic key.

Today, this point doesn't seem worth mentioning because all relevant crypto algorithms are standardized on a national or international level, and all are publicly available for everyone to read and analyze. However, when it comes to engineering software and devices, some developers still break with this principle. They invent their own "crypto" procedures and argue that security is achieved "because nobody knows how it works." They sometimes do this for performance reasons, but more often it's the result of a lack of solid crypto knowledge. However, the phrase "can be stolen by the enemy" could also be interpreted as "can be reverse engineered by an attacker," which would break the security of such a "solution."

If you catch yourself considering the implementation of a custom function probably including some magic values and XOR operations to achieve security, stop thinking about it immediately! It's called *security by obscurity* and it will only get you into trouble.

Levels of Security

Cryptographic algorithms have several parameters and properties that describe and differentiate them, but one is central: their *security level* that's indicated by a certain bit length—for example, 64-bit, 80-bit, or 256-bit. This practical gauge allows you to compare algorithms and their cryptographic strength. But what does it actually mean if a specific algorithm has a 128-bit security level?

The level describes the effort an attacker needs to expend in order to break the algorithm's protection goal. Usually, that effort involves testing large sets of data for a correct solution, such as a secret decryption key. If an algorithm has a 128-bit security level, the *search space* for an attacker is 128 bits large, which means that the attacker has to perform a maximum of 2^{128} tries in order to identify the needle in the haystack.

For well-designed symmetric ciphers, the key length can be translated directly into an algorithm's security level. However, security levels are subject to change if cryptographers find algorithmic flaws. In that case, the algorithm's security level might become significantly less than the key length.

In addition, keep in mind that attackers continuously make performance gains. Modern *brute-force* attacks make use of thousands of cloud instances to efficiently search for a key. In recent years, attacks on 64-bit secrets have been successful, increasing the need for a solid choice of security level.

If you want to engineer secure and long-lasting devices, keep up with the current recommendations of crypto security levels (see *https://www.keylength.com*). As a rule of thumb at the time of writing, a 128-bit security level is considered suitable for practical security engineering, and 256-bit is typically used for high-security applications.

WARNING *Although the security level of symmetric ciphers often equals their key length, that's not always the case. In addition, security levels for asymmetric crypto are completely different; keys with 2,048 bits might offer only 112-bit security, for example, as you'll see later in this chapter.*

Symmetric Ciphers

The origin of symmetric cryptography dates back to the famous Roman named Caesar, who is said to have used a simple letter-substitution cipher to make messages incomprehensible. Since then, the basic principle of symmetric crypto hasn't changed. It follows the idea that a *plaintext* message can be encrypted to a *ciphertext* by using the encryption algorithm Encrypt() and a *cryptographic key*, as illustrated in Figure 2-1.

Figure 2-1: The basic principle of symmetric cryptography

The decryption operation Decrypt() uses *the same secret key* to reverse the encryption and yield the original message, hence the term *symmetric cryptography*.

Data Encryption Standard

Fast-forward 2,000 years. In many cases, symmetric encryption is now handled by *block ciphers* that take one block of plaintext and encrypt it to a block of ciphertext. One of the first publicly standardized block ciphers was the *Data Encryption Standard (DES)*, also known as the *Data Encryption Algorithm (DEA)*. It's based on a so-called *Feistel network* and has only a 56-bit key. Today, with dedicated hardware, this key space can be completely searched within hours, which makes it absolutely insecure for modern applications.

Triple DES (3DES) is an extension of DES that uses three 56-bit keys and applies DES three times to a plaintext or ciphertext. Given the total key length of 168 bits, the block size of 64 bits, and known cryptographic weaknesses, 3DES is considered to achieve only a 112-bit security level and should no longer be used in new designs.

Some modern crypto libraries still provide DES and 3DES. However, if you don't have very good reasons—for example, indispensable backward compatibility—do not use any DES-based algorithm.

Advanced Encryption Standard

The first choice for symmetric encryption is currently the *Advanced Encryption Standard (AES)*, originally named *Rijndael*. This successor of DES was standardized as Federal Information Processing Standard (FIPS) 197 and ISO/IEC 18033-3 after a cryptographic competition process that was organized by NIST lasted from 1997 to 2000. AES is based on a substitution-permutation network (SPN), has a block length of 128 bits, and can be operated with three key lengths: 128-bit, 192-bit, and 256-bit.

As shown in Figure 2-2, AES operates on a 4×4 byte matrix, known as the *AES state*.

Byte 0	Byte 4	Byte 8	Byte 12
Byte 1	Byte 5	Byte 9	Byte 13
Byte 2	Byte 6	Byte 10	Byte 14
Byte 3	Byte 7	Byte 11	Byte 15

Figure 2-2: A matrix visualization of the AES state

Depending on the selected key size, this state is processed for a certain number of rounds: 10 for 128-bit keys, 12 for 192-bit keys, and 14 for 256-bit keys. Here's the basic encryption process based on the main AES functions:

Key expansion The original key is expanded to multiple 128-bit subkeys, one for each round plus an initial one.

Initial round As a preparation step, the function AddRoundKey() is applied to the input plaintext to obtain a new state.

Main rounds Depending on the key lengths, 9, 11, or 13 main rounds are performed with the following operations happening consecutively: SubBytes(), ShiftRows(), MixColumns(), and AddRoundKey().

Final round In the last round, only SubBytes(), ShiftRows(), and AddRoundKey() are called. MixColumns() is omitted.

The four operations that enable this strong encryption are pretty simple. The SubBytes() function substitutes each byte in the AES state with a corresponding byte resulting from a lookup table called an *S-box*, as shown in Figure 2-3.

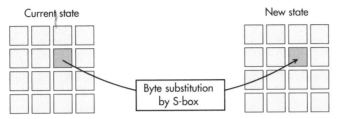

Figure 2-3: The SubBytes() transformation

Figure 2-4 shows that the ShiftRows() transformation shifts the second row of the AES state matrix 1 byte to the left, the third row 2 bytes to the left, and the fourth row 3 bytes to the left. The first row remains unchanged.

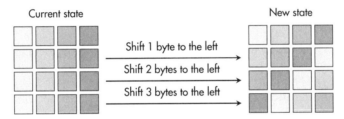

Figure 2-4: The ShiftRows() transformation

The MixColumns() operation applies a linear transformation to each column of the AES state matrix, as depicted in Figure 2-5. This yields 4 resulting bytes representing the new state of each column, respectively.

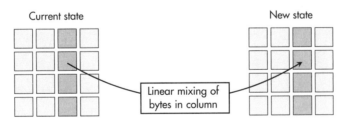

Figure 2-5: The MixColumns() transformation

Every round, the AddRoundKey() operation XORs each byte of the AES state with the corresponding byte of a given round key, as illustrated in Figure 2-6.

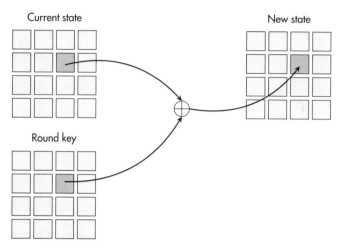

Figure 2-6: The AddRoundKey() transformation

For decryption, the order of subkeys is reversed, and the inverse functions of SubBytes(), ShiftRows(), MixColumns(), and AddRoundKey() are called.

After more than 20 years and extensive research, nobody has discovered an attack on the AES architecture that has practical relevance. It's available in all major crypto software libraries, and systems as small as 8-bit microcontrollers can use it with reasonable performance. AES is used for disk encryption in laptops, but also for payload encryption in secure internet communication. Whenever it comes to symmetric encryption, you should choose AES unless you have serious reasons not to do so.

Modes of Operation

Since AES is a block cipher, it naturally encrypts or decrypts only a single block, but many applications have much more input data than just one 128-bit block. Therefore, AES has to be used in a certain *mode of operation* that defines the procedures to encrypt and decrypt multiple blocks of data. The modes introduced here are defined in NIST's *Special Publication 800-38A*.

Electronic Codebook Mode

Some of you might wonder, "Why not just encrypt the data block by block?" That trivial approach is exactly what the *Electronic Codebook (ECB) mode* does. It takes the first 128 bits of a message as the first plaintext block, encrypts it to the first 128 bits of ciphertext, and continues in the same way with as many chunks of 128-bit data as available, as shown in Figure 2-7.

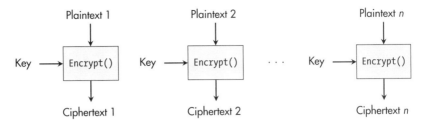

Figure 2-7: Encryption in ECB mode

However, the problem with this approach is that equal input data blocks are encrypted to equal ciphertext blocks. Therefore, the relation between blocks, which can also carry sensitive information, is preserved. Figure 2-8 illustrates this phenomenon.

(a) Original image   (b) Encrypted with ECB   (c) Encrypted with CTR

Figure 2-8: Comparing ECB and Counter (CTR) modes

When images are encrypted in ECB mode, the plaintext pixels with the same values are still mapped to ciphertext pixels with identical values. The image information is still comprehensible. For other operation modes, such as Counter mode, things look different, as explained in "Counter Mode" on page 34.

Cipher Block Chaining Mode

The *Cipher Block Chaining (CBC) mode* breaks the relation between plaintext and ciphertext by XORing the ciphertext of the first block with the plaintext of the second block, and so on. Figure 2-9 shows the basic principle.

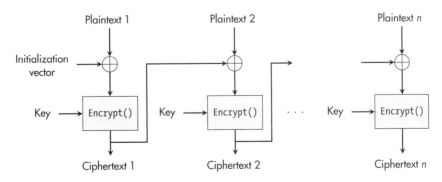

Figure 2-9: Encryption in CBC mode

From a security point of view, CBC mode is significantly better than ECB mode, but it has a new drawback: the dependency between subsequent encryptions makes parallel implementations less efficient, which limits performance.

Counter Mode

An interesting mode that doesn't permit a relation between ciphertexts but facilitates high-performance, multicore implementations is called *Counter (CTR) mode*. As illustrated in Figure 2-10, the plaintext blocks themselves aren't encrypted, but the concatenation of a *nonce (number used once)* and a counter value starting at 0.

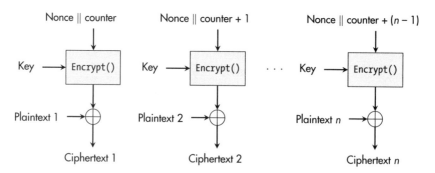

Figure 2-10: Encryption in CTR mode

The result of this encryption is then XORed with the plaintext to obtain a ciphertext. For every further plaintext block, the counter value is incremented by one to support changing ciphertexts, as shown in Figure 2-8c. This approach even provides another advantage: both encryption and decryption utilize the Encrypt() function of the used block cipher. There's no need to implement Decrypt().

In contrast to ECB mode, CBC and CTR modes require an additional input parameter: an *initialization vector (IV)* or a nonce. The rationale for both is to make every encryption unique, so they should never be used twice. Further, decryption is possible only if the receiver also has access to the corresponding IV or nonce. But since it doesn't carry confidential data, transmitting it in cleartext is okay along with the ciphertext.

WARNING *In practice, just setting an IV or a nonce to 0 or a fixed random number is tempting. However, doing so will significantly weaken the strength of this cryptographic primitive. Spend the additional effort to implement a suitable generator for unique values.*

Together with the operation modes CBC and CTR, AES enjoys great popularity. However, other, more interesting symmetric ciphers might be helpful if you have special requirements. For example, the modern stream ciphers Salsa20 and ChaCha20, developed by cryptographer Daniel J. Bernstein, have simple designs and provide high performance in pure software implementations. If your hardware doesn't support AES but you need to get the highest performance possible, these algorithms might be worth looking at.

Hash Functions

Hash functions are somewhat exotic in the pool of cryptographic algorithms. On their own, they don't aim for one of the classic protection goals. Their objective is to map more or less arbitrarily large input data to a fixed-length, binary sequence called a *hash value*, or *digest*.

However, the design of such functions isn't trivial. They have to fulfill a set of strong requirements:

Preimage resistance   The term *preimage* refers to the correct input data to a hash function that maps to a given hash value. This requirement says that an attacker shouldn't be able to find such suitable input data for an existing hash value. This is why hash functions are also called *one-way functions*. Nobody should be able to invert them.

Second preimage resistance   Further, a malicious actor who has access to a message and its hash value shouldn't be able to find a *second preimage*—namely, another message that maps to the same hash.

Collision resistance   Naturally, hash-value collisions must exist because the input space of a hash function is larger than its output space. The strongest assumption for hash functions is that finding any two messages that map to the same hash value should be *practically impossible*.

By design, hash functions don't use a secret key, which means that everyone can use them and apply them to all data at hand. Therefore, we have to determine the security level of hash functions differently. The security level is described as the amount of difficulty in finding collisions, which is again a kind of search-space problem, similar to finding the correct key for an encryption algorithm.

Based on the so-called *birthday paradox* and the *rho method*, cryptographers have shown that, for well-designed hash functions, we can estimate the security level to be half of their output size. For example, for a hash function with 160-bit output, the security level estimate is around 80-bit.

At this point, you might wonder why we need hash functions and their cryptographic mapping process for device security. The reason is simple: they're part of many security applications like digital signature generation and verification, key-derivation algorithms, secure password storage, and many more.

The first practical implementations of hash functions emerged in the 1990s. MD4, MD5, and SHA-1 are three prominent representatives. However, in the meantime, researchers have discovered ways to find collisions for those three (and others), so you shouldn't use those legacy algorithms in modern designs anymore.

Currently, the most widely used family of hash functions is SHA-2, the successor to SHA-1. It's described in the *FIPS 180-4* standard and has four members: SHA-224, SHA-256, SHA-384, and SHA-512. The numbers represent the output lengths of these functions, so SHA-224 is very similar to SHA-256 except for different initial values and the truncation of the final hash value to 224 bits. The same applies for SHA-384 in relation to SHA-512.

SHA-256 processes 512 bits (sixteen 32-bit words) in 64 rounds. It exhibits a 128-bit security level against collisions and is, therefore, a secure and efficient option. SHA-512 is intended for high-security areas like federal and military purposes. It works on 1,024 bits (sixteen 64-bit words) for 80 rounds and exhibits a lower performance compared to SHA-256.

Since the SHA-2 family is based on an architecture similar to MD5 and SHA-1, cryptographers are skeptical about its long-term security. In 2007, NIST announced a cryptographic competition in order to find a candidate to be standardized as SHA-3. One important requirement was that the design of the algorithm should be based on primitives other than SHA-2. Five years later, the *Keccak* algorithm was named as the winning hash function. Subsequently, it has been published as the new SHA-3 standard in *FIPS 202*.

SHA-3 is also available in four versions: SHA3-224, SHA3-256, SHA3-384, and SHA3-512. Again, the lengths of their output values in bits is denoted by the numbers after the hyphen in their names. Their performance and security level is comparable to those of their SHA-2 counterparts, but they're based on a completely different algorithmic foundation, as intended by NIST.

NOTE *Even if SHA-3 is the newer standard, you don't need to migrate from SHA-2 to SHA-3 soon. They are comparable, so you are free to decide which to use depending on the libraries you need and application requirements you have.*

Message Authentication Codes

A common misconception about encryption is that it protects against manipulation. It doesn't. Even if you use AES and a state-of-the-art mode of operation, and an attacker can't read anything from the resulting ciphertext, that attacker is still able to manipulate single bits or whole messages without being detected by the block cipher. Encryption protects only confidentiality, not integrity.

A *message authentication code (MAC)*, also known as a *message integrity code (MIC)*, is another primitive from the symmetric cryptography tool belt, and it's meant to protect message integrity and authenticity. It creates an *authentication tag* from a message and a secret key. Afterward, everyone in possession of the secret key can verify the correctness of a message and its corresponding authentication tag.

A popular method for generating MACs is a *hash-based message authentication code (HMAC)*. The HMAC construction, also known as a *keyed hash function*, is defined in RFC 2104. The following formula shows its composition:

$$HMAC = hash((key \oplus opad) \parallel hash((key \oplus ipad) \parallel message))$$

The *inner padding (ipad)* is a byte string, 0x3636...36, containing the same number of bytes as the input block size of the used hash function. It is XORed with a key of at least the security level of the underlying hash function. The result is concatenated with the message to protect before it is hashed altogether. The digest of this operation is then appended to the XOR between the same key and the *outer padding (opad)*, a byte string 0x5c5c...5c of the same length as the ipad. Hashing the resultant bytes leads to the final HMAC value.

As an example, if SHA-256 is chosen as an HMAC's hash function, the cryptographic algorithm is then called HMAC-SHA-256. The length of the inner and outer padding is 512 bits, or 64 bytes. The key should be at least 128 bits long, and the HMAC length is 256 bits, or 32 bytes.

NOTE   *In practice, you might come across HMAC constructions that are built upon MD5 or SHA-1. Even if collision attacks have been demonstrated for these hash functions, they're still valid to be used for practical HMAC implementations because an attacker would have to acquire an enormous number of authentication tags resulting from the same single secret key to break a specific instance.*

A *cipher-based message authentication code (CMAC)* uses a block cipher in CBC mode to compute MACs. A variant that's based on AES, called *AES-CMAC*, is specified in RFC 4493. There, the message to protect is processed with AES in CBC mode except for the last message block, which is specifically treated for security reasons. The final ciphertext is taken as the authentication tag, and all other ciphertexts are discarded.

This solution isn't as popular as the HMAC construction, but it might be interesting from a performance point of view, especially on devices that have built-in AES accelerators.

Authenticated Encryption

For secure communication, confidentiality, integrity, and authenticity are common protection goals. In the previous sections, we considered how we can use block ciphers and MACs to achieve these goals, but two practical questions still remain: "How do we combine them?" and "Can combinations of ciphers and MACs be more efficient than using them separately?"

Strategies and Requirements

When combining encryption and MAC generation, we can use three strategies. All three assume the use of secure ciphers and MAC algorithms and that each of them uses its own key, but differ in the order of the performed operations:

Encrypt-and-MAC   This approach generates a ciphertext and an authentication tag from the same plaintext in parallel, which could yield a performance advantage. However, applying a MAC algorithm to plaintext might lead to information leakage about the plaintext by the authentication tag because MAC algorithms are not designed to protect the confidentiality of their input data. However, for modern MACs like HMAC-SHA-256, this problem doesn't exist. A second issue is that the ciphertext's integrity isn't protected. An altered ciphertext has to be decrypted first to detect the manipulation, which could allow an attacker to exploit implementation weaknesses in the decryption routine.

MAC-then-encrypt   In this variant, an authentication tag is generated from the plaintext and appended to it. The result is then encrypted to obtain the final ciphertext. In this case, the MAC algorithm can't leak any information, but the ciphertext can still be manipulated without a possibility to detect it before decryption.

Encrypt-then-MAC   This is a strong strategy for integrity and confidentiality protection of messages. First, the plaintext is encrypted before the MAC is generated from the resulting ciphertext. With this approach, the authentication tag can't leak any information about the plaintext, and at the same time, we can verify the correctness of the ciphertext bits before decrypting the given data.

Crypto practitioners are always on the lookout for performance gains because security measures should have as little performance overhead as possible. Therefore, it's not surprising that the field of *authenticated encryption (AE)* emerged from the combination of ciphers and MACs to enhance processing speed.

In comparison to "normal" ciphers, AE algorithms take plaintext and compute both ciphertext and an authentication tag during encryption. At decryption, the integrity of the ciphertext and authentication tag are verified before proceeding.

An interesting extension of AE is called *authenticated encryption with associated data (AEAD)*, which allows you to integrate additional plaintext data into the process of generating the authentication tag. Examples are sequence numbers or metadata that don't require confidentiality. The integrity of this associated data is achieved while binding it to the yielded ciphertext.

Galois Counter Mode

Today, the most popular AEAD algorithm is the AES cipher operated in the special *Galois Counter mode (GCM)*, which follows the encrypt-then-MAC principle and is specified in NIST's *Special Publication 800-38D*. Figure 2-11 depicts its basic functionality.

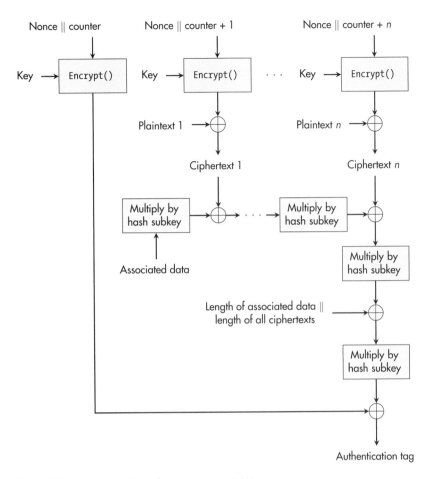

Figure 2-11: An authenticated encryption in GCM

The confidentiality protection is very similar to CTR mode, except GCM doesn't use the result of the first encryption to process plaintext, but rather does it in the final step of authentication-tag generation. The MAC generation is based on the hash function GHASH, which basically consists of a series of multiplications in a binary Galois field with a fixed parameter, the *hash subkey*. This subkey is derived by encrypting the all-zeros plaintext block with the AES key used for encryption.

The nonce or initialization vector of GCM is meant to be a unique 96-bit binary string. GCM is pretty fragile regarding nonce reuse, which means that an attacker can forge authentication tags if they have access to two authentication tags that were generated using the same key and nonce. Therefore, the implementation of a robust nonce generation is essential for GCM.

Besides AES-GCM, you might encounter many more AE algorithms in the field. Examples are the Counter with CBC-MAC (CCM) mode as detailed in NIST's *Special Publication 800-38C* and the Offset Codebook (OCB) mode designed by Phil Rogaway. The combination of the stream cipher ChaCha20 and the MAC algorithm Poly1305, both designed by Bernstein, also serves as a common AEAD solution. It's especially efficient in software-only implementations and has been specified in RFC 8439.

Further, the CAESAR competition (*https://competitions.cr.yp.to/caesar -submissions.html*) that ran from 2013 to 2019 yielded another set of innovative AEAD designs—for example, lightweight implementations on resource-constrained devices or high-performance applications.

Asymmetric Cryptography

In contrast to using a single secret key, the basic idea of *asymmetric cryptography* is having a pair of keys and using each key for only a distinct operation that complements the other. For example, everyone uses one key, called a *public key*, to encrypt data (Figure 2-12). The second key, called a *private key*, belongs to a single entity, and only that entity is able to decrypt the previously generated ciphertext by using its private key. Asymmetric cryptosystems are also known as *public-key cryptography*.

Figure 2-12: Encryption with asymmetric cryptography

However, asymmetric cryptography is useful for more than confidentiality protection. The private-key operation can also generate a *digital signature*, which is a kind of checksum for given data that only the unique private key of a specific entity can compute. Everyone in possession of the corresponding public key would be able to verify this signature, which protects not only the protected data's authenticity but also its integrity, because manipulations of the data or signature would lead to a verification failure. Figure 2-13 illustrates the basic idea.

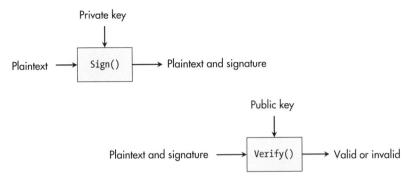

Figure 2-13: The generation and verification of a digital signature

These fundamentally different opportunities have paved the way for many security features we've come to take for granted, like secure communication over the internet. To understand the basics of the two most popular representatives of asymmetric cryptography, there is no way around a little bit of math, as I'll show in the next section.

The RSA Cryptosystem

The first and still most common asymmetric crypto scheme was published in 1977 and is named after its inventors: *Rivest-Shamir-Adleman (RSA)*. To achieve the typical asymmetry between public and private operations, RSA implements a *trapdoor function*. With this approach, you can transform data A to data B easily, but deriving data A from data B is practically impossible unless you know the trapdoor.

Basic RSA Math

RSA is based on modular arithmetic, which means integer calculations that wrap around if they reach a limit called the *modulus*. The following formula describes all the magic behind RSA encryption:

$$y = x^e \bmod n$$

The *modular exponentiation* of the *x* plaintext and *e*, the *public exponent*, compute the *y* ciphertext. The *n* denotes the modulus.

Decryption works in a very similar way:

$$x = y^d \bmod n$$

The modular exponentiation processes the y ciphertext with d, the *private exponent*, to obtain the x plaintext. However, the naive way of exponentiation, which means performing $d - 1$ multiplications by y, is completely impossible for d being a number with thousands of bits. You can overcome this obstacle with an algorithm called *square-and-multiply*. That algorithm basically operates bit by bit on the binary representation of the exponent. In every step, the algorithm performs a squaring operation, but if a given bit is 1, it carries out an additional multiplication, making RSA a practically usable crypto mechanism.

The numbers n and e are usually considered part of the public key, and d corresponds to the private key in RSA. Their described behavior is possible only because d and e have a special relation that is established during RSA key generation. In its first step, two large prime numbers p and q have to be chosen randomly. Their multiplication leads to the modulus $n = pq$. Using n, you can derive the result of Euler's phi function $\Phi(n)$:

$$\Phi(n) = (p - 1)(q - 1) = pq - p - q + 1 = (n + 1) - (p + q)$$

This value is essential for the RSA cryptosystem and its security because the inverse relation between e and d is achieved in a group modulo $\Phi(n)$:

$$ed \bmod \Phi(n) = 1$$

In practice, $e = 65537 = (10000000000000001)_2$ is a common choice because of its shortness and the low number of 1 bits, both contributing to higher performance with the square-and-multiply algorithm. After e is chosen, the final step of key generation is to compute d as the inverse of e modulo $\Phi(n)$.

Knowing these details, it might become clearer why RSA is often mentioned in the same sentence with the *integer factorization problem*. This mathematical consideration suggests that finding the factors of large numbers is difficult. The modulus n would be such a large product. RSA is secure because it's hard to find p and q from a given n. However, if someone discovers a solution to this problem, an adversary could calculate $\Phi(n)$ from the factorized values p and q and compute the inverse of e modulo $\Phi(n)$, and RSA would be broken.

Compared to symmetric schemes, the mathematical basis of the RSA cryptosystem makes it more difficult to estimate its security level. In *Special Publication 800-57* from 2020, crypto experts from NIST judged the security levels of RSA as listed in Table 2-1.

Table 2-1: Security Estimation of RSA

Security level	Key size
$\leq$ 80-bit	1,024-bit
112-bit	2,048-bit
128-bit	3,072-bit
192-bit	7,680-bit
256-bit	15,360-bit

Two important properties are obvious. The required key sizes are much longer than the achieved security level. The relation between them isn't linear, but the security level rises significantly more slowly in comparison to the invested key bits. At the time of writing, 2,048-bit is a common setting, but for long-term usage, 4,096-bit RSA keys are recommended.

Real-World RSA Usage

The basic structure of RSA, however, is not perfectly suitable for practical encryption because attackers in possession of two ciphertexts would be able to create a new ciphertext that is the correct encryption of the multiplication of the two original plaintexts. The *Optimal Asymmetric Encryption Padding (OAEP)* scheme was developed to avoid this weakness. In connection with RSA, it's called *RSA-OAEP* or *RSAES-OAEP* and is specified in NIST's *Special Publication 800-56B*.

In a nutshell, OAEP uses a random string and two hash functions to process the plaintext, often a symmetric key, and generates a padded plaintext version that is subsequently used for RSA encryption. For decryption, the ciphertext is decrypted as in standard RSA, but then the initial message and random value have to be recovered by using the two hash functions mentioned before. Finally, the computation result has to be verified for its correct structure before you can use the plaintext.

A similar problem also exists for digital signatures with the basic RSA equations. Based on a valid signature for a specifically prepared message, attackers would be able to create a valid signature for a message of their choice. The *Probabilistic Signature Scheme (PSS)* defined as RSASSA-PSS (RSA Signature Scheme with Appendix) in RFC 3447 prevents such attacks.

PSS injects additional random padding into the input data of the signature scheme—namely, the hash value of the message to be signed. Again, two hash functions and a predefined encoding are necessary to generate a padded version of the message's hash. During verification, the intermediate values have to be restored and the padding has to be checked for correctness in order to validate a signature.

Diffie-Hellman Key Exchange

When only symmetric cryptography was available, people had to exchange keys over *secure channels*—in person, with sealed letters, or over an already protected communication line. The process was pretty inconvenient and had several practical pitfalls.

Luckily, in 1976, Whitfield Diffie and Martin Hellman published their idea on how to establish a *shared secret* between two parties that are able to communicate only over an *insecure channel*, which is now commonly known as the *Diffie-Hellman (DH) key exchange*. Instead of generating a key at a specific location and then applying a *key-transport* mechanism (for example, RSA encryption), DH creates the shared key by using a *key-agreement* protocol between two entities.

The Mathematical Beauty

The math behind DH is based on a group $\mathbb{Z}_p^*$, where all operations are performed modulo a prime p and the primitive element is denoted as g. Figure 2-14 illustrates the process of establishing a shared secret.

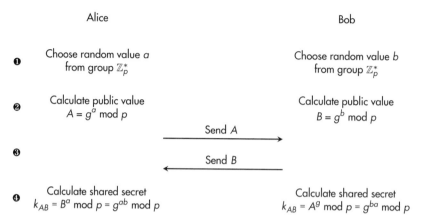

Figure 2-14: The steps in a Diffie-Hellman key exchange

First, both parties, commonly named Alice and Bob, choose secret numbers a and b, respectively ❶. Then, they derive the corresponding public values A and B ❷ and exchange them ❸. Afterward, they raise the public value of the other party to the power of their own private value ❹ to obtain the shared secret k_{AB}.

The security of DH relies on the *discrete logarithm problem (DLP)*: it's hard to obtain a from $A = g^a \bmod p$. Deriving the private number a from the publicly transferred value A clearly would break the security of this protocol. However, since that's practically impossible, attackers eavesdropping on the DH protocol don't receive any helpful information. The achieved security level in relation to DH key sizes is practically the same as for RSA.

Man-in-the-Middle Attacks

This basic version of DH is also called *anonymous Diffie-Hellman* because Alice and Bob can't verify each other's identity. This fact can be exploited by an adversary through a *man-in-the-middle (MITM)* attack: a malicious actor intercepts the communication between the original parties, drops their exchange of public values A and B, and instead performs one DH protocol run with Alice and one with Bob. In the end, Alice and Bob think that their key agreement was successful and they can communicate securely. However, they now both share a key with the attacker, who is able to read and manipulate all information flowing between them.

The solution to this problem is the introduction of *authenticated Diffie-Hellman*, which is based on the assumption that Alice and Bob each have a long-term public-key pair they can use to prove their identities to each other by exchanging digitally signed values of *A* and *B*. In this case, an MITM attacker would be unable to slip in between without being noticed. In variations of this approach, other protocol data is signed and verified, but it's always essential to authenticate the other party before computing and using the shared secret.

A second property of DH is that you shouldn't regard the values *a* and *b* as long-term keys. Reusing them for multiple key-agreement runs violates the common requirement of *perfect forward secrecy (PFS)*. This means that session keys established during a key exchange should still be secure, even if long-term keys are compromised in the future. You should consider the private numbers *a* and *b* to be *ephemeral keys* and use them only once. The corresponding version of DH is often called *Diffie-Hellman Ephemeral (DHE)*.

You can find details on Diffie-Hellman variants and other key-agreement schemes in NIST's *Special Publication 800-56A*.

Elliptic-Curve Cryptography

RSA and DH provide many meaningful mechanisms for asymmetric cryptography, but they come with two strong downsides: long keys and significant performance demand. The field of *elliptic-curve cryptography (ECC)*, founded in 1985, promised to provide asymmetric cryptography with noticeably reduced drawbacks.

However, about 20 years passed before it was widely used in practice. The math behind ECC is rather complex compared to RSA and DH, and the adoption of ECC was impeded by the Certicom company, which held a series of patents that had to be licensed in case of ECC usage. Luckily, most of those patents have expired by now.

The Math Behind the Curves

In a nutshell, *elliptic curves* are considered to be a group of points with x- and y-coordinates—for example, denoted as $P(x, y)$. The values of x and y are integers of a group modulo a prime p, often denoted as $GF(p)$, a *Galois field*. The equation of an elliptic curve describes all the points that are part of it.

In cryptography, only a few curve equations are of practical relevance. The following is used for *Weierstrass curves* like P-256 standardized by NIST and has parameters *a* and *b*:

$$x^2 = x^3 + ax + b$$

Montgomery curves use parameters *A* and *B*, and they're especially known because of the prominent member Curve25519. The following equation describes them:

$$By^2 = x^3 + Ax^2 + x$$

Edwards curves, with their parameter *d*, are another interesting type of curve, and Ed448-Goldilocks is based on it. Here's the general equation for these curves:

$$x^2 + y^2 = 1 + dx^2y^2$$

You can process points on elliptic curves in three ways:

Point addition   Add two points *P* and *Q* to obtain a new point *R* on the same curve: $R = P + Q$.

Point doubling   Multiply a given point *P* by 2 to obtain a new point *R*: $R = 2P$.

Scalar multiplication   Take a point *P* and multiply it with an integer (scalar) *k* to yield a new curve point *R*: $R = kP$.

The scalar multiplication in ECC is similar to the modular exponentiation for RSA. Also, the naive approach to scalar multiplication, which means adding a point *k* − 1 times, is infeasible for *k* being a large number with hundreds of bits. Therefore, a similar algorithm to square-and-multiply, namely *double-and-add*, has to be used to compute it efficiently. Putting it simply, *k* is processed bit by bit, and for every bit position, a point doubling is performed. If a bit is 1, an extra point addition is executed. Altogether, this enables the practical usage of ECC crypto primitives.

Elliptic curves are designed in a way that the *elliptic-curve discrete logarithm problem (ECDLP)* is difficult. The name suggests that it's similar to the DLP that's the foundation of DH, and it is. However, in the ECC world, you can describe the problem as finding the scalar *k* given points *P* and $R = kP$. Table 2-2, derived from NIST's *Special Publication 800-57* from 2022, shows the striking difference of the ECDLP compared to the underlying problems of RSA and DH.

Table 2-2: Security Estimation of ECC

Security level	Key size	Key size of RSA/DH (for comparison)
≤ 80-bit	160-bit	1,024-bit
112-bit	224-bit	2,048-bit
128-bit	256-bit	3,072-bit
192-bit	384-bit	7,680-bit
256-bit	512-bit	15,360-bit

ECC achieves the same security level with much lower key sizes. Additionally, with increasing key lengths, the corresponding security level rises *linearly*, so doubling the curve size from 256-bit to 512-bit also leads to twice the security level.

The Agony of Choice

In contrast to many other cryptographic algorithms, ECC requires an implementer to choose not only a key size but also a specific elliptic curve to be used. Certain mathematical requirements have to be fulfilled by "safe" curves, which is why it's reasonable to choose one from the common, standardized options that have undergone rigorous analysis.

On the other hand, a criterion that you can consider in the selection process is the origin of the curve parameters. Although the US National Security Agency (NSA) created the prime curve P-256, and the NIST standardized it in 2000, it's one of the most popular curves in practice. Its parameter b is a 256-bit number, and only the NSA knows how and why it was chosen. The same is true for the other NIST curves: P-192, P-224, P-384, and P-521. It might not be a critical issue, but maybe a relevant one, for devices operating in critical infrastructures.

Curve25519 is currently the most popular and most trustworthy elliptic curve. It was proposed by Bernstein in 2006 and is prominent because of two properties. First, it has a strong focus on high performance in software implementations. Second, it doesn't rely on randomly chosen or obscure curve parameters. In the future, Edwards curves like Ed448-Goldilocks and Curve41417 also might be of interest because they offer a security level above 200-bit.

Practical Applications of ECC

One of the most common applications of ECC is a digital signature based on the *Elliptic-Curve Digital Signature Algorithm (ECDSA)* as defined in *FIPS 186-5*. The basic setting for this use case is that two parties have agreed on a specific curve and its parameters. The signing entity holds the private key d, a secret integer, and the verifier has access to the corresponding public key $P = dG$, where G is the base point of the selected curve.

For signature generation, the signer hashes the message, chooses a random ephemeral key, and processes both together to obtain a unique signature consisting of two values with a total size of twice the curve order—for example, 512 bits, or 64 bytes, for a 256-bit curve. (The details of the verification process are rather complex and beyond the scope of this book.)

In general, ECDSA signatures are preferable to RSA signatures for performance and security reasons, except for a single case: if the signature verification has the highest priority, and signature generation happens only rarely—for example, when signing a firmware image once in the development process—and verification is time-critical because it happens during the device's boot process.

Besides digital signatures, ECC is an inherent part of modern key-exchange and key-agreement schemes as described in NIST's *Special Publication 800-56A*. They're also known as *Elliptic-Curve Diffie-Hellman (ECDH)* and *Elliptic-Curve Diffie-Hellman Ephemeral (ECDHE)*. There, the modular exponentiation of DH is replaced by a scalar multiplication based on an elliptic curve. The rest is pretty similar to DH. Again, this leads to a significant performance gain compared to classical DH, which is especially interesting when you need to perform a high number of key-agreement handshakes regularly, such as a server handling lots of connections.

Last but not least, you can use ECC for public-key encryption, but it's rarely used in practice. The *Elliptic-Curve Integrated Encryption Scheme (ECIES)* is meant for exactly that purpose. In a nutshell, it uses a recipient's public key to generate a shared ECDH secret and derives a symmetric key from it. This key is then used to encrypt a message by an AE cipher, producing a ciphertext and an authentication tag.

Summary

This chapter started off with crypto fundamentals like Kerckhoffs's principle that a cryptographic key should be the only secret in a cryptosystem, followed by a discussion that security levels are merely a description of the potential search space an attacker has to face.

I covered the area of symmetric encryption based on the popular AES algorithm and common operation modes in detail because it's omnipresent in security. Hash functions like SHA-256, integrity-protecting MAC algorithms, and efficient AE schemes like AES-GCM complete the modern toolbox of symmetric cryptography.

The introduction of asymmetric cryptography based on RSA and DH has enabled amazing possibilities to protect communication and devices: public-key encryption, digital signatures, and secure key agreements over insecure channels. Further, the field of ECC has enhanced the performance of these mechanisms significantly.

Post-quantum cryptography goes beyond the scope of this book, but it might be a topic that will challenge existing asymmetric crypto schemes in the future, and it will be inevitable if a universal quantum computer is built. NIST's standardization process for post-quantum cryptography (*https://csrc.nist.gov/projects/post-quantum-cryptography*) is still ongoing but worth following.

If you're interested in learning more about the inner workings of cryptography, Jean-Philippe Aumasson's *Serious Cryptography* (No Starch Press, 2017; second edition forthcoming) and *Understanding Cryptography* by Christof Paar and Jan Pelzl (Springer, 2009) are good resources.

PART II

DEVICE SECURITY
BUILDING BLOCKS

If you want to engineer a car, you obviously need an engine and body, some tires and seats, and probably at least one window. If you set your sights on engineering a secure device, you also want to have some essential building blocks.

Modern security would not be possible without a reliable source of random numbers and cryptographic operations that are optimized for the processors of your choice. Further, since many crypto algorithms rely on secrets, a decent storage option for this confidential data is required. Last but not least, unique and secure device identities in combination with secure communication channels are mandatory for every connected device. Since the devil is in the details for all these topics, this second part of the book dedicates one chapter to each of them.

3

RANDOM NUMBER GENERATORS

Randomness is the natural counterpart of determinism. While we want most device functionalities to follow the latter, *random number generators (RNGs)* are meant to extract the former. But is it even possible to yield random numbers within an integrated circuit (IC)? And if so, can we even describe "good" randomness with practical requirements?

Some people argue that true randomness is present only in quantum-mechanical processes (and they might be right), but quantum experiments are usually hard to carry out within a standard complementary metal–oxide semiconductor (CMOS) chip. On the other hand, many security applications absolutely require a source of random numbers to reach their intended protection level.

This chapter starts with applications that demand randomness in order to be regarded as secure. It introduces a common way to extract randomness within a microchip and the idea behind *true randomness*. Additionally, I explain the concept of *pseudorandomness* and why it's necessary for practical scenarios. Finally, I provide three simple tools you can use to evaluate sets of random numbers in order to find possible implementation flaws.

The Need for Randomness

Many security concepts rely on randomness. For example, when secrets like passwords, cryptographic keys, or unique tokens are generated, they serve as confidential data that is available only to a specific entity. Naturally, the result of this generation process has to be completely unpredictable. Otherwise, the search space for that secret would be narrowed, reducing the security level and making attacks more efficient, as discussed in Chapter 2.

Challenge-response authentication, which is part of many popular security protocols, is a second use case where randomness is essential. With this type of authentication, a verifier sends a random, unforeseeable challenge to the entity claiming a given identity to initiate the authentication process. This random value then must be processed with a unique secret to prove the claimed identity. However, if the challenge could be known in advance or possibly be recurring, the attacker would be able to prepare for this situation and acquire the expected response by other means.

Since secret keys and secure communication are essential for many IoT devices, the need for RNGs within these devices is pretty obvious. However, in most cases, a software solution can't solve this need, so it has to be integrated in the hardware, usually the main processor of a device or a dedicated security chip. Therefore, an RNG requirement should be part of every processor-purchasing process when aiming for device security.

NOTE *In practice, some software libraries, such as Mbed TLS, explicitly require you to define a source of randomness to be used for security operations. They won't work without it.*

The Nature of Randomness

Although randomness is a natural thing, it's quite difficult to describe. A simple explanation is that randomness is obtained from an experiment for which the outcome can't be predicted before it's executed, like a coin toss. Even if that experiment has been executed a million times, we wouldn't find any pattern or characteristic repetition in the results, and couldn't derive any certainty about the output other than by purely guessing.

The measure for this uncertainty and unpredictability is called *entropy*. It's also used in other disciplines like physics or information theory to describe the amount of disorder or information contained in a system or data. In the RNG context, entropy describes the number of bits that can be regarded as *truly* random. A bad RNG might produce only 2.4 bits of entropy per byte, which means that more than 5 bits of information about a single RNG output byte could be guessed with high certainty.

At this point, it's probably clear that we desire 8 bits of entropy per byte for a high-quality RNG. However, entropy itself or its absence is hard to measure, so RNG experts rely on statistical evaluations of preferably large amounts of collected random bits to identify flaws and assess their design optimizations. Two of these statistical requirements are independence and uniform distribution.

Independence means that every randomness-generating experiment should be separate from previously run experiments. Therefore, the value of output bits doesn't have a *conditional* probability of occurrence, so it doesn't have any relation to the output bits that have been extracted before. Figure 3-1 shows four binary datasets.

(a)   (b)   (c)   (d)

Figure 3-1: A 2D visualization of random bits possibly containing patterns

In Figures 3-1a and 3-1d, our brain will immediately detect patterns, which means the binary data repeats. These are clearly less random than the others. Looking closer, Figure 3-1c exhibits a subtle pattern, while Figure 3-1b doesn't show any visually detectable relation between the depicted bits.

We could also state that the requirement of a *uniform distribution* for random bits demands that the probability of every symbol an RNG can generate has to be equal. Figure 3-2 shows the random bits resulting from four symbol distributions.

(a)   (b)   (c)   (d)

Figure 3-2: A 2D visualization of random bits possibly containing a bias

With the naked eye, we can see that Figures 3-2b and 3-2c contain more white squares than black ones. Specifically, 70 percent of the area is white in Figure 3-2b, and 80 percent is white in Figure 3-2c. Distinguishing between Figures 3-2a and 3-2d is more difficult, but looking at the numbers, the situation becomes clear. Figure 3-2a has a black-white relation of 45 to 55, whereas Figure 3-2d is perfectly 50-50.

True Random Number Generators

The main task of a *true random number generator (TRNG)*, sometimes also called a *nondeterministic random bit generator (NRBG)*, is no less than the extraction of "true" randomness. We can implement an *entropy source* as described in NIST's *Special Publication 800-90B* that (at microscopic scale) performs experiments and outputs their results as random bits to achieve true randomness. Metaphorically, imagine a nanoscale person tossing a coin regularly and controlling transistors according to the results of heads or tails.

Physical sources for entropy could be a photon transmission upon a semi-transparent mirror, the observation of a radioactive atomic disintegration process, or even a wall of lava lamps (*https://blog.cloudflare.com/randomness -101-lavarand-in-production*). However, these ideas are all hard to implement in CMOS designs, which means chip manufacturers usually rely on physical effects related to thermal and electronic noise available in ICs.

Ring Oscillators

A common circuit to extract and accumulate such noise is a *ring oscillator (RO)*. It consists of an odd number of inverters that are connected in a ring-like structure. On power-up, the gates drive their outputs to the inverted level of their input signals. Figure 3-3 shows a three-inverter RO.

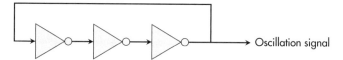

Figure 3-3: A basic RO circuit

Assuming the input of the leftmost inverter is *high*, its output will be *low*, the output of the second inverter will be *high*, and the last output signal *low* again. Feeding back the final output to the first input line results in a mismatch, which causes all inverters to change their outputs accordingly. As you probably noticed, this stable circuit will never settle but will oscillate at a certain frequency.

In a perfect world, the RO output signal would be absolutely deterministic, as would its oscillation frequency. However, in reality, the behavior depends on the physical characteristics of the implementation and the physical state it's in. Both lead to *jitter* in the RO signal, which, in turn, causes the frequency to vary, sometimes a bit higher, sometimes a bit lower. In short, the signal and its frequency are subject to noise. Although we are still able to partly predict the RO's behavior, some characteristics do originate from randomness. In many cases, this is the first step toward "true" randomness in microchips.

Since a single oscillator provides only "a little bit" of entropy, many oscillators usually are combined to create a TRNG. Figure 3-4 shows a simple way these oscillator signals could be sampled by flip-flops, be combined by an XOR operation, and then be sampled again to obtain a single random bit with high entropy.

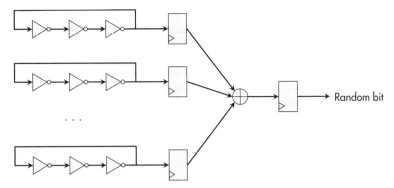

Figure 3-4: A basic TRNG architecture using multiple ROs

However, in commercial devices, we can hardly characterize any of these internal design decisions and the actual entropy of these circuits. We have to trust the chip manufacturer. The previous paragraphs are just meant to give you an idea of where that "true" randomness might come from.

The Health Status of Entropy Sources

The health status of the entropy source *should be available* to TRNG users because it's necessary to inform the system in case of a nonfunctional entropy source. Otherwise, the device might rely on random numbers that are effectively all zeros. For high-quality TRNGs, therefore, at least three test procedures monitor the correct functionality of their entropy source:

Startup test   Some entropy sources have to successfully run through an initialization phase in order to generate high-quality random bits. For example, for oscillator-based circuits, the intended oscillation must get going and not be stuck in a non-oscillating state. Therefore, TRNGs must implement a startup test that carefully monitors the startup phase of its entropy source and raises an error if it fails.

Total failure test   Environmental influences, such as changes in temperature, supply voltage, or intentional attacks, can lead to the sudden loss of the correct functionality of an entropy source. The total failure test watches the entropy source's output bits for such events and issues an alarm upon occurrence.

Online test   While the two previous tests monitor entropy sources for a complete outage, the online test continuously observes the distribution of the generated random bits to identify drifts and biases. If they exceed a certain limit, this might also be a reason to notify an OS or an application.

Although TRNGs are the only way to extract "true" randomness and are inevitable for secure devices, they also have disadvantages. They rely on physical processes that naturally depend on environmental circumstances that can cause changes in behavior or even errors. Also, extracting and collecting raw entropy bits takes time and usually doesn't fulfill high-performance demands. The next section introduces primitives that lack "true" randomness but perform much better.

Pseudorandom Number Generators

Pseudorandom number generators (PRNGs) are kind of the opposite of TRNGs and are also called *deterministic random bit generators (DRBGs)* because, in contrast to TRNGs, their behavior is completely deterministic and they don't contain an entropy source. Both characteristics are advantages of PRNGs because they make them reliable and robust against environmental impacts, while at the same time allowing for high-speed implementations.

Key requirements for PRNG algorithms are *backtracking resistance* and *prediction resistance*. Both assume that an attacker got access to the current state (output) of a PRNG. The former requirement then demands that the adversary is unable to derive any previous state value for this information, while the latter requires that the attacker is unable to predict future output values of the PRNG algorithm. These claims might remind you that hash functions are one-way functions or that block cipher encryptions can't be reversed without the corresponding key—and you'd be right. These algorithms are pretty suitable for the task at hand.

In *Special Publication 800-90A*, experts from NIST recommend three PRNG constructions. *Hash_DRBG* uses an approved hash function that's meant for the desired security level to process initial and intermediate state data to derive pseudorandom output bits and obtain subsequent states. *HMAC_DRBG* and *CTR_DRBG* use keyed hash functions and block ciphers in Counter mode, respectively, where the corresponding keys are not fixed but updated regularly as part of the PRNG operations.

Maybe you've heard about linear feedback shift registers (LFSRs) and Mersenne Twister PRNGs and wonder why they aren't recommended here although they are highly efficient. They do yield random *looking* sequences, but they're not cryptographically secure because their architecture relies only on linear combinations, which can't provide prediction resistance. To put it simply, any attacker who is able to observe a certain number of output values can derive future values.

NOTE   *You might stumble across* Dual_EC_DRBG, *a PRNG that was originally meant to be cryptographically secure. However, it contains a potential backdoor that might have been inserted deliberately. Choose your cryptographic primitives carefully!*

In addition to making a solid choice for a PRNG algorithm, *seeding* is one of the most important parts of PRNG usage. With seeding, a PRNG is initialized with data that has enough entropy to fulfill the desired security goal. For example, if a 128-bit security level is required, the PRNG has to be seeded with a bit string that has at least 128 bits of entropy. Also, this information has to be treated as confidential and may never be revealed to an attacker.

Optionally, we can implement regular *reseeding*, which means that the entropy pool of a PRNG instance is updated with "fresh" entropy. Further, we can individualize PRNG initialization by adding a unique value such as a device serial number, a nonce, or a timestamp. However, be careful, as this additional data is always considered as *having no entropy at all*, because it can be publicly available without compromising security.

Practical RNG Constructions and Usage

After reading the preceding chapter, you might have already guessed that you can achieve the best RNG solution for secure devices by combining TRNGs and PRNGs. The former extracts entropy continuously (and slowly), which is used for seeding and subsequently reseeding a PRNG that reliably provides almost arbitrary amounts of random bits to OSs and applications.

If your device runs an OS, chances are the OS developers already took care of the hard parts. But even if so, architects and developers still need to keep the following topics in mind.

RNG Selection

Even if an OS provides a strong RNG, not all frameworks and programming languages use it by default. Usually, it must be selected explicitly or the corresponding API has to be used in your code. Otherwise, you rely on non-cryptographic PRNGs that may break device security.

Error Handling

As mentioned earlier, TRNGs can fail. In addition, OS-provided RNGs might return errors, so make sure to take these return values seriously and handle them accordingly. The last thing you want is a device that works with supposedly random data that actually contains nothing but zeros without anybody noticing.

Boot-Time Entropy

Some procedures take place during the boot process or immediately afterward, such as Secure Shell (SSH) key generation at the initial device startup. However, at boot time, a device might not have collected a lot of entropy yet, or maybe none at all. In turn, this might lead to identical or at least similar secret keys on several devices, which is absolutely not desirable. Keep in mind that critical key-generation processes need to wait until a defined amount of entropy is available.

Case Study: Random Numbers from Hardware to Python

In this case study, I analyze the hardware RNG features of an STM32MP157F device, explain how the Linux RNG works, and point out why you still have to be careful to use the correct RNG in Python.

Hardware RNG and Entropy Source

Looking at ST's *Reference Manual RM0436* for STM32MP157F devices, a lot of information is available about the integrated RNG. At the beginning of the corresponding section, ST writes that the implemented RNG can be used as a basis for a NIST-compliant DRBG construction and that it was successfully tested with the AIS-32 test suite of the German Federal Office for Information Security (BSI).

WARNING *Be careful, as the implemented RNG itself is not equal to a NIST DRBG. A later part of the reference manual states that an approved PRNG must be added on top of this TRNG if a NIST-compliant DRBG with a 128-bit security level is required.*

Looking closer at the manual, you'll read that the implemented TRNG uses two analog noise sources, and that each contains three free-running ROs that are XORed to mix their outputs. The XOR result is then sampled by a dedicated clock signal and postprocessed to remove a possible bias of the raw bits. Further, a conditioning stage "increases the entropy rate," but that process isn't described in more detail. The final output contains 128 bits of random data that's provided to the 32-bit Advanced High-performance Bus (AHB) by a first-in, first-out (FIFO) buffer.

Regarding the continuous monitoring of the noise sources, ST has implemented a repetition count test. For example, an error is raised if a noise source outputs more than 64 bits with the same value or 32 repetitions of the same 2-bit pattern. A status register available over AHB shows the errors that occurred.

The good news at this point is that the selected microchip provides a hardware RNG. As usual, evaluating the quality of this module for users is difficult, but if we trust a manufacturer and its security competencies, this hardware RNG can be a valuable asset.

Hardware RNG Integration in Linux

In Linux, a hardware RNG can be integrated by the hw_random framework that consists of a hardware-specific driver and a generic kernel interface creating the corresponding */dev/hwrng* device. If CONFIG_HW_RANDOM is enabled in the Linux kernel configuration and the vendor-provided driver works correctly, you can check the availability and selection of your hardware RNG, as shown for my STM32MP157F device in Listing 3-1.

```
# cat /sys/class/misc/hw_random/rng_available
optee-rng
# cat /sys/class/misc/hw_random/rng_current
optee-rng
```

Listing 3-1: Checking hardware RNG availability

Further, if rng-tools is installed on your Linux system, you can run statistical tests on the integrated hardware RNG as shown in Listing 3-2.

```
# rngtest -c 1000 < /dev/hwrng
rngtest 6.15
...
rngtest: starting FIPS tests...
rngtest: bits received from input: 20000032
rngtest: FIPS 140-2 successes: 999
rngtest: FIPS 140-2 failures: 1
rngtest: FIPS 140-2(2001-10-10) Monobit: 0
rngtest: FIPS 140-2(2001-10-10) Poker: 0
rngtest: FIPS 140-2(2001-10-10) Runs: 0
rngtest: FIPS 140-2(2001-10-10) Long run: 1
rngtest: FIPS 140-2(2001-10-10) Continuous run: 0
rngtest: input channel speed: (min=117.995; avg=137.966; max=149.035)Kibits/s
rngtest: FIPS tests speed: (min=14.638; avg=28.942; max=29.434)Mibits/s
rngtest: Program run time: 142228806 microseconds
```

Listing 3-2: Running statistical tests on data from an RNG hardware device

The tests originate from NIST's *FIPS 140-2* cryptographic requirements document. The mathematical details aren't relevant here, and a small number of failures are nothing to worry about. Notice that this hardware RNG source supplies random numbers at a rate of around 138Kb per second.

Linux RNG Architecture

Like any other major OS, Linux has its own RNG concept and PRNG implementation. It was first introduced in 1994 and, back then, its architecture was based on SHA-1 operations because strong encryption algorithms were part of US export restrictions.

However, since version 5.17 of the Linux kernel, SHA-1 was completely removed from the code. PRNG instances now rely on the ChaCha20 cipher, while the compression function of the *entropy pool* is implemented as the hash-update operation of *BLAKE2s*, a hash function also based on ChaCha. Version 5.18 introduced various additional improvements for the Linux RNG (for example, regarding boot-time entropy).

The entropy pool is an internal 256-bit memory buffer that collects data from a set of noise sources and is used to feed the base instance of a ChaCha20 PRNG. If a hardware RNG is available on the given platform, as we've seen for the STM32MP157F device, its provided entropy can be integrated into the entropy pool by the add_hwgenerator_randomness interface. Its entropy content estimation depends on the entropy quality value provided in its driver code. For my device, that value is given as 900, which means that each RNG bit delivers an entropy of around $900/1,024 = 0.879$ bits.

Further noise sources may contribute to entropy collection. If spinning hard disks or similar block devices are available in your system, add_disk_randomness might positively add to your entropy pool. However, since my STM32MP157F-DK2 board runs on a microSD card, this mechanism doesn't contribute anything. Further, key presses and mouse movements can be used to extract a certain amount of noise and enhance the internal pool by add_input_randomness, but user interaction is usually rare in embedded system usage. Also, device drivers can provide random data possibly available during device initialization to add_device_randomness in order to integrate it into the entropy pool. However, it's treated as having zero entropy by default.

The proc filesystem provides information about the instantiated entropy pool, like its size and current entropy estimation level in bits, as shown in Listing 3-3.

```
# cat /proc/sys/kernel/random/poolsize
256
# cat /proc/sys/kernel/random/entropy_avail
256
```

Listing 3-3: Printing entropy pool information

Keep in mind that older Linux systems are based on another RNG architecture that would show a pool size of 4,096 bits instead of 256 at this point.

In the same path, the file *bootid* provides a unique, random identification number for the current runtime, as demonstrated in Listing 3-4. It changes for the next boot.

```
# cat /proc/sys/kernel/random/boot_id
e67a7d3e-3825-4019-ad86-940a7c8748df
```

Listing 3-4: Showing the boot identification number

In contrast, Listing 3-5 shows that reading *uuid* yields a new *universally unique identifier (UUID)* for each access.

```
# cat /proc/sys/kernel/random/uuid
703a31fe-fd53-44d4-8a85-075416a107ea
# cat /proc/sys/kernel/random/uuid
10f38bb8-66a8-4951-b9b4-db89db438ba8
# cat /proc/sys/kernel/random/uuid
6abf0dd4-2d0b-421b-b04e-8f02f994149b
```

Listing 3-5: Reading UUIDs from the Linux RNG

From user space, random numbers can be retrieved in multiple ways:

Reading from */dev/random*   The behavior of the device file */dev/random* is *blocking*. That means if the ChaCha20 PRNG didn't receive 256 bits of entropy yet, it won't return any data.

Reading from */dev/urandom*   The *nonblocking* nature of */dev/urandom* allows random numbers to be read from this device no matter the status of the initial entropy collection, making it a popular choice for developers.

Using the `getrandom` system call   This system call can be parameterized to define its behavior. With its flag set to zero, it behaves like */dev/random*, but if the flag is set to `GRND_INSECURE`, it returns random numbers just as */dev/urandom* does.

In kernel space, the get_random_bytes function can be used to access a PRNG instance and get random numbers from it. This function doesn't depend on the status of the ChaCha20 PRNG seeding and the entropy pool.

A simple one-liner to write 1MB of random data into a file is shown in Listing 3-6.

```
# dd if=/dev/urandom of=rand_file.bin bs=1M count=1 iflag=fullblock
1+0 records in
1+0 records out
1048576 bytes (1.0 MB, 1.0 MiB) copied, 0.0638873 s, 16.4 MB/s
# ls -l rand_file.bin
-rw-r--r-- 1 root root 1048576 ... rand_file.bin
```

Listing 3-6: Generating a file that contains 1,048,576 random bytes

Calling rngtest with */dev/urandom* as shown in Listing 3-7 practically demonstrates the advantage of combining a hardware random source with a reliable software PRNG.

```
# rngtest -c 1000 < /dev/urandom
rngtest 6.15
...
rngtest: starting FIPS tests...
rngtest: bits received from input: 20000032
rngtest: FIPS 140-2 successes: 999
rngtest: FIPS 140-2 failures: 1
rngtest: FIPS 140-2(2001-10-10) Monobit: 0
rngtest: FIPS 140-2(2001-10-10) Poker: 0
rngtest: FIPS 140-2(2001-10-10) Runs: 0
rngtest: FIPS 140-2(2001-10-10) Long run: 1
rngtest: FIPS 140-2(2001-10-10) Continuous run: 0
rngtest: input channel speed: (min=85.917; avg=185.867; max=190.735)Mibits/s
rngtest: FIPS tests speed: (min=12.203; avg=28.918; max=29.756)Mibits/s
rngtest: Program run time: 763735 microseconds
```

Listing 3-7: Running RNG tests on /dev/urandom

The statistics are still fine, but the speed is increased to around 186Mbps. That's a factor of more than 1,000 compared to the raw hardware RNG.

Cryptographically Secure Random Numbers in Python

Even though we have a device that comes with a hardware RNG that was properly integrated into Linux, and the Linux RNG is behaving correctly, we still can fail at cryptographically secure random number generation on the application level. In this case study, we take a look at Python, but the same is true for many other programming languages and environments.

Python tutorials usually name the random module for random number generation. However, its documentation clearly points out that this is a PRNG based on the Mersenne Twister algorithm that's meant, for example, for modeling and simulation purposes, but isn't suitable for cryptographic usage.

To use the OS-provided RNG, the os module provides the os.urandom() function. However, the recommended way in Python 3.6 or newer is to use the secrets module that's meant specifically for extracting cryptographically secure random numbers and that chooses the most secure randomness source on your system.

Listing 3-8 shows a script that takes a number of bytes and a filename from the command line arguments, generates the respective number of random bytes by using the token_bytes() function of the secrets module, and writes them to the given output file.

```
import sys
import secrets

n_bytes = int(sys.argv[1])
output_file = sys.argv[2]

print('Generating', str(n_bytes), 'random bytes ...')
random_bytes = secrets.token_bytes(n_bytes)

print('Writing random bytes to', output_file, '...')
with open(output_file, "wb") as f:
  f.write(random_bytes)
```

Listing 3-8: Using Python's secrets module to create a file with random bytes

Finally, this case study demonstrated the variety of layers in hardware and software to consider when generating random numbers for cryptographic purposes.

Case Study: Practical Tools for a Randomness Quick Check

If you're in charge of developing and testing a new RNG design, you'll want to use a variety of statistical analysis algorithms as described in NIST's *Special Publication 800-22* or provided by the Dieharder suite, but only very few people on this planet actually design new RNGs.

However, many people *use and process* random numbers, which can lead to practical implementation mistakes, especially on the application level. Some of these mistakes can be found by applying relatively simple tools. This case study explains two such approaches and demonstrates how to discover common problems with them.

Simple Tools for Distribution Analysis and Pattern Recognition

At the beginning of this chapter, we saw that bias (or a nonuniform distribution of any kind) and recurring patterns are two indicators of low-quality random numbers. This section describes a simple means to analyze basic data features, but they are far from professional statistical analysis. They serve a sole purpose: getting hints that something is wrong in the random number generation process, most probably in the last stage (namely, in an application).

Listing 3-9 shows a short script that takes a file as a command line argument, reads it, and plots a histogram showing the frequency of occurrence for all possible byte values. In the perfect case, the histogram should show a flat line, which means that all bytes are equally likely to occur within the file.

```
import sys
import matplotlib.pyplot as plt

file_to_analyze = sys.argv[1]

print('Reading', file_to_analyze, '...')
with open(file_to_analyze, "rb") as f:
  data = f.read()

hist_data = bytearray(data)

print('Plotting distribution of bytes ...')
fig1, ax1 = plt.subplots(figsize=(15, 5))
ax1.hist(hist_data, bins=range(256+1), align='left', color = "gray")
ax1.set_title('Distribution of Bytes')
ax1.set_xlabel('byte value')
ax1.set_xticks([0, 32, 64, 96, 128, 160, 192, 224, 256])
ax1.set_ylabel('frequency of occurrence')
plt.show()
```

Listing 3-9: A Python script to plot the distribution of bytes for a given file

For illustration, I generated a file with 1MB of random data by using the Linux RNG and ran the script on it. Figure 3-5 shows the corresponding distribution. It's not a flat line, but the frequencies are pretty close to one another.

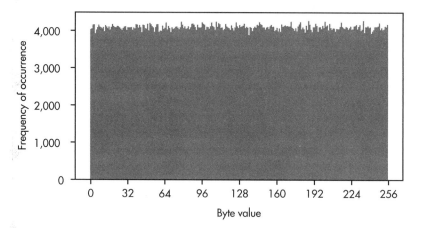

Figure 3-5: The distribution of byte values from the Linux RNG

Pattern detection is a bit more complicated than bias analysis because patterns can be of various types. However, some applications are optimized for exactly that task: compression tools. These algorithms run through data and try to find repeating sequences, build up dictionaries, and remove redundancy. Applied to random data, every success in compression means that the dataset has entropy deficiencies. Although compression tools don't tell us what the problem is, they can clearly state that the information content of a file is less than expected from random data.

Listing 3-10 shows a simple script to invoke the common Linux compression tools bzip2, gzip, and xz on a file presumably containing random data.

```
import sys
import subprocess
import os

file_to_analyze = sys.argv[1]

print('Compressing', file_to_analyze, '...')
run = subprocess.run('bzip2 -k ' + file_to_analyze, shell=True)
run = subprocess.run('gzip -k ' + file_to_analyze, shell=True)
run = subprocess.run('xz -k ' + file_to_analyze, shell=True)

print('Compression test results:')
print('{:<28}'.format(file_to_analyze),            '-->',
    '{:>9}'.format(os.path.getsize(file_to_analyze)), 'bytes')
print('{:<28}'.format(file_to_analyze + '.bz2'), '-->',
    '{:>9}'.format(os.path.getsize(file_to_analyze + '.bz2')), 'bytes')
```

```
print('{:<28}'.format(file_to_analyze + '.gz'), '-->',
    '{:>9}'.format(os.path.getsize(file_to_analyze + '.gz')), 'bytes')
print('{:<28}'.format(file_to_analyze + '.xz'), '-->',
    '{:>9}'.format(os.path.getsize(file_to_analyze + '.xz')), 'bytes')
print('')
```

Listing 3-10: A Python script to test random data with typical compression tools

Again, 1MB of data from the Linux RNG serves as a positive example here. As shown in Listing 3-11, all the compression tools yield larger files than the original one. This is expected because the content can't be compressed and, at the same time, header information for the used compression format is added to the files.

```
data_urandom.rnd            -->    1048576 bytes
data_urandom.rnd.bz2        -->    1053538 bytes
data_urandom.rnd.gz         -->    1048771 bytes
data_urandom.rnd.xz         -->    1048688 bytes
```

Listing 3-11: The results of a compression test on the Linux RNG

Problem 1: Output Space Restriction by Modulo

In some cases, restricting the output space of a random variable is needed—for example, to the range of 0 to 99—because that range is required for a given application. A trivial approach to limit the results of an integer operation is to use the modulo operator. To obtain an integer from 0 to 99, we could just compute all random numbers modulo 100.

To test that case, I added that operation to the Python example from Listing 3-8. Figure 3-6 shows the resulting distribution of bytes.

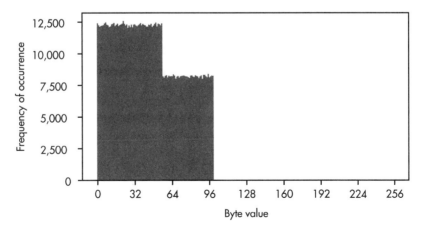

Figure 3-6: The distribution of bytes when restricting with a modulo operation

While we would expect a drop to 0 at byte values 100 or higher, a strange drop in probability occurs at value 56. However, that means the given application would generate values from 0 to 55 with *significantly higher probability*. This is unacceptable from a security point of view.

For Python, a robust solution would be to use the randbelow() function from the secrets module to obtain uniformly distributed and cryptographically secure random numbers within a certain integer range.

Problem 2: Custom PRNG Designs

Sometimes we have to rely on applications that are black boxes. We can't assess the internals of the software, let alone the quality of random number handling. However, it might well be the case that an application instantiates its own PRNG, probably for performance reasons or for ease of use. Maybe it's even seeded by a strong OS-provided RNG. However, if the custom PRNG exhibits a weak design, security problems might result.

For this test case, I implemented a weak PRNG on purpose. It's more or less a modified 16-bit counter, seeded by the Linux RNG. It's not very reasonable but also not completely unrealistic; developers can be creative. As in the first case, I extracted 1MB of test data from this PRNG instance and plotted its distribution of bytes as shown in Figure 3-7. It shows a perfect distribution. Although that could already be suspicious, it doesn't directly indicate a weakness.

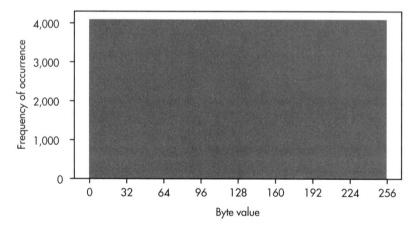

Figure 3-7: The distribution of bytes from a custom PRNG

However, after applying the compression tests explained previously, it becomes clear that something must be wrong. Listing 3-12 shows the output.

```
data_custom_prng.rnd        -->     1048576 bytes
data_custom_prng.rnd.bz2    -->       86756 bytes
data_custom_prng.rnd.gz     -->      997143 bytes
data_custom_prng.rnd.xz     -->       84648 bytes
```

Listing 3-12: The results of a compression test on data from a custom PRNG

Two of three compression tools reduced the file size by a factor of more than 12. This change is significant. It still doesn't tell us what exactly is wrong with the application at hand, but it calls for a discussion with its developers.

Summary

Randomness is a tricky beast. However, after reading this chapter, it should be clear that randomness is absolutely necessary for security and that it deserves careful consideration regarding the involved hardware and software components.

I explained some of the basics of entropy sources in CMOS microchips and how they create "true" randomness from noise—for example, the noise present in oscillation circuits. Further, I discussed the need for PRNGs and their beneficial properties like reliable behavior and high-speed data delivery. Both TRNGs and PRNGs are relevant and should be implemented in combination to build a secure and reliable RNG for embedded systems.

In the first case study, I walked through the layers of randomness in a real-world system—starting from the integrated physical noise sources in STM32MP157F devices to their integration in the Linux kernel to the complex architecture of the Linux RNG itself. Finally, I added that even on the application level, incorrect handling of RNGs and their data can lead to weaknesses. If you are interested in the details of Linux RNGs and their evolution over time, refer to the regular Linux RNG analysis documents from the German BSI.

Simple and pragmatic tools for identifying some problems with RNGs and their output data, especially in third-party software, concluded this chapter in a second case study.

4

CRYPTOGRAPHIC IMPLEMENTATIONS

In Chapter 2, I gave an overview of cryptographic algorithms, their parameters, and typical use cases. However, a mathematical algorithm is still a long way from the secure and efficient *implementations* of cryptography.

In the majority of applications, cryptography doesn't play a leading role. It's more like a necessary evil to protect device and business assets. Therefore, developers and product managers would love to have cryptographic implementations that run in no time, occupy no memory, and consume no energy. Of course, that's not possible, but it's a significant discussion point in many cases. Inefficient implementations might even lead to the elimination of security features, lower product quality, or at the very least, annoyed comments from colleagues who aren't focused on security.

In this chapter, I'll discuss the requirements for cryptographic implementations and selection options for developers. The following sections introduce examples of algorithmic optimizations for symmetric and asymmetric crypto. The final case study analyzes and discusses performance characteristics of crypto implementations in hardware and software on an STM32MP157F device.

Implementation Context and Requirements

Developers choose the central microchip early in the product design and architecture development phases because many further decisions depend on it. The microchip might be a single-core microcontroller, a homogeneous or heterogeneous multicore system, a field-programmable gate array (FPGA), or even a system-on-chip (SoC) that combines processors, peripherals, and possibly FPGAs within a single package.

If a typical processor is selected, several parameters influence general performance, including crypto performance. These parameters start with the *instruction set architecture*, or *ISA* (for example, ARM, RISC-V, or MIPS), and the data width (8-bit, 16-bit, 32-bit, 64-bit, or even more). The number of cores and their maximum frequencies are also of significant relevance. Specifically for cryptographic operations, it's interesting to see whether dedicated crypto instructions are available, like Intel's AES New Instructions (AES-NI) extension, or whether the given chip comes with a crypto coprocessor.

In systems intended for industrial, automotive, or datacenter applications, considering microchips that include an FPGA part might be interesting as a way of benefitting from the high-performance properties or the real-time guarantees digital hardware designs can provide. Besides the maximum supported frequency, FPGAs have specific characteristics like the number of lookup tables, flip-flops, blocks of random access memory (RAM), multipliers, and similar options that might set the limits for cryptographic implementations.

No matter which type of processing unit you choose, it requires internal and/or external memory. Usually, both volatile memory like RAM and nonvolatile memory like flash memory, memory cards, or solid-state drives (SSDs) are necessary. Besides their size, which affects cryptographic implementations on only very resource-constrained devices, their read and write speeds might influence the overall performance of a crypto application.

Last but not least, the transmission speed of wired and wireless interfaces of the device (for example, Wi-Fi, Bluetooth, Ethernet, and proprietary buses) limits the bandwidth for communication, including cryptographically protected channels.

NOTE *Sometimes in practice, the device and hardware architecture is already more or less fixed when cryptographic performance is discussed, and you have to make the best of it. However, don't shy away from contributing crypto performance requirements at an early stage. For example, if your intended application requires thousands of signatures per second, that requirement definitely must be considered for hardware selection.*

Looking at this problem from the application side, you might impose several types of requirements on crypto implementations. While *latency* describes the time of processing a single data block from input to output, *throughput* defines the amount of data that can be processed in a given time.

For software implementations on resource-constrained devices, it might be necessary to limit the static code size of the compiled binary that has to be stored in volatile and/or nonvolatile memory. Further, the dynamic memory usage during runtime can be a relevant factor. On the other hand, FPGA implementations have to statically instantiate digital components, which is why, in addition to performance, the efficiency of digital hardware designs for crypto are usually compared by the number of occupied FPGA resources.

As several IoT devices are battery-powered and some even rely on energy harvesting, the energy consumption of cryptographic implementations also can be a valid requirement.

All information about the implementation context of a device is relevant for solid and efficient crypto decisions. And in some cases, finding reasonable compromises between resource consumption and security might be necessary.

Selecting Crypto Implementations

We've seen many implementation issues over the past decades that have led to vulnerabilities. If you don't want to have such valuable but exhausting experiences yourself, take a look at existing optimized and mature cryptographic libraries like OpenSSL, LibreTLS, Mbed TLS, and wolfSSL, just to name a few from the embedded system area.

However, this issue leads us to a question many developers face during development: How do you choose a specific crypto library for a device or an application? The decision depends to a large extent on your specific requirements, if already explicitly stated, and the frameworks and programming languages you work with. The following list describes four typical situations:

Freedom to choose   Sometimes only the intended protection aim is stipulated—for example, that communication should be protected by authenticated encryption, without further details. This might be the case for a company-internal feature that has no external dependencies. In such situations, several cryptographic algorithms could be considered. For example, both AES-GCM and ChaCha20-Poly1305 might be suitable options. Performance evaluation on the target device makes sense in this scenario. Test both algorithms with a set of parameters and various crypto libraries to obtain a preferably efficient solution.

Strong performance requirements   In some cases, cryptography is essential and has to fulfill high demands regarding performance—for example, if an application requires thousands of digital signatures per second. Since ECDSA is faster in signature generation than RSA, the algorithm should probably be ECC based. However, you still have to choose the type of curve. Testing a set of curves from available crypto libraries on the given hardware is the way to go when choosing the best-performing configuration. If your requirements can't be reached, replacing the hardware or implementing a custom, optimized solution might be options.

Strong resource constraints   Devices based on small microcontrollers are present in a large part of the IoT. However, those components usually exhibit significantly weaker performance characteristics compared to Linux-based devices. Although much state-of-the-art cryptography can be run on these processors, requirements regarding latency, throughput, number of connections to serve, and many more have to be selected carefully. Practical evaluations on the target hardware are essential.

Fixed algorithm and security level   If algorithm and key size are fixed in advance (for example, because of compatibility concerns), the scope is significantly reduced. However, if the specific implementation is not fixed, a quick performance comparison between libraries might still be valuable and unlock performance potential.

Even though this chapter has a strong focus on performance, latency and throughput are by far not the only quality characteristics to consider for cryptographic implementations. Especially for security applications, the following two properties can make a significant difference, even if they result in lower performance:

Transparency and clarity   Readable, comprehensible, and documented code is wonderful. It reduces mistakes, assumptions, and misconceptions. Further, those properties lead to trustworthiness for the developers and their products. That is even truer for cryptographic implementations. Spaghetti code, optimization to the utmost degree that makes the code completely incomprehensible, and torn structures can be reasons to neglect implementations despite their outstanding performance.

Support and maintenance   Open source software has enabled the development of incredible projects. However, some projects are not well-documented nor supported. If vulnerabilities are found and reported, there might not be anyone to fix them right away. Of course, the same can be true for commercial and closed source software. The point is, you need to pay attention to how a specific library was maintained in the past and to any warning signs that might indicate loss of maintenance in the near future, especially for cryptographic libraries.

WARNING   *Do not develop your own crypto implementations unless you have very good reasons to do so!*

Whatever crypto algorithm you select, issues might arise someday in the future because of quantum computing or new cryptanalytic successes. Therefore, it makes sense to follow the approach of *crypto agility*, which means that algorithms (for example, a block cipher) can easily be replaced by another one of the same type.

AES Implementation Options

In this section, I want to shed light on options to consider if you have to configure or analyze an AES implementation. AES is used as an example here, but since many other symmetric ciphers and hash functions also exhibit a round-based structure and similar operations, you might be able to translate these insights to other algorithms.

Basic Architecture

A fundamental consideration is the operation width of processed data. In optimal software implementations, the width is chosen to utilize the data width of the underlying hardware. However, a mismatch can lead to issues. For instance, 8-bit implementations on 32-bit central processing units (CPUs) lack performance, and 32-bit implementations on 8-bit CPUs might not compile or lead to inefficient transformations.

In FPGA implementations, the operation width of an implementation can be arbitrarily selected. If slower performance is acceptable and the focus is on using few resources, an 8-bit implementation is suitable. On the other hand, if high performance is required, we would probably like to operate at a 128-bit data width. If a *balanced* implementation (one with a reasonable trade-off between required resources and performance) is desired, a 32-bit architecture can be a solid choice.

AES needs to expand a given key to a set of round keys. This key expansion can be performed once in the beginning to improve performance during bulk data encryption and decryption. However, the second option is to perform it on the fly, just before the corresponding round key is needed for operations. Advantages in dynamic memory consumption are gained because only a single round key has to be stored in memory instead of all round keys.

For round-based algorithms like AES, implementing a loop structure to run through the necessary rounds seems natural. However, continuously handling and checking a loop variable reduces the maximum performance. Even if a comparison and a conditional branch don't take seconds, they will impair overall throughput. The term *loop unrolling* describes an approach you might find in high-speed implementations: a loop is replaced by a sequence of code representing all AES rounds in order to achieve a performance boost at the expense of a larger binary size.

Optimized Operations

The AES S-box is usually represented as a table that is meant to perform a nonlinear substitution. Therefore, it's often implemented as a constant lookup table in software implementations. However, it isn't the only option. If static tables don't fit your requirements, you could generate the substitution tables dynamically in RAM. Also, for digital hardware designs, a Boolean circuit implementation known as a *Canright S-box* can be used.

One of the most popular approaches to implementing AES in an optimized way combines the round operations SubBytes(), ShiftRows(), and MixColumns() to obtain a highly efficient sequence of four table lookups and four XOR operations per column per round, sometimes also known as the *T-tables* implementation. It requires four tables containing 256 4-byte words that add up to a memory requirement of 4KB for encryption and decryption, respectively. Further optimizations can lower the required table memory to 1KB at the cost of three additional rotation operations per column per round.

NOTE   *Keeping these basic options in mind can help you estimate performance characteristics of given implementations, but it might also allow you to derive the implementation details of a given device when looking at its performance data.*

Clearly, platforms offering dedicated instructions for AES acceleration or specific crypto coprocessors enable further performance optimizations. Some crypto libraries are already prepared to support these optimizations—for example, the popular AES-NI instructions. However, on embedded systems, it's not unusual that you have to expend effort to utilize hardware acceleration in your application.

While performance gains are certainly the most common motivation for hardware crypto usage, in some cases it might also improve power consumption of your device or at least take some load off the main CPU.

Implementation Characteristics of RSA and ECDSA

Implementations of asymmetric cryptography like RSA and ECDSA are different from those of symmetric cryptography. The asymmetric options don't exhibit a round structure filled with a set of transformations, but instead build on mathematical problems that require arithmetic operations on large numbers. Therefore, real-world performance of these algorithms depends to a certain extent on the efficiency of *multiple-precision arithmetic*, also known as *bignum arithmetic*.

The first obstacle these libraries have to overcome is the simple fact that typical processors support 32-bit and 64-bit data operations, but RSA, for example, is based on integers with lengths of 2,048, 4,096, or even more bits. This problem can be solved by splitting those long numbers into an array of *limbs*, usually equal to the maximum data width of the CPU.

RSA Optimizations

While general bignum libraries support a comprehensive set of arithmetic operations on large numbers, cryptographic algorithms usually require only a small subset. As shown in Chapter 2, the main operation of RSA is the modular exponentiation—for example, for encryption and signature verification: $y = x^e \bmod n$. With a naive approach, performing this calculation on integers with thousands of bits wouldn't be possible. Using the square-and-multiply algorithm enables this computation in the first place.

RSA has two cases to consider that have very different properties. First, the verification and encryption operations use the public exponent $e = 65537 = (10000000000000001)_2$, which leads to pretty high performance. The reason for this is that its length of 17 bits with a leading and a trailing 1 in binary representation leads to only 16 squarings and a single multiplication operation based on the square-and-multiply algorithm. As you'll see later in this chapter, this not only is drastically faster than the decryption and signing functions, which have to handle integers with the full key length of RSA, but also beats ECDSA verification speed.

RSA's private-key operation can't be optimized in the same way, but an approach called the *Chinese remainder theorem (CRT)* reduces runtime roughly by a factor of 4. This is possible because CRT exploits that $n = pq$, which allows it to obtain the result of the exponentiation modulo n from two exponentiations, modulo p and modulo q, respectively. This leads to computational savings because p and q are only roughly half the size of n.

An important aspect of the square-and-multiply algorithm for RSA performance is that its complexity has a cubic dependency on the bit lengths of the processed exponents. You can feel the painful effect of this relation when you migrate from 2,048-bit RSA to a more future-proof 4,096-bit RSA, because the doubling in key length leads to a runtime increase by a factor of around $2^3 = 8$, which might just vaporize all your runtime requirements.

ECDSA Specifics

Since ECDSA operates on elliptic curves that process significantly smaller numbers, the private-key operations are substantially faster than their RSA counterparts. However, different types of curves facilitate different implementations and optimizations. Although the choice of a suitable curve involves mathematical and trust considerations, performance should not be completely ignored in this process because considerable differences exist across all options.

FPGA implementations and internal hardware to support asymmetric cryptography are much less common than for symmetric cryptography. You can find them in dedicated security ICs that, for example, provide authentication by digital signatures, as well as in SoC devices that support digital signature verification to protect their boot process. However, you usually won't know a lot of details about these implementations, and you won't have arbitrary access to their interfaces.

Case Study: Crypto Performance on an STM32MP157F Device

In this case study, I explore the performance of a diverse set of symmetric and asymmetric cryptographic algorithms on an STM32MP157F device and discuss what you can learn from the results. Measuring performance with high accuracy is difficult for complex embedded systems that have feature-rich OSs. Therefore, all results should be regarded as ballpark figures.

The SoC at hand is based on an ARM Cortex-A7 dual core running at up to 800 MHz. It comes with two types of cryptographic coprocessors. The *CRYP1* core offers DES, Triple DES, and AES in different operation modes. The hashing module *HASH1* provides acceleration of SHA-1, MD5, SHA-224, SHA-256, and corresponding HMAC operations. Both run at approximately 266 MHz.

In the following test cases, the OpenSSL command line tool is used to assess performance because it's often available on Linux systems and its software implementations are already highly optimized and suitable for our task.

The call `openssl speed -elapsed -evp` *algorithm-to-test* is always used to run the tests. The -elapsed option defines that throughput is calculated on the basis of elapsed wall-clock time instead of CPU time spent in user space. The latter would distort the results, especially when using hardware support. The -evp flag stands for *envelope* and enables a generic high-level crypto interface that can use software as well as hardware implementations, depending on availability.

The resulting console output always includes the compilation parameters as shown in Listing 4-1 and a list of test results in bytes per second for the following set of input data sizes: 16 bytes, 64 bytes, 256 bytes, 1,024 bytes, 8,192 bytes, and 16,384 bytes.

```
version: 3.0.5
...
options: bn(64,32)
compiler: arm-ostl-linux-gnueabi-gcc  -mthumb -mfpu=neon-vfpv4
-mfloat-abi=hard -mcpu=cortex-a7 --sysroot=recipe-sysroot -O2 -pipe -g
-feliminate-unused-debug-types ...
-DOPENSSL_USE_NODELETE -DOPENSSL_PIC -DOPENSSL_BUILDING_OPENSSL -DNDEBUG
CPUINFO: OPENSSL_armcap=0x3
```

Listing 4-1: The compiler parameters and metadata of the given OpenSSL tool

For clarity and comprehensibility, the terminal outputs of all the tests are reduced to the main relevant numbers.

Parameter Choice for Symmetric Encryption

Let's consider a use case that requires confidentiality protection for sensor values that should be encrypted in chunks of 50KB. Say that your team members already selected AES as the block cipher, but the key size and the operation mode have not been fixed yet.

The first analysis compares the performance of AES in CTR mode with keys of 128, 192, and 256 bits in order to get a feel for the numbers. Listing 4-2 shows the results obtained on an STM32MP157F device: the top line shows the size of the input data chunks, and the second line shows the throughput in kilobytes per second associated with that specific input data size.

```
# openssl speed -elapsed -evp aes-128-ctr
...
type              16 bytes    64 bytes    ...    8192 bytes  16384 bytes
AES-128-CTR       15102.09k   19198.53k   ...    22915.75k   22943.06k
# openssl speed -elapsed -evp aes-192-ctr
...
type              16 bytes    64 bytes    ...    8192 bytes  16384 bytes
AES-192-CTR       13517.07k   16734.31k   ...    19327.66k   19360.43k
# openssl speed -elapsed -evp aes-256-ctr
...
type              16 bytes    64 bytes    ...    8192 bytes  16384 bytes
AES-256-CTR       12158.66k   14689.77k   ...    16711.68k   16728.06k
```

Listing 4-2: The performance differences depending on the AES key size

The first general point you might notice is that throughput increases if the input data size rises. This is due to necessary overhead that loses relevance for larger input data.

For our example, the last column is the one of interest because we want to handle input data of around 50KB. There, we can see that AES-128-CTR achieves roughly 22.9MBps, while AES-256-CTR reaches only 16.7MBps. This is a performance reduction of approximately 27 percent, or a processing-time increase of approximately 37 percent. This makes absolute sense because AES-128 has to compute only 10 rounds, while AES-256 needs 14 rounds, and therefore 40 percent more. However, considering this relation in terms of security level, we gain 128 bits of security while investing approximately only 37 percent more performance. The upgrade could be worth it.

The second interesting point is the operation mode's influence on the performance. While CTR, CBC, and GCM mode differ in security, they also exhibit different performance characteristics. In Listing 4-3, you can see that CTR mode shows a performance of approximately 8 percent above CBC mode for larger input sizes, which might be a reason to choose CTR over CBC in many cases.

```
# openssl speed -elapsed -evp aes-256-ctr
...
type              16 bytes    64 bytes    ...    8192 bytes  16384 bytes
AES-256-CTR       12157.72k   14690.37k   ...    16708.95k   16722.60k
# openssl speed -elapsed -evp aes-256-cbc
...
type              16 bytes    64 bytes    ...    8192 bytes  16384 bytes
AES-256-CBC       11962.59k   14429.91k   ...    15515.65k   15515.65k
# openssl speed -elapsed -evp aes-256-gcm
...
type              16 bytes    64 bytes    ...    8192 bytes  16384 bytes
AES-256-GCM       9052.80k    10844.44k   ...    12126.89k   12113.24k
```

Listing 4-3: The impact of the AES operation mode on encryption throughput

GCM provides authenticated encryption, which means that it yields not only ciphertext but also an authentication tag for integrity protection. The processing efforts for the latter lead to a performance decrease of approximately 28 percent. However, if you have to add a MAC generation algorithm to AES-CTR (for example, an HMAC-SHA-256), this would likely cost you more than 28 percent.

If security has a higher priority than throughput, going with AES-256-GCM would still result in a reasonable performance of 12.1MBps. However, if performance is your key feature, you can achieve the minimal security requirement of confidentiality protection with AES-128-CTR at almost twice the speed—namely, 22.9MBps.

At this point, you might remember that software implementations of the ChaCha stream cipher often outperform those of AES. And since you are probably the type of person who wants to bring your product to perfection, you should check whether the software at hand supports this algorithm, as shown in Listing 4-4.

```
# openssl list -cipher-algorithms | grep -i chacha
ChaCha20
ChaCha20-Poly1305
ChaCha20 @ default
ChaCha20-Poly1305 @ default
```

Listing 4-4: The availability of the ChaCha cipher in the given OpenSSL tool

Running speed tests on ChaCha20 and ChaCha20-Poly1305 yields the results shown in Listing 4-5.

```
# openssl speed -elapsed -evp ChaCha20
...
type              16 bytes    64 bytes    ...   8192 bytes  16384 bytes
ChaCha20          21168.64k   36814.83k   ...     57442.30k    57507.84k
# openssl speed -elapsed -evp ChaCha20-Poly1305
...
type              16 bytes    64 bytes    ...   8192 bytes  16384 bytes
ChaCha20-Poly1305 16054.38k   28477.87k   ...     47390.72k    47300.61k
```

Listing 4-5: The performance tests for the ChaCha20 and ChaCha20-Poly1305 ciphers

If your team is willing to switch from AES to ChaCha20, it can get 256-bit security and authenticated encryption at data rates of 47.3MBps or more. Therefore, ChaCha20 might be worth a second thought.

Software vs. Hardware Implementation for SHA-256 Hashing

Imagine that your device generates logfiles split at 100MB and that you want to sign those files for integrity and authenticity protection before they leave the device. Since the input data size is relatively high, the performance of the signing operation is mainly determined by the hashing step and not the asymmetric signing at the end. Therefore, comparing the software implementation of SHA-256 and the accelerator that comes with the *HASH1* hardware module of the STM32MP157F device might be worthwhile.

Listing 4-6 shows all hash functions supported by hardware and available through their corresponding drivers.

```
# cat /proc/crypto | grep stm32-sha*
driver     : stm32-sha256
driver     : stm32-sha224
driver     : stm32-sha1
```

Listing 4-6: The SHA algorithms supported by the STM32MP157F hardware

The hardware acceleration can be made available to the OpenSSL command line tool, by loading the cryptodev kernel module and then adding -engine devcrypto to the speed test parameters. Listing 4-7 shows the basic comparison between OpenSSL's software implementation of SHA-256 and the hardware-supported operation.

```
# openssl speed -elapsed -evp sha-256
...
type            16 bytes    ...   1024 bytes   8192 bytes  16384 bytes
sha-256         2868.42k    ...     24365.74k   27598.85k   27841.88k
# modprobe cryptodev
# openssl speed -elapsed -evp sha-256 -engine devcrypto
Engine "devcrypto" set.
...
type            16 bytes    ...   1024 bytes   8192 bytes  16384 bytes
sha-256          127.87k    ...      5835.78k   29996.37k   42592.94k
```

Listing 4-7: A comparison of SHA-256 performance in software and hardware

For small input data like 16 bytes, the software solution outperforms the hardware by a factor of 22. This occurs because the test data has to be moved from user space to kernel space to hardware and back, which comes with significant overhead. However, with increasing data size, this effect becomes increasingly irrelevant. It seems that the STM32MP157F hardware has performance advantages for input data of 8KB and larger.

NOTE *Even if most hardware suppliers call their crypto modules "accelerators," they aren't guaranteed to accelerate anything. It might well be that the use of hardware even slows the crypto operations in your specific case. Make sure you test performance before you make a choice.*

The standard data sizes of the OpenSSL command line tool stop at 16KB, but for our specific use case, it would be interesting if even higher throughput rates could be achieved when hashing a 100MB file. The commands in Listing 4-8 add the options -bytes 104857600 and -seconds 60 to the calls to tell OpenSSL to use input chunks of 100MB and do the hashing for roughly one minute.

```
# openssl speed -elapsed -evp sha-256 -bytes 104857600 -seconds 60
...
type           104857600 bytes
sha-256            27566.90k
# openssl speed -elapsed -evp sha-256 -engine devcrypto -bytes 104857600
    -seconds 60
Engine "devcrypto" set.
...
type           104857600 bytes
sha-256            68021.40k
```

Listing 4-8: The performance analysis for hashing 100MB of data with SHA-256

The resulting numbers show that the software implementation doesn't benefit from large input data, but the hardware implementation can enhance its throughput to about 68.0MBps.

Sanity checks are small steps that can reduce mistakes, misconceptions, and even vulnerabilities. I definitely recommend doing them when it comes to using hardware crypto.

First, I want to know whether the hardware is actually used or a software fallback steps in and sets me on the wrong track. Second, my confidence in the chosen solution would increase if the performance numbers given by the chip manufacturer somehow match my experimental data. Listing 4-9 shows a pragmatic way to answer those questions.

```
# time openssl speed -elapsed -evp sha-256 -bytes 104857600 -seconds 60
You have chosen to measure elapsed time instead of user CPU time.
Doing sha-256 for 60s on 104857600 size blocks: 16 sha-256's in 60.87s
...
type           104857600 bytes
sha-256            27562.37k
real   1m 1.79s
user   1m 0.94s
sys    0m 0.75s
# time openssl speed -elapsed -evp sha-256 -engine devcrypto -bytes 104857600
    -seconds 60
Engine "devcrypto" set.
You have chosen to measure elapsed time instead of user CPU time.
Doing sha-256 for 60s on 104857600 size blocks: 39 sha-256's in 61.19s
...
type           104857600 bytes
sha-256            66831.94k
real   1m 2.26s
user   0m 0.18s
sys    0m 2.08s
```

Listing 4-9: A sanity check for SHA-256 hardware hashing

The prefixed `time` command analyzes execution time of the subsequently called process in terms of three classes: elapsed wall-clock time (`real`), processing time spent in user space (`user`), and time used for process-specific kernel space operations (`sys`).

The software-only analysis took 1 minute and 1.79 seconds, of which 1 minute and 0.94 seconds were spent in user space and only 0.75 seconds were used for kernel operations. The "missing" 61.79 − 60.94 − 0.75 = 0.10 seconds can probably be attributed to the OS scheduling other processes or performing independent OS tasks.

Looking at the hardware-assisted run, the situation looks completely different. The speed test lasted 1 minute and 2.26 seconds, but only 0.18 seconds are allotted to user-space computations and 2.08 seconds were spent in kernel space. Despite these low numbers, 39 blocks of 100MB input data were processed by SHA-256.

The first conclusion is that 62.26 − 0.18 − 2.08 = 60.00 seconds aren't represented in the results. Besides the previously mentioned scheduling and OS-related tasks, this amount of time also includes delays when waiting for hardware components to process and return data. In *Reference Manual RM0436* for STM32MP157F devices, ST explains that the processing time of one 512-bit intermediate block for SHA-256 takes 66 cycles. Therefore, an estimation of the time required for pure hardware operations in this specific case can be calculated as follows:

$$39 \times \frac{104,857,600 \times 8}{512} \times \frac{66}{266,500,000 \text{ Hz}} = 15.82 \text{ seconds}$$

This number is at least in the right order of magnitude, but it still indicates that 60.00 − 15.82 = 44.18 seconds are "lost" in OS tasks, drivers, and further hardware processes like bus transfers. If performance is your utmost goal, profiling and optimizing driver implementations could be a next step.

Comparison of Software Performance of Asymmetric Crypto

Operations for asymmetric cryptography are computationally expensive. However, it's important to get an idea of *how* costly they are and how the available options differ in performance.

The first analysis outputs in Listing 4-10 show the significant impact of key lengths in RSA implementations.

```
# openssl speed -elapsed rsa1024 rsa2048 rsa4096
...
                   sign      verify   sign/s  verify/s
rsa 1024 bits 0.004880s 0.000204s    204.9    4897.8
rsa 2048 bits 0.028736s 0.000672s     34.8    1487.6
rsa 4096 bits 0.178246s 0.002454s      5.6     407.5
```

Listing 4-10: An RSA performance analysis with keys of 1,024, 2,048, and 4,096 bits

While the deprecated RSA-1024 completes almost 205 signatures per second on my STM32MP157F device, the state-of-the-art version with 2,048-bit keys yields only 35 signatures per second. By doubling the key length, we have to accept a performance drop by a factor of approximately 6. Moving to the 4,096-bit variant leaves us with only five to six signatures per second, which means that the signing operation takes more than 178 milliseconds, although this device is already running at 800 MHz.

On the other hand, clearly the signature verification, equivalent to the encryption operation, shows a drastically higher performance for all key sizes because it utilizes the short RSA public exponents.

When it comes to ECDSA, the OpenSSL tool provides a large set of curves. Listing 4-11 gives a performance overview for some of the most popular NIST curves in use.

```
# openssl speed -elapsed ecdsap224 ecdsap256 ecdsap384 ecdsap521
...
                            sign     verify    sign/s  verify/s
224 bits ecdsa (nistp224)   0.0090s  0.0074s    110.8    134.6
256 bits ecdsa (nistp256)   0.0010s  0.0028s    982.3    355.5
384 bits ecdsa (nistp384)   0.0322s  0.0243s     31.1     41.1
521 bits ecdsa (nistp521)   0.0773s  0.0567s     12.9     17.6
```

Listing 4-11: The signing and verification performance of selected NIST curves

We can instantly see that NIST curve P-256 is tremendously faster than the other curves because of its highly optimized structure and implementation. Further, ballpark estimations of performance cost factors (for example, for RSA) are hard to provide. Measuring a specific implementation on a specific platform is usually the way to go.

Regarding the comparison of ECDSA and RSA, NIST's P-224 and RSA-2048, which have a similar security level, differ in signing performance by roughly a factor of 3 to the benefit of ECDSA. But in terms of verification speed, RSA-2048 is more than 11 times faster than the P-224 curve.

Finally, alternative elliptic curves are often considered because of trust issues with the NIST selection, but performance can also be a positive aspect, as presented in Listing 4-12.

```
# openssl speed -elapsed ed25519 ed448 ecdsabrp256t1 ecdsabrp512t1
...
                                  sign     verify    sign/s  verify/s
256 bits ecdsa (brainpoolP256t1)  0.0099s  0.0084s    101.5    119.1
512 bits ecdsa (brainpoolP512t1)  0.0420s  0.0317s     23.8     31.6
                                  sign     verify    sign/s  verify/s
253 bits EdDSA (Ed25519)          0.0008s  0.0021s   1301.0    478.7
456 bits EdDSA (Ed448)            0.0059s  0.0120s    169.4     83.1
```

Listing 4-12: Alternative elliptic curves with interesting performance

The Brainpool curve P512t1 exhibits better performance than NIST P-521 for a similar level of security. Further, Bernstein's Ed25519 (Curve25519) shows outstanding performance, even higher than that of NIST P-256.

Assuming you are free to choose an asymmetric signature algorithm for your application, Ed25519 would be a pretty interesting candidate from a performance point of view. If backward compatibility with RSA is a requirement, RSA-2048 might currently be a solid choice, but make sure that RSA-4096 is also feasible on your device to be prepared for future updates.

Summary

Performance is not everything. However, when it comes to the implementation of cryptographic algorithms, it's a property you should never neglect. In addition to security itself, performance is one of the fundamental quality characteristics of crypto.

Some embedded systems have strong restrictions regarding processing power, memory size, or power consumption, which makes optimized implementations a necessity. Otherwise, crypto might lose in a trade-off discussion. Other devices serve dedicated purposes in networking or data processing and require high-speed crypto implementations. Sometimes performance requirements can be met by the use of efficient software libraries, but other scenarios demand specific, digital hardware designs in FPGAs (which is an engineering field of its own) or hardware coprocessors built exactly for this task.

Be aware that even if your chosen crypto algorithms are secure from a mathematical point of view and exhibit nice performance characteristics, they're not necessarily robust against implementation attacks like side-channel analysis and fault injection. *The Hardware Hacking Handbook* by Jasper van Woudenberg and Colin O'Flynn (No Starch Press, 2021) is full of practical examples and insights on how to break and secure crypto implementations. *Power Analysis Attacks: Revealing the Secrets of Smart Cards* by Stefan Mangard, Elisabeth Oswald, and Thomas Popp (Springer, 2007) is also a classic for diving deeper into this field.

Also, keep in mind that such advanced protection measures often come with a reduction in crypto performance. Make sure to determine as soon as possible in your development life cycle whether your product requires specifically hardened crypto implementations.

5

CONFIDENTIAL DATA STORAGE AND SECURE MEMORY

Embedded systems store and process a variety of data. Some of this data is trivial because it is the same on many platforms or can be guessed or derived easily. However, a certain amount of data, usually known as *sensitive*, *secret*, or *confidential* data, requires careful treatment.

The information that this data carries is valuable, and its disclosure would likely lead to negative consequences. One example is *intellectual property* forged into software algorithms, proprietary protocols, and application content. Further, *cryptographic material* like secret keys and passwords contain critical information by nature. A device's *lifetime data* like sensor data, log entries, and sent or received messages might also fit into this category.

This chapter starts by looking at data that should be stored in a confidential manner and the dilemma of how to keep secrets in embedded systems. Next, I'll describe your options for storing confidential data from the OS level to the hardware to obfuscated software, and the corresponding pros and cons. A case study in this chapter will then walk through using encrypted file containers on an embedded system running Linux.

Confidential Data

The identification of confidential data and the awareness of related threats is always the first step toward its protection. The following examples are meant to create the necessary mindset.

Imagine that your research department invents a superefficient engine-control algorithm that runs a car on significantly less fuel than competing products. Although you probably filed a patent, that might not be enough to protect your device from piracy and copycats. The value of the invention becomes reality only if you implement it in your control device. There, it's likely available as a compiled software executable or maybe as part of a kernel module. Both are stored in the device's filesystem, and if an attacker can read the filesystem, they can reverse engineer your algorithm and directly benefit from your research investment. This situation is clearly one you'll want to avoid, which means you must protect the confidentiality of the control algorithm's implementation.

Some household and consumer devices contain a lot of media content like pictures and videos, and their production is anything but cheap. Storing them in plain sight in a device's filesystem is rarely a good idea. Attackers might copy them, upload them to their favorite online platform, and reuse them for their own purposes, which could not only cause financial losses but also damage the reputation of your product and company.

At first glance, the need to protect cryptographic material seems to go without saying. However, many devices store the private keys corresponding to their certificate-based authentication in their standard filesystems. Reading and copying these keys opens the door for impersonation attacks. In addition, especially on the application level, the passwords that control user authentication are sometimes stored in plaintext within configuration files or software binaries. Of course, extracting a password allows an adversary to authenticate successfully with the device because the credential wasn't stored in a way that protects confidentiality.

In some cases, the really interesting data is generated during a device's lifetime. Think, for example, of the privacy implications for biometric data that a product may collect through fingerprint readers or location data that creates movement profiles of users. This information often has a high confidentiality requirement, maybe even by laws like the European GDPR. Failure of protection can lead to fines up to €20 million or 4 percent of a company's total global turnover.

Stored data history in a device can reveal even more. For example, in industrial production environments, the data history might allow attackers to reconstruct machine utilization and output figures, which could be valuable information for competitors. Again, confidentiality protection would be a crucial device feature.

Almost every modern device contains data that deserves confidentiality protection. Make sure to keep that in mind when doing your threat and risk analysis.

The Dilemma of Keeping Secrets on Embedded Systems

Embedded systems often include a toxic combination of properties. First, they have to be able to boot and run without user interaction, which means that everything relevant for correct operation has to be stored within the device, including all secrets. Second, attackers can usually obtain a device for themselves and analyze it thoroughly. This analysis includes not only network-based investigations but also physical eavesdropping on communication lines within the product and the extraction of nonvolatile memory contents like firmware images and filesystem partitions for reverse-engineering purposes. From a theoretical point of view, confidentiality protection for secrets in a device that can be analyzed on all levels can't be guaranteed.

However, from a more pragmatic perspective, the question always is, "How much effort does an adversary have to spend to reach a comprehensive understanding of the device at hand, including its secrets?"

Let's consider the intellectual property example I mentioned previously. Imagine you're responsible for keeping the software implementation of a highly sophisticated algorithm secret, although it has to be stored and used within your device. Some people might immediately think that reading the firmware from flash memory, identifying the executable, and reverse engineering the algorithm is highly complicated, so they assume they don't need any protection measures.

That assumption might be true for attackers like script kiddies. However, consider criminals seeking financial gain. For them, dumping flash memory and mounting a filesystem doesn't seem like too much work. Further, free and open source tools like Radare2 and Ghidra enable everybody with interest to do at least basic software reverse engineering. If confidentiality has an increased priority in your product, these attackers should definitely be in scope.

Of course, some cases are much simpler to attack. For devices that store their firmware on removable media like a microSD card that many off-the-shelf laptops can read, flash dumping isn't even necessary. If the confidential information, such as an RSA private key, is stored in a directly reusable format like Privacy-Enhanced Mail (PEM), an "attack" could be performed in no time, even by a script kiddie. Also, not every executable even needs to be reverse engineered. *Code lifting attacks*, for example, just take the binary as is, copy it to another device, and run it. If it fulfills its purpose, there's no need to access its proprietary details.

Secure Filesystem Approaches

At this point, you might wonder, "Is there such a thing as an encrypted filesystem? That would solve all our problems." There is, but it doesn't make the problem go away completely. Three common options are available that provide confidentiality protection for files: encrypted stacked filesystems, native filesystem encryption, and encrypted block devices.

Encrypted Stacked Filesystems

A *stacked filesystem* is an additional filesystem structure on top of an existing one, which means that standard filesystems like ext3 aren't touched and the encryption happens in a layer above. In this case, the content and the names of files are encrypted—for example, for all files in a specific directory. However, the number of files and their metadata is readable.

Stacking filesystems also comes with a certain performance overhead, and filenames might be subject to additional restrictions. For years, EncFS, which uses the Filesystem in Userspace (FUSE) framework, has been a popular and easy-to-use example of this approach, but it seems that development has stalled. An aspiring successor might be gocryptfs.

A competitor that operates in kernel space is eCryptfs. While eCryptfs might be a bit harder to configure, it exhibits better performance in certain cases. However, its development is also stalled. File-based encryption (FBE) with stacked filesystems seems to be out of fashion.

Native Filesystem Encryption

Today, filesystems like ext4, F2FS, and UBIFS directly support the encrypted storage of files. Compared to filesystem stacking, this allows for more efficient integration and operation.

Popular users of this native FBE approach include the Android and Chrome OSs. The underlying features are implemented in the Linux kernel and use the kernel's crypto API for encryption. The user-space tool for configuring and managing encrypted directories is called fscrypt.

Encrypted Block Devices

File-based approaches always leave folder structures and metadata unencrypted. A common way to avoid this information leakage is *full-disk encryption (FDE)*. In Linux, this means that the encryption layer lies below the filesystem, on the block device level. It doesn't matter whether this block device is a whole disk, a partition, or a file container; it's encrypted as a whole, and its content isn't distinguishable from random information.

The most common representative of this class for Linux is dm-crypt, which is based on the device mapper infrastructure and uses the kernel's crypto API. The cryptsetup user-space tool can create encrypted volumes, and it supports the popular Linux Unified Key Setup (LUKS) container format that enables various key-management functionalities for encrypted volumes.

The TrueCrypt successor VeraCrypt is another popular tool, which, for example, also enables the chaining of two ciphers to enhance decryption resistance.

Recommendations

Encrypted data storage clearly doesn't have a lack of options. Whether FDE or FBE fits your needs largely depends on your device and its corresponding security requirements.

If, from your point of view, the location, number, and size of files already convey sensitive information to an attacker, FDE is probably the solution that leads to the highest possible security. However, FBE offers more flexibility—for example, for hosting a heterogeneous set of files within the same filesystem so that some data is always available and readable to all processes, but confidential data is decrypted selectively per directory. It could also have application-specific keys, which allows for more fine-grained confidentiality protection.

The Passphrase

No matter which implementation you choose, one big problem will always remain: all the tools require a passphrase to either directly unlock protected directories and volumes or to unlock a key file subsequently used to unlock encrypted data. Even the word *passphrase* indicates that this concept is meant for users to enter credentials as we do on our PCs at boot time.

However, most embedded systems don't have active users sitting in front of them, able to enter a passphrase to unlock hard-disk encryption when booting up. The usual next question is, "Where to hide the secret that unlocks encryption?"

Secure Memory in Hardware

Every now and then, I hear people (and companies) say that *secure memory* implemented in hardware is the solution to the embedded system credentials problem. However, that's only partially true.

One advantage of hardware-based secure memory is that it implements a strong physical segmentation between the classic nonvolatile memory, where the firmware is stored, and a dedicated security module, which can be reached only by a specific interface. Further, it allows for tamper detection or resistance, and the stored bits might be buried deep inside a chip, making hardware attacks difficult and requiring sophisticated equipment.

However, this approach also has downsides. Most obviously, only small amounts of data, usually cryptographic keys, can be stored in such protected memory. In addition, these secrets often *have to leave* the security module to serve their purpose, like unlocking a LUKS container. In such cases, attackers might capture the keys on their way over a communication line.

In the past, this issue has been practically exploited when external security modules transferred secrets to a main CPU and adversaries eavesdropped on the physical PCB traces. Other attacks actively communicate with the secure memory and, for example, ask it to encrypt, decrypt, or sign arbitrary data for an attacker. So merely *having* a secure memory doesn't enhance your device's security significantly; it also must be *integrated* securely.

As usual, whether the use of secure memory makes sense depends on the specific application and implementation details. Often, it at least adds another layer of required attacker knowledge—namely, observing secure memory communication at device runtime instead of "only" extracting secrets from firmware or filesystems. Let's consider the options regarding secure memory.

External Secure Memory

The "traditional" way of adding a secure memory device to your design is by integrating a dedicated microchip to your device's PCB and connecting it to the main microprocessor. The most prominent player in this area is the Trusted Platform Module (TPM).

You can purchase discrete TPMs from a variety of manufacturers like Infineon, NXP, and ST. They're well established in the PC world because Microsoft Windows made them a hard requirement. A basic use case is that a user can unlock a TPM key, which is then used to unlock volumes protected by BitLocker. Of course, this is a simplified view of the process, and that's where the problem comes in.

A TPM is much more than secure memory. It comes with authorization layers, with key hierarchies, and with a specification that's more than 1,000 pages for the current TPM version. Although tools are available to make use of TPMs under Linux, like `tpm2-tools` and `ibm-tss`, using a TPM seems to be too complex for average products and development teams.

Fortunately, secure microcontroller manufacturers provide interesting alternatives that target automotive, industrial, and IoT applications. Similar to a TPM, products like Infineon's OPTIGA Trust X, NXP's EdgeLock SE050 family, and Microchip's ATECC608B come with a broad set of crypto algorithms, from symmetric ciphers like AES, to hash functions and HMACs, to asymmetric crypto like RSA and ECDSA. Of course, they also provide secure memory for cryptographic keys. Their promise is that these devices require much less integration effort for IoT products.

In summary, a TPM used only as secure memory is like breaking a butterfly on a wheel. Leaner alternatives might be more suitable for the embedded system world. However, when deciding whether to use a dedicated hardware security module, you should also consider the topics of secure device identity and secure communication, as discussed in Chapters 6 and 7. In any case, make sure you understand the implications that secret keys might be communicated over interfaces accessible to physical attackers.

NOTE   *The TPM 2.0 specification provides a means to encrypt the communication between host CPU and TPM, which adds complexity for attackers but also for engineers.*

Internal Secure Memory

In contrast to discrete hardware components that have to be designed in and soldered to a PCB, security modules and secure storage facilities are already deeply integrated into the main CPU of a device.

Known as *integrated TPMs* or *firmware TPMs*, these alternatives to dedicated hardware TPMs are offered by chip vendors like AMD and Intel. Besides reduced PCB integration costs, the striking advantage of this concept is that on-chip communication is much harder to capture than signals running across a PCB. Of course, the complexity issue of TPMs stays the same.

On the other side, modern SoCs often offer one-time programmable (OTP) memory that can be used to store at least a master key. A common example is the cascaded encryption concept of NXP's i.MX series. There, an OTP master key (OTPMK) is programmed to the device during production. Subsequently, this key is used to encrypt a data encryption key (DEK) to obtain a so-called DEK *binary large object (BLOB)*. In turn, developers can then use the DEK to encrypt application data.

Figure 5-1 shows the procedure running on a device from the master key OTP reading to the application data decryption.

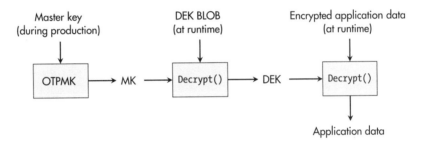

Figure 5-1: The decryption cascade from NXP's i.MX series

This procedure adds security to a device because keys and confidential data are not stored in plaintext and, at the same time, the necessary keys are loaded directly to the device's cryptographic acceleration and assurance module (CAAM) where the decryption is performed, which means only the decrypted user data leaves this internal module at runtime.

Secrets in Application Code

Additional hardware or security-enhanced main CPUs are not always an option because of their cost or because legacy hardware can no longer be upgraded. Is storing the keys in plain view inevitable? Not necessarily.

We can still move keys from the structured field of a filesystem into the more crowded form of an executable. Again, this approach demands further capability from potential attackers—namely, binary reverse engineering. Even if adversaries learn that a specific executable is responsible for unlocking an encrypted volume, they can't extract the unlocking key immediately.

NOTE *Yes, security by obscurity is actually appearing in a security engineering book. At some point in real-world device engineering, you have to clutch at straws.*

The term that describes such countermeasures is *obfuscation*. Its sole purpose is to make software reverse engineering harder, and this can be accomplished in several ways:

- Replace common operations with complex but equivalent ones
- Overcomplicate control flow by rearranging command order without breaking functionality
- Insert redundant, unnecessary code and data
- Store parts of the code or data in encrypted or encoded form and decrypt or decode it only at runtime
- Add randomness to data structures and control flows
- Integrate anti-debugging measures that thwart analysis
- Split secrets into multiple parts, store them in different places, and assemble them only at runtime

This list isn't comprehensive, and each bullet point can be implemented in a variety of ways and with many degrees of creativity. If you can't do it yourself, tools are available that provide automatic code obfuscation functionality. However, such tools must be treated with caution because each given obfuscation tool might also have a corresponding counterpart, a *de-obfuscation* tool, that reverts the added complexity and leaves attackers with code they can analyze much more efficiently.

In 2002, an idea called *white-box cryptography* appeared in academic discussions as a way to overcome the problem of hiding secrets in software. This approach aims to perform cryptographic operations in software without revealing the underlying secret. That means the used cryptographic key diffuses into the operations of a crypto algorithm.

The first concepts of white-box cryptography transformed ciphers with hardcoded keys into key-dependent table lookups and injected random values into the internal calculations that would mask data at some point and demask it later. However, not surprisingly, this led to significant overhead in binary size and performance, and those implementations were also broken by cryptanalysis. Although academia has not yet found a perfect solution to the problem, many software companies use some kind of white-box cryptography in their products—for example, in mobile apps allowing users to download the binary and analyze it.

No matter whether you apply custom obfuscation, commercial tools, or academic white-box crypto approaches, you should always keep in mind one attacker approach when hiding secrets in software binaries: code lifting. In these cases, binaries are used "as is"—for example, to unlock a LUKS container. The secret key itself isn't of interest to attackers if they just have to use the executable as a key to an encrypted vault. This might happen in place, or the file of interest might be extracted and executed in an attacker-controlled environment.

Secure Password Storage

Password-based authentication is a common method for verifying legitimate users at login, but it's also used to unlock encrypted volumes and containers. Naturally, passwords are confidential data. Storing them in plaintext within a file or an executable for comparison during verification makes an attacker's life easy. Once extracted, they can be used successfully to access confidential data. However, traditional encryption, as discussed as a protection measure for other classes of data, is usually not appropriate here. The specific verification process of passwords allows for implementing a different secure storage approach: *password hashes*.

The one-way property of hash functions is useful in prohibiting attackers from retrieving a password from its hash value, even if extracted from the device. The verification still works because a given password can be efficiently hashed and compared to the stored value. However, in this trivial case, attackers could precompute *rainbow tables*, which are large collections of hash values for millions of passwords, maybe even all possible passwords with, for example, 10 characters. To protect against such attacks, a random *salt* is added to the password-hashing process that makes every hash unique and renders all rainbow tables useless.

Linux currently, still by default, uses a function based on SHA-512 hashes to generate salted user-password hashes. Also, the Password-Based Key Derivation Function 2 (PBKDF2) was standardized more than 20 years ago in RFC 2898. It's based on HMACs using hash functions like SHA-1, SHA-256, or SHA-512. Both approaches are definitely better than plaintext password storage, but modern attackers use graphics processing units (GPUs), FPGAs, and dedicated application-specific integrated circuits (ASICs) to break password hashes literally with brute force.

Therefore, for future-proof products, the use of modern representatives of this field is recommended. Typical examples are scrypt, standardized in RFC 7914 from 2016; its successor yescrypt; and Argon2, which won the Password Hashing Competition in 2015. These algorithms share the common goal of enhancing cracking resistance by parameterizable password-hashing algorithms that consider dimensions like computation time, necessary memory, and required number of parallel CPU threads, which is meant to discourage even attackers who have access to a variety of hardware resources and computing capacity.

NOTE *Even if confidentiality is the main protection goal for a password, the consequences of someone being able to change it are severe. Replacing the password hash of the root user with one of a known password is a pretty common attack that opens all doors for an adversary. You should seriously consider integrity protection for password storage, as discussed in Chapter 8.*

Case Study: Encrypted File Containers on Linux

In this case study, let's assume that one of your legacy devices doesn't have any secure storage for confidential data implemented. While visiting an international fair, members of your engineering team recognize that a currently unknown competitor uses one of your proprietary GUI applications and the associated media content that you produced with great effort to fit the needs of your target audience.

Back home, you discuss the issue with your team and management. After an initial investigation, it becomes clear that stealing the data required nothing more than opening your device and reading the contents from flash memory, which your competitor obviously succeeded in doing. To limit future damages, you decide to establish at least a basic protection by using LUKS containers. Your current flash memory device has a capacity of 256MB. The basic Linux system and all associated tools occupy roughly 136MB. Your proprietary executables together with their data and configuration files sum up to roughly 19MB, while the high-quality video content consumes 73MB.

You want to protect the latter two classes of data. Because memory requirements are rather tight on your platform and you'd like to separate code from media, you plan on creating a 25MB container for executables and files containing intellectual property, and a 90MB container for video files.

Crypto Benchmarking

As a first step, you add cryptsetup to your device's root filesystem to be able to work with LUKS containers. You also enable CONFIG_CRYPTO_SERPENT and CONFIG_CRYPTO_TWOFISH in your Linux kernel config because you've heard that cryptsetup supports them and you wonder whether they might outperform AES on your STM32MP157F SoC. Listing 5-1 shows the results of cryptsetup's own performance-benchmarking tool.

```
# cryptsetup benchmark
# Tests are approximate using memory only (no storage IO).
PBKDF2-sha1        59148 iterations per second for 256-bit key
PBKDF2-sha256      92695 iterations per second for 256-bit key
PBKDF2-sha512      58618 iterations per second for 256-bit key
PBKDF2-ripemd160   49201 iterations per second for 256-bit key
PBKDF2-whirlpool   14021 iterations per second for 256-bit key
argon2i      4 iterations, 65536 memory, 4 parallel threads (CPUs)
             for 256-bit key (requested 2000 ms time)
argon2id     4 iterations, 65536 memory, 4 parallel threads (CPUs)
             for 256-bit key (requested 2000 ms time)
#      Algorithm |     Key |   Encryption |    Decryption
          aes-cbc     128b       36.9 MiB/s       36.8 MiB/s
      serpent-cbc     128b        9.0 MiB/s       10.4 MiB/s
      twofish-cbc     128b       11.1 MiB/s       12.0 MiB/s
          aes-cbc     256b       36.9 MiB/s       37.0 MiB/s
      serpent-cbc     256b        9.1 MiB/s       10.5 MiB/s
      twofish-cbc     256b       11.3 MiB/s       12.0 MiB/s
```

aes-xts	256b	18.4 MiB/s	17.0 MiB/s
serpent-xts	256b	9.0 MiB/s	10.4 MiB/s
twofish-xts	256b	11.5 MiB/s	12.0 MiB/s
aes-xts	512b	15.3 MiB/s	13.1 MiB/s
serpent-xts	512b	9.6 MiB/s	10.5 MiB/s
twofish-xts	512b	12.0 MiB/s	12.0 MiB/s

Listing 5-1: The benchmarking results offered by `cryptsetup`

At first, this output shows that multiple functions for password storage are analyzed to give you an idea about which parameters of the specific function might be reasonable choices for your device. You want to set parameters like iteration count to valucs that lead to acceptable performance on your device (for example, unlocking within two seconds) but leave an attacker with maximum cracking effort. In this case, since you don't have specific requirements, you stick with the default of LUKS2 volumes: Argon2.

The encryption/decryption benchmark shows that AES is the fastest algorithm no matter whether you use it in CBC mode or XTS (XEX-Based Tweaked-Codebook Mode with Ciphertext Stealing). It also seems that AES-CBC performance is accelerated by the STM32MP157F crypto hardware. On the other hand, XTS is the default and recommended operation mode for `cryptsetup` and hard disk encryption in general. Since you highly value performance and don't want the container encryption to impact any device functionality, you choose AES-CBC, and since there's practically no difference between 128-bit and 256-bit keys, you go with a 256-bit key.

NOTE *You might wonder how XTS can use 512-bit keys with AES. In short, it doesn't! It requires two keys (in this case, two 256-bit keys, which add up to 512 bits), but the security level is 256-bit.*

Container Creation

After determining the crypto parameters, you can start by creating random files and corresponding key files for your two containers. The container for executables takes 25MB, and the one for media is based on a 90MB file, as shown in Listing 5-2. Both keys are initialized with 32 bytes, which equals 256 bits.

```
# dd if=/dev/urandom of=executables.enc bs=1M count=25
# dd if=/dev/urandom of=media.enc bs=1M count=90
# dd if=/dev/urandom of=executables.key bs=32 count=1
# dd if=/dev/urandom of=media.key bs=32 count=1
```

Listing 5-2: A random initialization of containers and key files

In the next step, as shown in Listing 5-3, you use `cryptsetup` to provide the basic structure of a LUKS container via the `luksFormat` command.

```
# cryptsetup -q -v --type luks2 --cipher=aes-cbc-essiv:sha256
    luksFormat executables.enc executables.key
# cryptsetup -q -v --type luks2 --cipher=aes-cbc-essiv:sha256
    luksFormat media.enc media.key
```

Listing 5-3: The creation of LUKS2 containers

Since you want to use Argon2 for passphrase verification, and you'd like to enjoy the robustness that comes with a second header copy in LUKS2, you select the second version of the header format with --type luks2. The earlier choice of AES in CBC mode with encrypted salt-sector initialization vector (ESSIV) is configured using --cipher=aes-cbc-essiv:sha256.

At this point, the containers and their structures are ready, but you can't store anything in these virtual vaults yet. The file containers need to be unlocked by luksOpen to create an ext3 filesystem inside. Note that after unlocking the LUKS container, as shown in Listing 5-4, it is mapped to the device */dev/mapper/dm_exec_enc*, which is then mounted to the newly created directory */mnt/exec_enc*. The same can be done for the encrypted media container with device */dev/mapper/dm_media_enc* and mount point */mnt/media _enc*, respectively.

```
# cryptsetup -v --key-file=executables.key luksOpen executables.enc dm_exec_enc
# mke2fs -t ext3 /dev/mapper/dm_exec_enc
# mkdir /mnt/exec_enc
# mount /dev/mapper/dm_exec_enc /mnt/exec_enc
```

Listing 5-4: Unlocking a container for filesystem creation and mounting

It seems like you're almost finished. Let's use luksDump, as shown for the executables' container in Listing 5-5, to check whether the right properties are set.

```
# cryptsetup luksDump executables.enc
...
Keyslots:
  0: luks2
    Key:        256 bits
    Priority:   normal
    Cipher:     aes-cbc-essiv:sha256
    Cipher key: 256 bits
    PBKDF:      argon2id
    Time cost:  4
    Memory:     65536
    Threads:    2
...
```

Listing 5-5: Double-checking container properties

The output completely matches our requirements.

Efficiency Analysis

Before you start populating the filesystem, let's take one last glance at the efficiency of this construction. The `fdisk` and `df` tools will help you understand how much memory is lost for the LUKS header and how much overhead is introduced by the ext3 filesystem. Listing 5-6 has the details.

```
# fdisk -l /dev/mapper/dm_exec_enc
Disk /dev/mapper/dm_exec_enc: 9 MiB, 9437184 bytes, 2304 sectors
...
# df -hT /dev/mapper/dm_exec_enc
Filesystem              Type  Size  Used Avail Use% Mounted on
/dev/mapper/dm_exec_enc ext3  4.5M   28K  4.0M   1% /mnt/exec_enc
# fdisk -l /dev/mapper/dm_media_enc
Disk /dev/mapper/dm_media_enc: 74 MiB, 77594624 bytes, 18944 sectors
...
# df -hT /dev/mapper/dm_media_enc
Filesystem               Type  Size  Used Avail Use% Mounted on
/dev/mapper/dm_media_enc ext3   66M   28K   62M   1% /mnt/media_enc
```

Listing 5-6: An efficiency check regarding memory usage

Unfortunately, this didn't turn out as planned. The 25MB container has only 4MB of space left to store data, and the other one with a size of 90MB leaves you with 62MB. It's clearly visible that the difference between the sizes of the containers and their corresponding devices in the device mapper infrastructure is approximately 16MB. Actually, if you had studied the LUKS documentation thoroughly, you'd have known that the headers of LUKS1 and LUKS2 consume 2MB and 16MB, respectively. While that's not an issue for hard disks with hundreds of gigabytes, it might turn out to be a pain point for memory-constrained embedded systems.

You can solve the issue by using LUKS1 headers and going without the LUKS2 improvements, which would be acceptable in practice, or even by using the "plain mode" of `cryptsetup` that doesn't store any metadata in memory. The latter choice might be the most efficient but comes with significant management limitations. LUKS1 would probably be a reasonable choice.

Listing 5-6 also shows that the ext3 filesystem reduces the available memory because of necessary allocation tables and journal data. However, for static storage of executables, configuration files, and media content, journaling might not be necessary, and you could also deploy an ext2 filesystem to squeeze out more bytes of available memory.

After repeating the whole process while changing `luks2` to `luks1` and `ext3` to `ext2`, the situation looks different, as shown in Listing 5-7.

```
# fdisk -l /dev/mapper/dm_exec_enc
Disk /dev/mapper/dm_exec_enc: 23 MiB, 24117248 bytes, 47104 sectors
...
```

```
# df -hT /dev/mapper/dm_exec_enc
Filesystem                   Type  Size  Used Avail Use% Mounted on
/dev/mapper/dm_exec_enc ext2   22M   14K   21M   1% /mnt/exec_enc
# fdisk -l /dev/mapper/dm_media_enc
Disk /dev/mapper/dm_media_enc: 88 MiB, 92274688 bytes, 180224 sectors
...
# df -hT /dev/mapper/dm_media_enc
Filesystem                    Type  Size  Used Avail Use% Mounted on
/dev/mapper/dm_media_enc ext2   81M   14K   77M   1% /mnt/media_enc
```

Listing 5-7: The memory usage efficiency with LUKS1 and ext2

A loss of 4MB and 13MB, respectively, still occurs, but the remaining space just fulfills the requirements of this case study.

NOTE   *If you find yourself in a similar situation in real life but can't reach your require-*
ments, you can still think about switching to native filesystem encryption (for ex-
ample, with ext4), or you can use compressed read-only filesystems like CramFS and
SquashFS.

After solving these unexpected, non-security-related problems, the final question of how to securely unlock the created containers remains. Since you don't have a secure element within your device and your main CPU doesn't provide OTP memory for this purpose, you may decide to hide the unlocking process in an executable within your *initramfs*, which is executed at boot. To be clear, you won't win a prize for "security by design" with such an approach, but it might set the bar higher for successful attacks.

You can consider including hardware-based system identifiers, as de-scribed in Chapter 6, to derive a device-unique unlocking secret instead of a global software-only solution that can be emulated easily off-device. Fur-ther, you might implement secret sharing methods like splitting the key-file contents into multiple pieces and dynamically combining them to obtain the final secret at runtime, which at least hampers simple static analysis attacks. In any case, you have to be aware that an attacker who obtained root privi-leges is able to circumvent all of that and access the decrypted filesystem at runtime. And for the next product generation, you'll make secure storage a priority from day one.

Read-Out Protection as a Low-Cost Solution

Some small embedded systems are low cost, don't have a secure memory, aren't able to run Linux, and can't afford external secure elements at all. These devices might be based on microcontrollers running a real-time oper-ating system (RTOS) or even only bare-metal software.

However, even those cases might have data that deserves a certain level of confidentiality protection. Since these devices often store all their code and data within internal flash memory, restricting read access to flash mem-ory might be a simple yet effective measure to protect sensitive information.

The activation of *read-out protection*—for example, by burning the corresponding fuses—leads to a device that can execute the internally stored code but denies requests to extract its nonvolatile memory contents.

Even so, be aware that physical attackers with suitable equipment can circumvent these basic protection features of low-cost microcontrollers and get access to your confidential data.

Summary

This chapter covered several classes of data that might require confidentiality protection, from intellectual property to media content to cryptographic secrets. Unfortunately, no perfect solution exists for storing such sensitive data in embedded systems. One reason for this dilemma is that, in comparison to a PC, embedded systems have no active users who keep the master secrets in their brains to enter them whenever needed.

Since all secrets have to be available in the same device at all times, the only thing we can do is hide those secrets in well-protected places, like secure elements, internal OTP memory, or within obfuscated software. All these solutions aim to increase the barriers an attacker has to break down for a successful compromise, but each comes with its own advantages and drawbacks.

Many approaches push secret disclosure and usage to the runtime phase of a device, which requires an adversary to take control of certain parts of a running device or even to execute custom code. Therefore, the quality and success of confidentiality protection have a strong relation to the runtime integrity of a device, which we'll discuss in Chapter 8.

6

SECURE DEVICE IDENTITY

For a long time, embedded systems ran anonymously in the shadows and didn't care about remote access, digital business models, or sharing their data with other devices and cloud services. However, these days, those scenarios have changed fundamentally.

Suddenly, maintenance staff are now logging into devices remotely and can't verify that they're working with the correct device by looking at physical indicators. In addition, pay-per-use business models have become more and more popular in industrial scenarios, and devices write their own bills. Being able to prove the origin of usage data and mapping it to a specific customer is essential in this case. Moreover, devices made by different manufacturers have started talking to one another and exchanging data. All these trends have a strong requirement in common: every device needs a unique identity, and every device must be able to prove it.

The first part of this chapter investigates which properties contribute to device uniqueness and can serve as a basis for identity as well as the closely linked processes of identification and authentication. Next, we'll look at how the implementation of device identity management is regarded from two angles: the on-device storage of a cryptographic identity and the life-cycle management on the manufacturer's side. The chapter concludes with two case studies that explore identity generation and provisioning.

Every Device Is Unique

Mass production of consumer goods and industrial components might convey the impression that all the products rolling off the line are identical, right up to every bit in their firmware. However, if that were the case, how would you be able to tell one device from another? Of course, products have had stickers with serial numbers on them for a long time, but what if a sticker falls off, is removed on purpose, or even replaced with a forged version?

For modern devices, a unique identity should be an integral part of the device itself, and the component should be able to actively prove its identity to third-party devices, repair shops, and cloud services of the original manufacturer, just to name a few examples.

From a theoretical point of view, every single device—even with identical PCBs, microprocessors, and RAM—is clearly unique, because all these units are subject to (if only small) individual differences in material, timely behavior, power consumption, and so on. Academia is already working on exploiting the uniqueness of these tiny physical features to establish device identities. The corresponding research area is focused on *physical unclonable functions (PUFs)*, which have recently even found their way into the first commercial products.

The following sections explore what might be available in current devices that makes them unique from a practical point of view and how these unique identities can be proven to other parties.

Identification and Identifiers

Clearly, the term *identification* is closely related to the word *identity*. However, take a minute to think about its exact meaning.

If we want to define the process of identification, we could say it's the "claiming of a given identity." For example, if you meet someone at a conference, you could say, "Hi, my name is Joe!" You claim that you are Joe. The same happens if your device collects some usage data—let's say in the course of one month—and then connects to your backend to provide the data for customer billing. It will probably start with "Hi backend, my name is XY1337-0815!" It claims to be a device with a certain "name."

Unique Identifiers

Regarding uniqueness, telling somebody you're Joe is clearly not enough. Several Joes might exist, maybe even at the same conference. Adding your last name might narrow it down, but your name still won't be unique, at least on a global scale. If you take place and date of birth into consideration, you'll be closer to having a set of data that uniquely identifies *you*. These properties are called *identifiers*. Humans have many more of them: hair color, eye color, size, weight, and so on.

Since devices usually don't have human-like names, manufacturers have to take another path for identification. For a long time, typical identifiers have been vendor-chosen values like model type, serial number, and date of production.

With the advent of the internet, the need for worldwide identifiers became clear. Back then, the concept of UUIDs, also known as *globally unique identifiers (GUIDs)*, was proposed. It's standardized in RFC 4122, among others, and is meant to provide 128-bit unique identifiers that don't require a central registration process. Although the probability of identifier collision is not zero, it's regarded as very close to zero in practice. The generation of UUIDs can, for example, be performed by the Linux RNG, as shown in Chapter 3.

From a cryptographic point of view, public keys generated by asymmetric crypto algorithms like RSA and ECDSA also can perfectly serve as identifiers. They might even be combined with a subject name and further attributes to obtain a unique device certificate for identification as, for example, standardized in the network authentication standard IEEE 802.1AR.

System Identities

While some devices consist of a single central component that constitutes the whole device and its identity, other product architectures are more modular and allow for partial replacements in case of defects or hardware upgrades. Discussing which components contribute to the device's identity and which don't is worthwhile for the latter cases. The physical parts of an embedded system provide a multitude of identifiers like media access control (MAC) addresses of network cards, Bluetooth chipsets, and Wi-Fi controllers, but also serial numbers and unique identifiers of CPUs, flash memories, and removable media.

Requiring a set of identifiers to be part of the system identity also means that the system identity has to be regenerated or reapproved if one of those parts changes. This requirement can be an advantage for manufacturers—for example, to force users to purchase spare parts of the same brand—because every exchange requires the acknowledgment of the manufacturer. However, system identities and forced manufacturer approval can also cause additional workload on the manufacturers' side. Further, if every little change requires a feedback loop with the original manufacturer, it could significantly limit operators' freedom to act in their daily business.

NOTE   *Sometimes a device's reliability is the utmost goal, and if its hardware breaks, it has to be immediately replaced by an operator. In such cases, allowing a device's identity to be transferable is reasonable—for example, with a removable memory card.*

Authentication and Authenticators

In everyday language, *identification* and *authentication* are sometimes used synonymously, but authentication means much more than merely claiming an identity.

If the validity and correctness of your identity are really important—for example, if you have to apply for a passport or register to vote—and you tell them "Hi, I'm Joe," they'll probably reply, "Hi, Joe, please show me your ID card." They'll make you *prove* your identity—the analog equivalent of a digital authentication process.

The term *authentication* means that you have to *confirm* the identity you claimed during identification some seconds before. To do so, you need to possess a valid *authenticator* corresponding to the given identity. For humans, authenticators can be ID cards, driver's licenses, and so on. For all these IDs, an authority at some point in time verified the human identity and subsequently issued a corresponding authenticator that's usually valid for a certain amount of time. During this validity period, the authority and others can use the provided authenticator to verify a specific identity.

For devices, typical authenticators are symmetric secret keys or asymmetric private keys, (temporary) authentication tokens, or passwords (in legacy cases). These authenticators were created and issued for a specific device (for example, during production), and they can be used to prove cryptographically the identity of that same device at a later time.

Authentication Protocols

Depending on the type of authenticator, the authentication process is performed in different ways. A common approach is a *challenge-response authentication protocol*. Figure 6-1 shows one form of a challenge-response handshake.

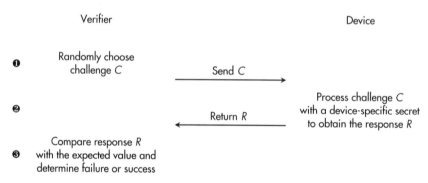

Figure 6-1: The typical steps during challenge-response authentication

The challenge-response authentication process starts with the generation of a random challenge *C* ❶ on the verifier side that is subsequently transmitted to the device. The device processes this unpredictable value with its secret authenticator and yields a response *R* that's returned to the verifier ❷. In the final step ❸, *R* is compared to its expected value to decide whether authentication was successful.

For symmetric secrets, the on-device algorithm processing the given challenge with the device-specific secret could be a hash function or an HMAC construction. However, the disadvantage is that the secret also has to be available in the verifier's database to compute the correct expected value and is not solely stored within the device.

In contrast, asymmetric cryptography allows for device-only authenticators that never leave the device, which is the most secure solution. Specifically, digital signatures based on RSA or ECDSA, as explained in Chapter 2, could be used to generate authentication responses from random challenges. In this case, the verifier would need only the corresponding public key in order to check the validity of the returned signature.

NOTE *In most cases, authentication is possible only with secrets. Therefore, confidentiality is a natural protection goal for all kinds of authenticators. If broken, device impersonation becomes a likely threat.*

Dedicated Authentication Chips

As introduced in Chapter 5, semiconductor manufacturers offer a variety of authentication chips that not only securely store authenticators but also provide an algorithmic means to perform a challenge-response handshake for authentication purposes.

This approach has two advantages. First, extracting the secret authenticator from the chip is a pretty difficult task for attackers. Second, since these chips usually come with integrated support for asymmetric cryptography, mainly digital signatures based on elliptic curves, the secret never has to leave the physical boundaries of the chip.

On the other hand, with this approach, you now have another component on your BOM, you need space on the PCB, and necessary software integration efforts of these devices vary among vendors. In addition, an attack vector is often overlooked—namely, the physical transfer of such an identity chip to another device. The simple 8-pin packages could be desoldered and integrated into a different original device or even into a custom attacker device. As in code-lifting attacks, adversaries might not care about the secret inside the chip if they can move the whole chip to their desired location.

Multifactor Authentication

For the authentication of human users, *multifactor authentication (MFA)* has gained a lot of attention over the last several years. Following the principle of defense in depth, MFA requires attackers to capture not only one authenticator, such as a password, but also at least a second factor, like a temporary token generated in a mobile app or by a hardware token. Since passwords are stored in human brains (or password managers) and additional authenticators often originate from an additional hardware device or at least a different communication channel, the necessary effort for successful attacks is significantly higher.

For device authentication, the situation is a little bit different because devices don't use brains and mobile apps for authenticator storage and generation. However, you could still consider a multifactor approach—for example, using one authenticator stored in firmware and a second one that originates from a dedicated authentication chip. The authentication process would then consist of two handshakes, one with the hardware component and one based on the device software, forcing attackers to compromise two different parts of your device if they want to get hold of its identity.

Besides additional explicit authenticators, you can use implicit, environmental parameters to strengthen device authentication. A common example is geographical limitations, also known as *geo-fencing*. In that scenario, device authentication (or general operation) succeeds only if the device's location matches a predefined area. One way to determine this parameter is the public IP address the device uses for internet communication. Of course, the security gain by these implicit authentication properties is maximized if an attacker who has compromised a device can't forge the parameters. They should be observable from the outside and not just claimed by the device itself.

Trusted Third Parties

In the past, the main verifier of a device's identity was the manufacturer of the same device. Proprietary (and eventually insecure) authentication processes did their job. However, in a multilateral digital ecosystem in IoT and IIoT scenarios, the need for cross-manufacturer device authentication becomes obvious.

This requirement means manufacturers have to trust authenticators of other devices, including competitors. Since one-to-one trust relations between manufacturers would lead to enormous management overhead, the concept of a *trusted third party (TTP)* is necessary, as shown in Figure 6-2.

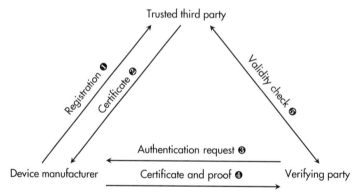

Figure 6-2: The role of a trusted third party in device authentication

In this approach, manufacturers register their device identities with the TTP ❶. After verification, the TTP certifies the given identity and returns a device-specific certificate ❷. Upon an authentication request in the field ❸, the device can provide the issued certificate and cryptographically prove that it is in possession of the corresponding authenticators ❹. However, at this point, the verifying party can't be sure that the given cryptographic data corresponds to the actual device identity. The verifier finally has to check the validity of the authentication ❺, either in direct communication with the TTP or by using data like public keys provided by the TTP. Afterward, a reliable trust relation with a previously unknown device can be established.

Certificates and Certificate Authorities

I've been using the term *certificate* to describe a digital document that's issued by a TTP to confirm a device's identity. Technically speaking, the most common implementations of this concept are X.509 v3 certificates based on asymmetric cryptography as specified in RFC 5280.

The purpose of these certificates is to bind a given public key to its corresponding subject, such as a device, and to a set of attributes including a validity period and a certificate serial number. A *certificate authority (CA)* digitally signs these values with its own private key. This CA is also included in the certificate, in the Issuer field. The result is the smallest version of a *certificate chain*, which means that a device certificate and its public key can be cryptographically verified, and if successful, the next certificate (namely, that of the CA) has to be verified. Authentication is trusted only if both verifications succeed.

In practice, a manufacturer might have its own product CA, which is certified by an intermediate CA of a TTP, which is again certified by an internationally recognized root CA. With that process, the rather complex hierarchical certificate chains are established that have to be verified up to their root, whenever a device needs to authenticate itself.

The *root certificates* aren't certified by anybody; they're self-signed and have to be available in some kind of root store on the verifier's side. This means that verifying parties also must unconditionally trust all their root certificates. Therefore, the root store requires strong integrity protection; otherwise, attackers can inject new trust relations by manipulating the stored certificates.

In several cases, a certificate can't be trusted until its actual end of validity—for example, because of a private-key compromise, device theft, or similar issue. For such situations, CAs maintain a *certificate revocation list (CRL)* that lists all certificates no longer trusted even though their validity period is not yet over. The *Online Certificate Status Protocol (OCSP)* is a common protocol for checking the revocation status of a certificate during authentication, as standardized in RFC 6960.

The whole architecture of verification, certification, and revocation, and the corresponding processes and services, are often referred to as the *public-key infrastructure (PKI)*. Since such a system demands significant maintenance and documentation efforts, small and medium-sized companies often hesitate to implement it themselves and rely on PKI service providers instead, which means TTPs.

Identity Life Cycle and Management

Now that we've covered the basic concepts of device authentication, this section establishes the need for reliable strategies for managing the *life cycle* of device identities. Life-cycle management has four main steps, as depicted in Figure 6-3: identity generation, its provisioning in manufacturer systems as well as within the device, everyday usage in the field, and the often-forgotten exchange or destruction of the same identity.

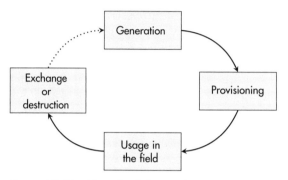

Figure 6-3: The life cycle of device identities

Don't treat life-cycle management as optional. Even if you've solved all the technical challenges regarding identifiers, cryptography, and secure memory, make sure your organization has answers regarding the organizational challenges ahead.

Generation

A device's identity can be generated in various places and at various times. The place and time you choose affect the security requirements and procedures of your production process. If you use electronics manufacturing services (EMS) to manufacture your product, a trustful and close cooperation with your service provider is essential.

Generating the identity on the device itself during production can be the most secure option of all, but only if the corresponding authentication secrets *never* leave the device. Asymmetric cryptography enables this use case because the generated private key might stay on the device, and its public counterpart can be made available to potential verifiers. Of course, you might also generate a symmetric secret on the device during the production process, but in that case, the key has to be exported later to enable identity verification.

While on-device generation has security advantages, it comes with operational and practical challenges. Imagine that a device "loses" its identity because the memory that stores it gets broken. If that was the single storage location, a new identity has to be generated after repair, which might lead to a conflict because a new entry is generated in your product database, but the hardware is actually old. Also, your customers would have to replace the old device identity with the new one in their asset management systems. If you as a manufacturer have an identity backup, this case could be handled easily, but at the cost of security.

A second disadvantage of on-device generation can be the late availability of product identities, because they are available only after a certain manufacturing step is completed. Sometimes that might be exactly what you want, but if your device identities have to be populated in your own IT systems to enable smooth operation from day one, you might want to prepare those processes with your device identities even before actual production.

WARNING *On-device identity generation based on RSA keys is a nondeterministic process and takes a variable amount of time. This limitation has to be considered when planning production processes, especially for low-performance devices.*

Generating an identity outside the device provides more flexibility in managing the device identity before production and in cases of repair. Authentication secrets are prepared in advance within an identity management system and provided to production in a second step. However, this means that these identities exist before the real device is even assembled and, of course, they already carry the protection goals of confidentiality and integrity. Information disclosure or data manipulation before production could have severe consequences for the security of your product.

A last point that might influence your on-/off-device generation decision is the involvement of a TTP. If you generate identities during production, they have to be registered, verified, and certified with a third party within a tight schedule. Of course, that's possible and desirable, and it's already implemented by leaders in this field, but it requires a significant amount of infrastructure and process management efforts.

Provisioning

Depending on the identity generation phase, the following provisioning step comes in two flavors with their own pros and cons. In both cases, the end result should be that the identity is provisioned on the device itself and within the product-tracking and identity management system of the manufacturer and the eventually involved EMS provider.

After on-device generation, all manufacturer systems have to be provisioned with the new identity, which requires a read-out step during production. For asymmetric crypto, only the public key or a corresponding certificate from a TTP has to be stored in the manufacturer's identity database. However, if backups of authentication secrets are desired, you can create them by extracting the private key at this point.

The offline generation of identities requires information flow in the other direction—namely, from an identity management system to the device to be produced. Clearly, a programming step is necessary, in which the secret and the attributes of the pregenerated identity are written to specific memory locations or hardware resources within the product. This step might be integrated in existing firmware programming procedures or similar processes.

In all these cases, when sensitive data is transferred to or from a device during provisioning, at least the integrity and often also the confidentiality of this communication should be guaranteed. Otherwise, authentication secrets might be disclosed, devices might end up with a manipulated identity, or the manufacturer's identity data might be corrupted.

NOTE *If your device identities are generated before production and are then sent to your EMS provider by email or on a USB stick by snail mail, consider carefully whether this meets your protection goals. If you're honest, it probably doesn't.*

Usage in the Field

The previously generated and provisioned identities are used for authentication in the field. So far, so good. Can we take any other precautions during everyday usage? Absolutely. An identity management system allows us to perform sanity and plausibility checks whenever devices authenticate with our systems.

Imagine your authentication logs show that the same device connects from two locations within a short time. This might be an indicator that somebody has stolen a device's identity and is using it for their own purposes. If such cases can be identified early and specific investigations follow in a timely manner, damage can be significantly limited.

Exchange or Destruction

Even if some devices (especially in industrial, military, or space applications) are meant to last forever physically, their authentication secrets usually don't. On the internet, a common validity period for web server certificates is 90 days (as, for example, implemented by Let's Encrypt at *https://letsencrypt.org*), which means that these identities have to be regenerated at least every three months.

Clearly, identity renewal in IoT and IIoT scenarios is still far away from such high frequencies. However, at least if X.509 certificates are used for authentication purposes, a validity period is a mandatory parameter that has to be specified, either by your company or by the TTP of your choice. Some manufacturers issue device certificates with a validity period of 20 years or more, but even if the chosen crypto is future-proof, it's hard to estimate whether such an identity will still be trustworthy after 15 years or more.

Some network products (for example, those from Cisco) support certificate management protocols like the *Simple Certificate Enrollment Protocol (SCEP)* or its more recent alternative, *Enrollment over Secure Transport (EST)*. Since this is new ground for IoT and IIoT devices, no common standard has been established as of this writing, but it's pretty clear that automation is key to continuous and reliable identity and certificate management.

NOTE *In 2022, manufacturers of security gateways for accessing the German health telematics infrastructure claimed that devices had to be physically replaced because the validity of their five-year cryptographic identities came to an end. Subsequently, the Chaos Computer Club (CCC) proved the opposite and, by its own account, saved the German healthcare system €400 million. This is just one example that emphasizes the importance of robust identity-renewal processes.*

The final step of an identity's life cycle is literally its destruction. While physical removal is not always possible, a manufacturer should at least be prepared to revoke the trust relation for a specific device if it reaches its end of life before the defined end of its validity period. A typical measure for this purpose is a CRL maintained by a CA or a trust status flag in your own manufacturer database.

Case Study: Identity Generation and Provisioning

In this case study, I investigate the availability of identifiers for an STM32-MP157F-DK2 and how to extract them in order to derive a system identity. Further, we'll see how to prepare a certificate signing request on this device that can subsequently be provided to a TTP, which in turn, is able to issue a valid device certificate.

Identifiers and System Identity

The STM32MP157F-DK2 evaluation kit is an embedded system that consists of several components. Many of these components come with their own identifiers that engineers might capture and use to create a comprehensive device identity.

A common identifier is the serial number of a device's main CPU. In this regard, ST's *Reference Manual RM0436* for STM32MP157F devices states: "The 96-bit unique device identifier provides a reference number, unique for a given device and in any context. These bits cannot be altered by the user." This unique ID (UID) is immutably stored in the OTP memory of the STM32-MP157F chip. Listing 6-1 shows that this UID is split into three 32-bit words that can be read from specific memory addresses.

```
Base address: 0x5C00 5000 (BSEC base address on APB5)
Address offset: 0x234 = UID[31:0]
Address offset: 0x238 = UID[63:32]
Address offset: 0x23C = UID[95:64]
```

Listing 6-1: The physical addresses of the UID in STM32MP157F devices

We can use the devmem2 command line tool to read physical memory addresses. As shown in Listing 6-2, the application outputs three 32-bit words representing the chip's identity, given a combination of base address and UID offsets.

```
# devmem2 0x5c005234
...
Read at address  0x5C005234 (0xb6fb0234): 0x0038003D
# devmem2 0x5c005238
...
Read at address  0x5C005238 (0xb6fb9238): 0x34385114
```

```
# devmem2 0x5c00523c

...

Read at address  0x5C00523C (0xb6f1423c): 0x36383238
```

Listing 6-2: Reading the CPU UID of my STM32MP157F device from physical addresses

On Linux systems, the serial number is also available from */proc/cpuinfo*. The output shown in Listing 6-3 confirms that the serial number is the same as that extracted from the raw memory locations before.

```
# cat /proc/cpuinfo | grep Serial
Serial : 0038003D3438511436383238
```

Listing 6-3: Capturing the CPU serial number available in Linux

However, the STM32MP157F chip is not the only one on the PCB. ST's *User Manual UM2637* describes a multitude of implemented communication interfaces. Besides classic Ethernet networking, the device includes an IC that provides Wi-Fi and Bluetooth capabilities. All these interfaces have unique MAC addresses that might be used to derive system identities. Listing 6-4 shows how to extract those values when running on Linux.

```
# cat /sys/class/net/eth0/address
10:e7:7a:e1:81:65
# cat /sys/class/net/wlan0/address
48:eb:62:c4:0a:08
# cat /sys/kernel/debug/bluetooth/hci0/identity
43:43:a1:12:1f:ac (type 0) 00000000000000000000000000000000 00:00:00:00:00:00
```

Listing 6-4: Extracting Ethernet, Wi-Fi, and Bluetooth MAC addresses in Linux

Finally, one part of the system can be removed and replaced easily: the removable media card. In my case, it's a microSD card that contains a *card identification (CID)*. This 128-bit value uniquely identifies an SD card. Among other information, it contains a manufacturer ID, a product serial number, and the date of production. Again, Linux provides a corresponding entry in its sysfs that can be read out as illustrated in Listing 6-5.

```
# cat /sys/block/mmcblk0/device/cid
275048534431364760dad3df9a013780
# cat /sys/block/mmcblk0/device/serial
0xdad3df9a
```

Listing 6-5: Reading the unique CID of an SD card

Besides the cid value, Linux provides the serial value for an SD card, which solely contains the memory card's serial number.

For this case study, let's assume your team has chosen to use the central CPU ID and the Wi-Fi MAC address as the two relevant system identifiers. They can be combined by a hash function, as shown in the next section.

Certificate Signing Request

A *certificate signing request (CSR)* is a data structure that requests a CA to certify that a given public key is bound to a specific identity, a device identity in this case. Linux offers several ways to generate a CSR and provide the necessary information. Listing 6-6 shows the imports necessary to accomplish RSA key generation and CSR creation with the help of the cryptography Python module. Also, the subprocess module is included to get system identifiers by using the available command line tools.

```
import subprocess
from cryptography.hazmat.primitives import serialization
from cryptography.hazmat.primitives.asymmetric import rsa
from cryptography import x509
from cryptography.x509.oid import NameOID
from cryptography.hazmat.primitives import hashes
```

Listing 6-6: The necessary imports from the cryptography and subprocess modules

The first part of the on-device identity generation is usually based on asymmetric cryptography (RSA, in this case). As shown in Listing 6-7, a random key pair can be created with a single line.

```
# Generate RSA key
key = rsa.generate_private_key(public_exponent=65537, key_size=4096 ❶)

# Write key to disk
with open('dev.key', 'wb') as f:
    f.write(key.private_bytes(
        encoding=serialization.Encoding.PEM,
        format=serialization.PrivateFormat.TraditionalOpenSSL,
        encryption_algorithm=
        serialization.BestAvailableEncryption(❷ b'PrivateKeyPassphrase'),
    ))
```

Listing 6-7: An on-device generation of an RSA key pair

For this case study, I decided to use an RSA key length of 4,096 bits ❶ to account for an (I)IoT device's lifetime of several years. To simplify this example, the generated private key is stored in the *dev.key* file and is protected by a standard passphrase ❷. In an actual production environment, the key should be stored in a secure way, as discussed in Chapter 5.

Listing 6-8 shows an example procedure of identifier collection and processing.

```
# Collect system data
❶ output = subprocess.Popen('cat /proc/cpuinfo | grep Serial',
            shell=True, stdout=subprocess.PIPE)
cpu_serial = output.stdout.read().split()[2]
```

```
❷ output = subprocess.Popen('cat /sys/class/net/wlan0/address',
            shell=True, stdout=subprocess.PIPE)
   wifi_mac = output.stdout.read().split()[0]


   # Hash collected system data
❸ digest = hashes.Hash(hashes.SHA256())
   digest.update(cpu_serial)
   digest.update(wifi_mac)
   system_id = digest.finalize()
❹ system_id = system_id[:4].hex()
```

Listing 6-8: Collection and processing of an on-device identifier

In the first step, the CPU serial number ❶ and the Wi-Fi MAC address ❷ of the produced system are read by the means Linux provides. Subsequently, the hash function SHA-256 ❸ is used to process those values and to derive a 4-byte system identifier ❹ that would change if the CPU or the Wi-Fi chip is replaced in the future. The SD card ID is neglected on purpose, because SD cards break every now and then, which would lead to an unnecessarily high demand for identity regeneration.

For a device certificate and a CSR, respectively, you need to specify a *common name* for the device, as shown in Listing 6-9.

```
   # Manufacturer data
   manufacturer = 'IoT Devices Corp'
   manufacturer_device_serial_no = 'IOTDEV-1337-08151234'


   # System name for CSR and certificate
❶ cert_common_name = manufacturer_device_serial_no + '-' + system_id


   # Generate CSR and sign with private key
   csr = x509.CertificateSigningRequestBuilder().subject_name(x509.Name([
       x509.NameAttribute(NameOID.ORGANIZATION_NAME, manufacturer),
❷  x509.NameAttribute(NameOID.COMMON_NAME, cert_common_name),
❸ ])).sign(key, hashes.SHA256())


   # Write CSR to disk
   with open('dev.csr', 'wb') as f:
       f.write(csr.public_bytes(serialization.Encoding.PEM))
```

Listing 6-9: An on-device CSR preparation

In this case study, the unique device name is the combination of the serial number given by the manufacturer and the hardware-dependent system identifier ❶. This string is used as an input to the CSR generation ❷, together with the manufacturer's name in the CSR's *organization* field. Finally, the device signs the CSR with its unique confidential private key ❸. Afterward, the CSR is stored in the *dev.csr* file.

The saved CSR file has to be transmitted to the CA responsible for certifying the identity of produced devices. Also, the manufacturer or EMS provider might extract the collected and generated device data in a database. As an example, Listing 6-10 shows the data from an STM32MP157F device.

```
Collected CPU serial number:   0038003D3438511436383238
Collected Wi-Fi MAC address:   48:eb:62:c4:0a:08
Derived system identifier:     f30cf858
Given device serial number:    IOTDEV-1337-08151234
Common name in certificate:    IOTDEV-1337-08151234-f30cf858
```

Listing 6-10: Example output of identifier data from my STM32MP157F device

As you can see, a 4-byte system identifier is generated from the listed individual identifiers and appended to the device serial number. This string is subsequently used as the common name for the generated CSR.

Certificate Authority

Before we issue the final certificate, let's look at what the CSR contains. Listing 6-11 shows how to display CSR contents with the openssl req command line tool.

```
$ openssl req -in dev.csr -noout -text
Certificate Request:
    Data:
        Version: 1 (0x0)
❶       Subject: O = IoT Devices Corp, CN = IOTDEV-1337-08151234-f30cf858
❷       Subject Public Key Info:
            Public Key Algorithm: rsaEncryption
                Public-Key: (4096 bit)
                Modulus:
                    00:d3:a0:14:fb:e1:0e:d0:74:3d:26:d4:ef:a1:ed:
                    ...
                    c9:2a:f5:46:e4:b2:ad:a9:5e:ee:cb:79:85:d9:1e:
                    9f:3e:57
                Exponent: 65537 (0x10001)
        Attributes:
            (none)
            Requested Extensions:
    Signature Algorithm: sha256WithRSAEncryption
❸   Signature Value:
        81:98:b1:e8:c2:fe:3a:55:32:39:2e:27:ce:2c:a8:54:bd:04:
        ...
        17:77:6c:a1:5b:4a:a7:ed:22:55:33:23:26:55:05:90:26:d2:
        90:7a:5e:34:65:80:32:4e
```

Listing 6-11: Example CSR for my specific STM32MP157F device

The subject ❶ is represented by an organization string (O) and a common name (CN) as specified in our CSR preparation script in Listing 6-9, followed by its corresponding RSA public key ❷. The device's digital signature ❸ can be clearly identified at the end of the given request. The CA can use it to verify whether the requesting subject actually has access to the private key corresponding to the given public key in the CSR.

CA and PKI infrastructures usually consist of complex processes with a variety of organizational and technical measures to ensure proper and trustworthy functioning. As shown in Listing 6-12, we create a test CA that's far from production-ready but okay for educational purposes. The term *quick and dirty* might be applicable here.

```
$ openssl genrsa -out ca.key 4096
$ openssl req -new -x509 -key ca.key \
            -subj "/C=DE/L=Augsburg/O=Super Trusted Party/CN=CA 123" \
            -out ca.crt
```

Listing 6-12: A quick generation of a test CA with openssl tools

We can generate the test CA with the help of the openssl genrsa tool. The first command in Listing 6-12 generates a 4,096-bit RSA key pair for the CA and stores it as *ca.key*. Since, in this case study, this is the root of the CA, the corresponding certificate has to be self-signed. The *ca.crt* certificate can be obtained by using the openssl req tool and telling it the CA's attributes—for example, the country (DE for Germany) and city it's located in (Augsburg), its organization's name (Super Trusted Party), and its common name (CA 123).

After the CA has registered and successfully verified the certificate request at hand, it takes the CSR data and adds attributes like the validity period. In Listing 6-13, you can see that the -days parameter is set to 3650, which means that the issued certificate is valid for 10 years.

```
$ openssl x509 -req -in dev.csr -CA ca.crt -CAkey ca.key -CAcreateserial \
            -days 3650 -out dev.crt
```

Listing 6-13: Generating a certificate from a CSR with the openssl tool

In the device certificate generation process, the CA decides on the length of the validity period, but of course that has an influence on your device identity life cycle. Make sure to choose this value deliberately.

Let's look at the final result of this demanding process. The openssl x509 tool is able to output the device certificate contents, as shown in Listing 6-14.

```
$ openssl x509 -in dev.crt -noout -text
Certificate:
    Data:
        Version: 1 (0x0)
        Serial Number:
          ❶ 45:3c:c3:30:c1:e3:c2:a9:49:5c:14:d6:16:5d:79:69:24:6c:31:66
        Signature Algorithm: sha256WithRSAEncryption
      ❷ Issuer: C = DE, L = Augsburg, O = Super Trusted Party, CN = CA 123
        Validity
            Not Before: Apr  5 11:18:13 2024 GMT
```

```
❸ Not After : Apr  2 11:18:13 2034 GMT
   Subject: O = IoT Devices Corp, CN = IOTDEV-1337-08151234-f30cf858
   Subject Public Key Info:
       Public Key Algorithm: rsaEncryption
           RSA Public-Key: (4096 bit)
           Modulus:
               00:d3:a0:14:fb:e1:0e:d0:74:3d:26:d4:ef:a1:ed:
               ...
               c9:2a:f5:46:e4:b2:ad:a9:5e:ee:cb:79:85:d9:1e:
               9f:3e:57
           Exponent: 65537 (0x10001)
   Signature Algorithm: sha256WithRSAEncryption
❹ Signature Value:
       75:d5:07:71:ec:fe:c6:27:fd:e2:a7:1c:fa:b9:89:b3:9c:0f:
       ...
       8d:fa:f6:f1:53:79:32:1e:a8:ec:6f:f7:03:57:2f:7b:f4:fb:
       45:77:6a:f8:c6:70:72:41
```

Listing 6-14: The certificate contents of a sample device

In comparison to the original CSR, you can see that the CA added a certificate serial number ❶ and its own data at the Issuer field ❷. The validity period ❸ is set to be 10 years from the moment of issuance. And, finally, all these attributes are signed by the CA ❹ together with the device's information and its public key. Now every entity that trusts the used CA is able to authenticate the produced device.

After issuing the certificate, it has to be provided to the device itself, but also to the manufacturer's identity management system. During production, this whole process of generation, certificate issuance, and provisioning should run with a high degree of automation and with precautions taken to minimize threats to confidentiality and integrity.

Case Study: RSA Key Generation in Production

Although ECDSA has some advantages over RSA, as discussed in Chapter 2, it's still widely used in certificates. However, if you work with RSA, be aware that RSA key generation is a nondeterministic process and might take varying amounts of time.

This second, brief case study investigates how much time is required during the production process to generate RSA keys of a given length. Listing 6-15 shows a simple way to analyze RSA key-generation times.

```
import time
from cryptography.hazmat.primitives.asymmetric import rsa

time_data = []
for n in range(16):
    start_time = time.time()
    key = rsa.generate_private_key(public_exponent=65537, key_size=4096)
```

```
elapsed_time = time.time() - start_time
print('Try', n, ': RSA 4096-bit key generation took',
    '{:.3f}'.format(elapsed_time), 'seconds!')
time_data.append(elapsed_time)
print('MIN:', '{:.3f}'.format(min(time_data)), 'seconds')
print('MAX:', '{:.3f}'.format(max(time_data)), 'seconds')
print('AVG:', '{:.3f}'.format(sum(time_data)/len(time_data)), 'seconds')
```

Listing 6-15: An RSA key-generation timing analysis

This example uses the cryptography Python module and the parameters from the previous case study. It performs 16 tries for simplicity, but a sound statistical analysis would require a larger number of test runs. Listing 6-16 shows exemplary results of RSA 4,096-bit key-generation times obtained by running the code from Listing 6-15 on my STM32MP157F device.

```
# python3 rsa_key_gen_time.py
Try 0 : RSA 4096-bit key generation took 59.920 seconds!
Try 1 : RSA 4096-bit key generation took 28.696 seconds!
Try 2 : RSA 4096-bit key generation took 72.872 seconds!
Try 3 : RSA 4096-bit key generation took 109.765 seconds!
...
Try 12 : RSA 4096-bit key generation took 48.925 seconds!
Try 13 : RSA 4096-bit key generation took 50.885 seconds!
Try 14 : RSA 4096-bit key generation took 90.907 seconds!
Try 15 : RSA 4096-bit key generation took 40.634 seconds!
MIN: 28.696 seconds
MAX: 109.765 seconds
AVG: 62.768 seconds
```

Listing 6-16: RSA key-generation timing results on my STM32MP157F device

The variation of generation times is not negligible. The RSA key generation may finish within 30 seconds but might also take 110 seconds or even more. This variation has to be considered in production scheduling, and since an upper bound doesn't exist for the generation time, you have to expect outliers that might take significantly longer.

Summary

There's no doubt that every single device is a physically unique object. With the help of identifiers like CPU serial numbers, MAC addresses, and values chosen by the manufacturer, we're able to represent this uniqueness in the digital space and provide a base for device identities.

However, merely claiming an identity isn't enough for most applications. Devices have to be able to cryptographically prove their identity with the help of unique and confidential authenticators like cryptographic keys. This process is called *authentication*. The secure storage of those authentication secrets is essential to prevent impersonation attacks. Chapter 5 provided some ideas for confidential data storage in hardware or software.

A common concept to establish trust in device identities is the registration of devices at third parties that verify their identities and issue digital device certificates. These can be used by anybody trusting the issuer to authenticate a device.

Besides the technical challenges of binding a digital identity to a device, a much broader field of organizational processes have to be specified to provide secure and reliable identity life-cycle management. These processes often involve EMS providers, TTPs, and your custom process specifics, which leads to a complexity that should never be underestimated.

The more you dive into this topic, the more "interesting" problems you will discover. For several years, researchers have been working on PUF implementations to exploit manufacturing process variations in order to derive implicit chip identities, and the first products on the market already contain such circuits. Further, identity management automation in on- and offline scenarios and corresponding protocols like SCEP and EST will certainly gain more attention in the future, providing a major step forward for managing secure device identities.

7

SECURE COMMUNICATION

In the past, many embedded systems operated in an *air-gapped* environment, not connected to any wired or wireless network. Although this practice is still present in some industries, it's slowly vanishing for the simple reason that none of the modern ideas like predictive maintenance, data-driven optimization, and remote access work without proper communication channels.

Even the first cryptographic methods in the days of Caesar aimed to protect communication, and 2,000 years later, the internet is inconceivable without secure communication. However, a significant number of *devices* still don't use secure protocols for data exchange with their administrators and other entities in their environment.

In this chapter, we'll first look at the set of requirements that's imposed on robust communication channels, followed by an introduction to the most common protocol to tackle these challenges and a corresponding practical case study. Afterward, we'll look at two areas where the standard solution doesn't help: non-IP communication and the need for redundancy.

All the Protection Goals

Communication is inherent to human nature. We exchange thoughts, provide assistance to others, and work together in teams. Every child who whispers something into somebody's ear is implicitly aware of confidentiality protection.

For written messages, confidentiality has been a topic for thousands of years, as the example of Caesar shows, and it's still present in postal privacy laws. For centuries, monarchs have used royal seals to guarantee the integrity and authenticity of documents, while replication of information by letterpress printing clearly targets availability—even if one "information source" fails, still others can be used to acquire that same "communication data."

Digital communication at internet scale has been practiced for roughly 30 years, and it's not surprising that it unites the demands for *all the protection goals* of previous communication approaches. Considering the specific field of (I)IoT device communication, confidentiality is apparently useful, because either proprietary values corresponding to intellectual property are transferred or personal data about humans is communicated that deserves privacy protection.

Also, integrity and authenticity are valued in many cases—for example, for control commands in industrial systems. In those scenarios, it's very important that the origin of communication is a legitimate party and that messages haven't been altered on the way. As mentioned before, typical (I)IoT devices rely on working communication channels. Disturbances—for example, those introduced by DoS attacks—threaten proper system operation and maybe even related business models.

Transport Layer Security

When we talk about data communication, we usually start by locating it within the *Open Systems Interconnection (OSI) model*. This model supports us in structuring stacks of communication protocols, as shown in Table 7-1.

Table 7-1: Communication Layers According to the OSI Model

Number	Layer	Description
7	Application	Application-specific communication data processing
6	Presentation	Translation between network data and application
5	Session	Session management for communication between nodes
4	Transport	Management of data transmissions between network nodes
3	Network	Management of a multiparticipant network
2	Data link	Transfer of data frames between two entities
1	Physical	Wired/wireless transmission over a physical medium

The Ethernet standard IEEE 802.3 is a typical example that specifies properties for layers 1 and 2. Often, Internet Protocol (IP) handles the network layer, while Transmission Control Protocol (TCP) and User Datagram Protocol (UDP) cover functionalities in layers 4 and 5. Application protocols like the common HyperText Transfer Protocol (HTTP) are represented by layer 7.

This section focuses on one of the most common protocols for secure communication: Transport Layer Security (TLS). It might seem obvious that it's located on layer 4 of the OSI model; however, encryption and decryption are usually attributed to layer 6. And since TLS also performs some kind of session management, we could say that it spans across layers 4 to 6 and, thereby, introduces a protection layer between raw packets distributed over a network and the application using the transmitted data in the end.

NOTE *TLS is application agnostic. Its payload might carry any application protocol like HTTP or even industrial protocols like Modbus.*

History

In the 1990s, while Netscape was working on a browser application of the same name, the need for secure internet communication became apparent. In 1995, Netscape published the predecessor of TLS, the Secure Sockets Layer (SSL) protocol in version 2.0. SSL 2.0 and SSL 3.0, released the following year, had significant security issues and should never be used in practice.

Unfortunately, many software applications as well as product marketing brochures use *SSL* and *TLS* synonymously. Usually, you can assume it's "a modern TLS version," but as a customer, I would have much more confidence if the manufacturer would show its security know-how by not mentioning SSL anymore, anywhere.

The new protocol name was introduced in 1999 with TLS 1.0 (which was an upgraded version of SSL 3.0), maybe to reduce association with the weaknesses of the previous SSL versions. TLS 1.1 fixed security issues with the CBC operation mode of block ciphers in 2006. However, both TLS 1.0 and TLS 1.1 were officially deprecated in March 2021 and should not be used in modern products.

Version 1.2 of TLS was specified in August 2008 and is still widely in use. It replaced the use of weak hash functions like MD5 and SHA-1 with their modern counterpart, SHA-256, and extended the support for authenticated encryption ciphers like AES-GCM. However, the complexity of TLS 1.2 became its own enemy, and correct configuration was not trivial. To minimize configuration mistakes and maximize security and performance at the same time, TLS 1.3 was published in 2018. Every new device should use that version by default.

TLS Basics

TLS is a set of client-server protocols that unite many modern cryptographic primitives introduced in Chapter 2. These are the two most important subprotocols in practice:

Handshake protocol   In this subprotocol, the cryptographic algorithms used to protect a communication channel are negotiated between client and server. Usually, at least one of them is authenticated to the other, but mutual authentication is also possible. Additionally, the handshake process establishes shared key material for the crypto algorithms used in the following communication. Any errors or tampering attacks at this stage lead to the termination of the connection.

Record protocol   This subprotocol is responsible for organizing and protecting the bulk of traffic between two endpoints based on the algorithms and parameters negotiated in the handshake protocol.

A further general property of TLS is that it uses X.509 certificates for authentication. However, in contrast to the device certificates mentioned in Chapter 6, the common name in these certificates usually corresponds to the device's IP address, its hostname, or its fully qualified domain name (FQDN). This is because the information is used to establish the basic connection to the device on the network layer in the first place, and the device then has to prove that it's the legitimate entity at this network node.

Never underestimate the complexity of TLS, and stick to secure defaults whenever you don't have specific requirements to change them. The following sections shed light on the main properties of the two TLS versions in use today.

TLS 1.3

TLS 1.3 is specified in RFC 8446 and is *the* version that product engineers should implement and use. Figure 7-1 illustrates the handshake process for mutual authentication that could, for example, be part of a machine-to-machine communication scenario.

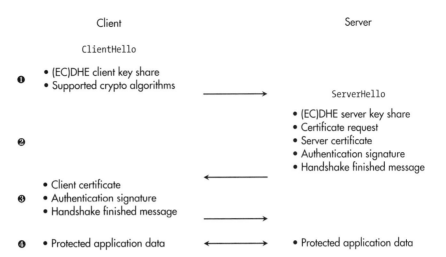

Client   Server

    ClientHello

❶   • (EC)DHE client key share
    • Supported crypto algorithms   ──────────▶   ServerHello

                                     • (EC)DHE server key share
                                     • Certificate request
❷   • Server certificate
                                     • Authentication signature
                                     • Handshake finished message

    • Client certificate   ◀──────────
❸   • Authentication signature
    • Handshake finished message   ──────────▶

❹   • Protected application data   ◀──────────▶   • Protected application data

Figure 7-1: A typical TLS 1.3 handshake with mutual authentication

In the first step, the client initiates the connection establishment by sending the ClientHello ❶ message to a server. This message contains the client's key share for a DHE or ECDHE key agreement scheme, its supported TLS version, and a list of available crypto algorithms and parameters. In response, the server provides its own data for the intended key exchange, its certificate, and a signature proving the possession of the corresponding private key. Further, it requests the client to authenticate itself and concludes the ServerHello ❷ of the handshake with a Finished message.

In the third part of the handshake, the client fulfills the server's certificate request by sending its certificate and a signature proving its identity ❸. After the client's Finished message, both parties can be sure about the other's identity and are prepared to securely exchange application data ❹.

Further Handshake Options

Besides key-agreement schemes like DHE and ECDHE that guarantee perfect forward secrecy but also consume significant performance, TLS 1.3 also provides a *pre-shared key (PSK)* option, which distributes keys to devices in an earlier process. However, this isn't the default variant and should be used only in exceptional cases and for solid reasons.

To reduce the necessity for the execution of a complete handshake, TLS 1.3 allows you to reuse PSKs from previous (EC)DHE handshakes if the client and server agree on it, which means costly asymmetric crypto operations can be spared and efficiency is enhanced.

If a client and server share a PSK, TLS 1.3 provides a zero round-trip time (0-RTT) mode that allows a client to send PSK-encrypted data with its first message, immediately enabling application data communication. However, this speed improvement comes at a price: perfect forward secrecy can't be guaranteed anymore, and the 0-RTT messages are not protected against replay of messages obtained earlier.

Selection of Crypto Algorithms

Compared to TLS 1.2, TLS 1.3 has significantly reduced the set of possible crypto algorithms to be used. This is a strong security enhancement, since it prevents *downgrade attacks* that try to influence crypto parameter negotiation to force the usage of weak algorithms. In the course of this cleanup, the *cipher suite*, a collection of supported crypto algorithms, was reduced to contain symmetric crypto only.

For this symmetric cryptography, TLS 1.3 requires the implementation of the TLS_AES_128_GCM_SHA256 cipher suite, which means that AES with a 128-bit key has to operate in GCM mode, and the hash function SHA-256 must be available to be used as an HMAC-based extract-and-expand key derivation function (HKDF), which is relevant to derive TLS secrets. The additional TLS_AES_256_GCM_SHA384 and TLS_CHACHA20_POLY1305_SHA256 cipher suites should also be implemented but aren't mandatory. Two cipher suites based on the CCM mode complete the five possible options for symmetric crypto in TLS 1.3, and they all belong to the class of modern AEAD algorithms.

Regarding digital signature algorithms and certificates, TLS 1.3 implementations must support RSA PSS and PKCS1 in combination with SHA-256, but also ECDSA based on the NIST curve secp256r1 and SHA-256. The mandatory curve for ECDHE is also secp256r1, but the RFC recommends the additional implementation of X25519. DHE based on finite field groups is also possible.

TLS 1.2

Although TLS 1.3 is the most recent version, many devices still rely on TLS 1.2 specified in RFC 5246, or at least support its use to maintain compatibility to legacy devices. However, this requires taking precautions to guarantee secure communication.

TLS 1.2 vs. TLS 1.3

A somewhat formal difference between TLS 1.2 and TLS 1.3 is that version 1.2 cipher suites include asymmetric as well as symmetric algorithms and parameters. For example, the TLS_DH_RSA_WITH_AES_256_CBC_SHA384 cipher suite specifies that DH (without the *E* for *ephemeral*) is used for key exchange; authentication is based on an RSA certificate; AES with a 256-bit key in CBC mode is used for payload encryption, and SHA-384 is the hash function used in the key-derivation scheme.

In addition to the different cipher suite format, TLS 1.2 supports and allows a much larger set of crypto algorithms, which can have negative consequences in several cases. Besides the possibility of choosing static key-exchange mechanisms based on RSA and DH, it's even possible to select cipher suites that explicitly allow anonymous DH key exchange, which means without any verification of the communication partner.

TLS 1.2 also allows you to select legacy ciphers like 3DES and Rivest Cipher 4 (RC4) or even the NULL cipher without payload encryption. Further, operation modes like CBC can be selected that don't lead to AEAD-compliant security.

The option to compress data before transmitting it over TLS was well-meant by the designers and is still available in TLS 1.2, but it facilitates vulnerability, as shown by the Compression Ratio Info-Leak Made Easy (CRIME) attack.

Besides those security-related differences, TLS 1.2 also misses some performance optimizations introduced by TLS 1.3 and the 0-RTT mode.

Secure Usage

The key to the secure configuration of TLS 1.2 lies in the strong restriction of its options. Your implementation must disallow deprecated ciphers like 3DES, RC4, weakened export ciphers, CBC operation mode, and (of course) the NULL cipher. Key exchange based on RSA key transport has to be denied as well as anonymous DH. Further, options like data compression have to be disabled to reduce the attack surface.

Looking at it the other way around, your configuration should enable only cipher suites that implement DHE and ECDHE key exchange and symmetric AEAD ciphers in combination with hash functions from the SHA-2 family, which means TLS 1.2 can be trimmed to behave similarly to TLS 1.3 and provide secure communication channels.

Requirements for Devices and Infrastructure

Assuming you've decided that TLS is the way to go for your device and you want to make things happen, you still have some requirements to consider before implementing a semi-secure communication helter-skelter. From a device perspective, you should analyze at least five aspects:

Private-key storage   If your device has to be able to authenticate itself by signing data with a private key, it needs a secure place to store that secret in a confidential way.

Certificate store   The verification of communication partners' identities is possible only if your device is in possession of corresponding public keys and root certificates. These files don't contain confidential information but need to be stored in an integrity-protected way because they represent your device's trust base.

Trustworthy source of randomness   Key-generation and key-exchange schemes in TLS require the availability of trustworthy random numbers. If your device generates "random numbers" based on a static value, this might have severe consequences for TLS security.

Reliable time base   Especially in industrial scenarios, but also in other application domains, devices often don't need a real-time clock. However, if you want to use TLS, your device has to be able to verify the validity period of certificates, which is clearly not possible if it's stuck in the 1980s time-wise.

Crypto performance   The TLS handshake performs several operations based on asymmetric crypto. Low-performance devices might reach their limit, for example, if they have to perform signing with RSA keys. The basic decision of RSA or ECDSA might have a strong impact on this point. It also makes a big difference if your device is meant to act as a client authenticating once a day, or if it has to handle hundreds of connection and authentication requests per minute as a server.

Not only does your device itself need to be prepared for TLS, but also your infrastructure and processes need to support it. A common example is the operation of a PKI to manage the generation, updating, and revocation of certificates.

Further, the real-time clock in your device probably depends on external time synchronization mechanisms like Network Time Protocol (NTP) and Precision Time Protocol (PTP), which require appropriate network services, master clocks, and the like.

Application Examples and Software Libraries

The most common use case for TLS is HyperText Transfer Protocol Secure (HTTPS), the protocol used throughout the internet. It's also known as *HTTP over TLS*, because that's essentially what's happening: TLS establishes a secure channel between a client and a web server. Within this channel, plain HTTP requests and responses are exchanged. In the same way, secure communication can be achieved for many other application protocols.

TLS is based on TCP, but is there a way to protect applications like Voice over IP (VoIP) or online gaming that rely on UDP or other stateless protocols? Yes, you can use a variant called *Datagram Transport Layer Security (DTLS)*. DTLS 1.2 and DTLS 1.3 are based on TLS 1.2 and TLS 1.3, respectively. They guarantee the same security as their TCP-based counterparts but can handle loss and reordering of packets.

When it comes to TLS implementations, OpenSSL is probably the most popular one on Linux systems as well as in the field of embedded systems. However, if either source code transparency or small footprint are of interest to your product, Mbed TLS might be worth a look. Further, implementations are available in a multitude of programming languages, such as Rustls for the Rust community.

Case Study: Secure MQTT Communication

Over the last few years as a professor, I've seen several student projects using the MQTT protocol, because it's pretty comprehensible and perfectly suits the needs of resource-constrained devices in IoT scenarios. It's used to transmit sensor values like temperature or pressure as well as to control messages like start and stop commands for actuators in a system.

However, if I ask for a secure communication channel for the obviously sensitive message content, I usually get responses like "But it's only a proof of concept!" or "There was no time left to tackle this complex topic." And, "Why do you always ask such painful questions?"

In this case study, I'll set up the Eclipse Mosquitto MQTT broker service on my STM32MP157F-DK2 board and configure it properly for secure communication based on TLS. Further, I'll dynamically test the implementation for misconfigurations.

Mosquitto Installation and Configuration

Because the toolchain for my STM32MP157F-DK2 device is based on the Yocto Project, I can simply add the mosquitto recipe from recipes-connectivity of the meta-networking layer to my image to install the broker software on my device. The version I get is 2.0.14. Of course, this comes only with a default configuration located at */etc/mosquitto/mosquitto.conf*.

In MQTT, the broker is a central component that receives messages and data published by clients and distributes this information to clients that subscribe to it. For clients, it's essential to share their data only with legitimate brokers and rely on messages only from brokers they trust. Therefore, MQTT brokers have to cryptographically authenticate to connecting clients.

As mentioned previously, TLS uses certificates for authentication, so the first step for broker authentication is to generate a corresponding certificate. I used Python and OpenSSL to create a CA and a MQTT broker certificate in a similar way, as described for device identities in Chapter 6. An important difference is the chosen common name in the certificate: it corresponds to the hostname *mqtt.iot-device-corp.com* under which the device can be reached within my network. This is important for hostname verification by the clients, so they can be sure to be connected to the correct host.

Armed with the CA certificate ca.crt, the broker certificate mqtt_broker.crt, and its corresponding private key mqtt_broker.key, we can configure the basic TLS settings for mosquitto as shown in Listing 7-1.

```
listener 8883
cafile /etc/mosquitto/certs/ca.crt
certfile /etc/mosquitto/certs/mqtt_broker.crt
keyfile /etc/mosquitto/certs/mqtt_broker.key
```

Listing 7-1: The basic TLS configuration for mosquitto

While plain MQTT is usually offered at port 1883, the version using secure communication based on TLS is typically provided at port 8883. Required certificates and keys can, for example, be stored in */etc/mosquitto/certs/*. So far, so good.

However, up until now, the system is configured only for server-side authentication. Client authentication would have to be managed by maintaining a password file on the device hosting the broker application (for example, at */etc/mosquitto/password_file*), which might be tedious, and the associated security level would be medium at best. But since TLS supports mutual certificate-based authentication, and Mosquitto is able to utilize that procedure for application layer usage, it's worth a look.

Listing 7-2 shows the two options that have to be added to *mosquitto.conf*.

```
require_certificate true
use_identity_as_username true
```

Listing 7-2: Important options for certificate-based authentication of MQTT clients

The first line makes the broker request a certificate for authentication from each connecting client, while the second line enables the use of the common name contained in the provided certificate as the username in the MQTT application.

It's important to note that, in this case, the client certificate has to be issued by the CA provided before by the `cafile` parameter. If you want to provide several trusted CAs to Mosquitto, the `capath` option is your friend. In my case, I just used the same CA as for the MQTT broker to create a further certificate, this time with the common name `mqtt-client123`.

The First Test Run

After starting `mosquitto` with the new configuration file, a brief `nmap` scan reveals that the MQTT broker is now available at port 8883, as shown in Listing 7-3.

```
$ nmap mqtt.iot-device-corp.com -p 8883
Starting Nmap 7.80 ( https://nmap.org ) at ...
Nmap scan report for mqtt.iot-device-corp.com (192.168.1.13)
Host is up (0.00067s latency).

PORT     STATE SERVICE
8883/tcp open  secure-mqtt

Nmap done: 1 IP address (1 host up) scanned in 0.03 seconds
```

Listing 7-3: An nmap scan showing open port 8883

To test the secure communication, I wrote a little Python script that uses the Eclipse Paho MQTT client library. Listing 7-4 shows the basic settings.

```
broker = "mqtt.iot-device-corp.com"
port   = 8883
client = mqtt.Client("mqtt-client123")
client.tls_set('ca.crt', 'mqtt_client.crt', 'mqtt_client.key')
client.connect(broker, port)
```

Listing 7-4: The basic Paho MQTT client configuration in Python

Besides obvious necessities like the hostname and the port of the MQTT broker, the client is also able to handle TLS settings like a trusted CA in *ca.crt*, and the client's authentication data located in the *mqtt_client.crt* and *mqtt_client.key* files.

In the test application, the client subscribes to the topic foo/bar, publishes some data to the same topic, and receives the information again from the broker, as shown in Listing 7-5.

```
❶ New connection from 192.168.1.7:46317 on port 8883.
❷ New client connected from 192.168.1.7:46317 as mqtt-client123
     (p2, c1, k60, u'mqtt-client123').
  ...
❸ Received SUBSCRIBE from mqtt-client123
     foo/bar (QoS 0)
  Sending SUBACK to mqtt-client123
❹ Received PUBLISH from mqtt-client123 (d0, q0, r0, m0, 'foo/bar', ... (2 bytes))
  Sending PUBLISH to mqtt-client123 (d0, q0, r0, m0, 'foo/bar', ... (2 bytes))
  ...
  Received DISCONNECT from mqtt-client123
  Client mqtt-client123 disconnected.
```

Listing 7-5: The mosquitto console output during a test

Clearly, a connection was successfully established on port 8883 ❶. Also, mosquitto directly uses the client certificate's common name (mqtt-client123) as the associated username ❷ for this connection. Both client commands, SUBSCRIBE ❸ and PUBLISH ❹, are correctly received and handled on the broker side as well.

Communication Security Analysis with Wireshark and SSLyze

The application seems to be working properly even though we already activated several TLS security features. That raises hope, but as security engineers, we'd prefer to base our trust on thorough analysis rather than gut feelings.

One of the tools for such analysis is Wireshark. It allows us to capture network communication traffic and analyze it for security properties. I first configured it to collect all exchanged data between the test station and the STM32MP157F device. Afterward, I filtered for TLS packets. Figure 7-2 shows a snippet of the result.

Time	Source	Destination	Protocol	Length	Info
1.420874455	192.168.1.7	192.168.1.13	TLSv1.3	583	Client Hello
1.653579873	192.168.1.13	192.168.1.7	TLSv1.3	1514	Server Hello, Change Cipher Spec,
1.653582909	192.168.1.13	192.168.1.7	TLSv1.3	769	Application Data, Application Data
1.675985824	192.168.1.7	192.168.1.13	TLSv1.3	1514	Change Cipher Spec
1.676015435	192.168.1.13	192.168.1.13	TLSv1.3	1514	Application Data [TCP segment of a
1.676019173	192.168.1.7	192.168.1.13	TLSv1.3	537	Application Data, Application Data
1.676687365	192.168.1.7	192.168.1.13	TLSv1.3	116	Application Data

Figure 7-2: The TLS messages exchanged during MQTT communication

You can see that a TLS handshake with its characteristic ClientHello and ServerHello messages took place. Afterward, encrypted Application Data packets were transmitted between client and broker.

As shown in Figure 7-3, Wireshark also provides the details of the TLS negotiation—namely, that the cipher suite TLS_AES_256_GCM_SHA384 was selected for bulk data transmissions. This, in turn, tells us that TLS 1.3 is used, because that specific cipher suite belongs to the most recent TLS version.

```
▸ Internet Protocol Version 4, Src: 192.168.1.13, Dst: 192.168.1.7
▸ Transmission Control Protocol, Src Port: 8883, Dst Port: 33629, Seq: 1, Ack: 518, Len: 1448
▾ Transport Layer Security
   ▾ TLSv1.3 Record Layer: Handshake Protocol: Server Hello
        Content Type: Handshake (22)
        Version: TLS 1.2 (0x0303)
        Length: 122
      ▾ Handshake Protocol: Server Hello
           Handshake Type: Server Hello (2)
           Length: 118
           Version: TLS 1.2 (0x0303)
           Random: 9dae67a600970ff963e4a8f84cc840d2f0ad6ac7181cc2a2...
           Session ID Length: 32
           Session ID: c31b232153c62ca321ad4984b993ece602ea85328d7d1586...
           Cipher Suite: TLS_AES_256_GCM_SHA384 (0x1302)
           Compression Method: null (0)
           Extensions Length: 46
         ▸ Extension: supported_versions (len=2)
         ▸ Extension: key_share (len=36)
```

Figure 7-3: The details of the TLS handshake

WARNING   *Be careful when analyzing the TLS version used in network traffic. The legacy Version field says it's TLS 1.2, but it's not.*

At this point, it seems that functionality and security measures work as expected. Let's use one more tool to finalize our confidence in this work. The SSLyze Python application is able to test TLS servers of all kinds regarding a variety of pitfalls and misconfigurations that would lower your product's security if they go unnoticed.

To start the TLS scan, simply enter the hostname and corresponding port: sslyze mqtt.iot-device-corp.com:8883.

The comprehensive results shed light on some interesting details. The extract shown in Listing 7-6 deals with certificate verification.

```
...
Certificate #0 - Trust
❶ Hostname Validation:        OK - Certificate matches server hostname
❷ Android CA Store (...):     FAILED - Certificate is NOT Trusted ...
  Apple CA Store (...):       FAILED - Certificate is NOT Trusted ...
  Java CA Store (...):        FAILED - Certificate is NOT Trusted ...
  Mozilla CA Store (...):     FAILED - Certificate is NOT Trusted ...
  Windows CA Store (...):     FAILED - Certificate is NOT Trusted ...
...
```

Listing 7-6: The `sslyze` console output regarding certificate verification

The good news is that I created the certificate correctly, which means that I included the correct server name of my device as the common name in the certificate ❶. However, many FAILED entries ❷ also occur. This happens because my certificate is not part of the popular certificate stores from Android, Windows, Mozilla, and the like, which was never the plan, but if you aim for broad trust compatibility of your certificates, this test might be important for you.

The main part of the results is about the cipher suites and TLS versions that a server accepts. The results in Listing 7-7 indicate that deprecated TLS versions and their corresponding cipher suites are all rejected by the implemented MQTT broker as intended. The default settings of mosquitto already seem to prohibit the use of these old protocols and ciphers.

```
...
 * SSL 2.0 Cipher Suites:
     Attempted to connect using 7 cipher suites; the server rejected all ...
 * SSL 3.0 Cipher Suites:
     Attempted to connect using 80 cipher suites; the server rejected all ...
 * TLS 1.0 Cipher Suites:
     Attempted to connect using 80 cipher suites; the server rejected all ...
 * TLS 1.1 Cipher Suites:
     Attempted to connect using 80 cipher suites; the server rejected all ...
...
```

Listing 7-7: The desired rejection of all deprecated cipher suites

As shown in Listing 7-8, the standard settings of mosquitto still support TLS 1.2, which is a good thing regarding backward compatibility, because many legacy devices in the field don't support TLS 1.3, but the list of supported cipher suites as given by sslyze exhibits some weaknesses.

```
...
* TLS 1.2 Cipher Suites:
    Attempted to connect using 156 cipher suites.

    The server accepted the following 20 cipher suites:
        TLS_RSA_WITH_AES_256_GCM_SHA384                256
        TLS_RSA_WITH_AES_256_CBC_SHA256                256
        TLS_RSA_WITH_AES_256_CBC_SHA                   256
        ...
        TLS_ECDHE_RSA_WITH_CHACHA20_POLY1305_SHA256    256  ECDH: X25519
        TLS_ECDHE_RSA_WITH_AES_256_GCM_SHA384          256  ECDH: prime256v1
        TLS_ECDHE_RSA_WITH_AES_256_CBC_SHA384          256  ECDH: prime256v1
        TLS_ECDHE_RSA_WITH_AES_256_CBC_SHA             256  ECDH: prime256v1
        ...
        TLS_DHE_RSA_WITH_CHACHA20_POLY1305_SHA256      256  DH (4096 bits)
        TLS_DHE_RSA_WITH_AES_256_GCM_SHA384            256  DH (4096 bits)
        TLS_DHE_RSA_WITH_AES_256_CBC_SHA256            256  DH (4096 bits)
        TLS_DHE_RSA_WITH_AES_256_CBC_SHA               256  DH (4096 bits)
        ...
```

Listing 7-8: The offered TLS 1.2 ciphers

The output shows that the implementation at hand still offers options that allow for RSA-based key exchange (TLS_RSA_WITH_...) and others that still use the CBC operation mode for AES encryption of application data. Both are not supported by TLS 1.3 and are not recommended anymore.

This insight allows us to adjust the *mosquitto.conf* file again by specifying the parameter ciphers, as shown in Listing 7-9.

```
ciphers ECDHE-ECDSA-AES256-GCM-SHA384:ECDHE-RSA-AES256-GCM-SHA384:
        DHE-RSA-AES256-GCM-SHA384:ECDHE-ECDSA-CHACHA20-POLY1305:
        ECDHE-RSA-CHACHA20-POLY1305:DHE-RSA-CHACHA20-POLY1305:
        ECDHE-ECDSA-AES128-GCM-SHA256:ECDHE-RSA-AES128-GCM-SHA256:
        DHE-RSA-AES128-GCM-SHA256
```

Listing 7-9: The restriction of TLS 1.2 ciphers in mosquitto.conf

This restricts the TLS 1.2 ciphers of mosquitto to only six modern options for RSA-based authentication and three for ECDSA certificates, which means the security of the MQTT communication at hand is enhanced one step further.

NOTE   *Mosquitto relies on OpenSSL for secure TLS communication. Enter* **openssl ciphers** *to list all ciphers offered by OpenSSL on a specific system.*

Regarding TLS 1.3, the recommended cipher suites are supported correctly, as shown in Listing 7-10.

```
...
* TLS 1.3 Cipher Suites:
    Attempted to connect using 5 cipher suites.

    The server accepted the following 3 cipher suites:
        TLS_CHACHA20_POLY1305_SHA256                    256  ECDH: X25519
        TLS_AES_256_GCM_SHA384                          256  ECDH: X25519
        TLS_AES_128_GCM_SHA256                          128  ECDH: X25519
```

Listing 7-10: TLS 1.3 support is available as intended

This is the base for future-proof device communication.

Secure Communication Without TLS

As mentioned multiple times in this chapter, TLS should be the default solution if your device needs to communicate securely. However, not all application scenarios and communication technologies allow TLS to be used.

For example, wireless communication for dedicated use cases like sensor or mesh networks might rely on proprietary protocols that don't include a TCP/IP stack. Further, some wired bus architectures like the controller area network (CAN) bus specify their own message format and data structures without relying on TCP/IP technology, and they might require a certain real-time behavior that can't be guaranteed with TLS. Also, very power-constrained devices like battery-powered remote control units for alarm systems, garage doors, and industrial cranes often use frequencies of 433 and 868 MHz within the license-free industrial, scientific, and medical (ISM) radio band, and they optimize message content and lengths for energy consumption, which renders a TLS handshake impossible.

However, it would be naive to conclude that these applications have to live without security measures because TLS doesn't fit. The issue just requires a different development approach. For those cases, usually no out-of-the-box solution exists, but custom, application-specific security protocols have to be developed. Of course, having extensive experience in cryptography, protocol design, and verification of such systems would be useful, but, in reality, that's rarely the case.

A pragmatic approach could be to regard TLS 1.3 and the cryptographic primitives it uses as a self-service store. If you're looking for specific protection measures (for example, to protect authenticity and integrity of commands sent by your remote control), digital signatures based on RSA or ECDSA would be a reliable solution. Whether you decide to work with certificates, as TLS does, or manage the raw public keys yourself depends on your requirements and possibilities.

Also, if your CAN bus traffic contains confidential messages, and integrity is also on your wish list, AES-GCM or ChaCha20-Poly1305 might be suitable candidates. If your scenario allows for management and distribution of pre-shared secrets, you can spare the costly key-exchange algorithms. If not, DHE or ECDHE, as used by TLS 1.3, might be the algorithms of your choice.

This sounds rather shallow and, to some extent it is, because you have to clarify hundreds of details on the way to your specific implementation. However, this information gives you some guidance as to where your journey needs to go.

Redundancy in Secure Communication

If you've made it to this point, you've read a lot about how secure communication can be achieved by using TLS and its magical crypto features to protect confidentiality and integrity of messages as well as authenticity of communication partners. However, at the beginning of this chapter, I said that communication demands all the protection goals, including availability. But to be clear: TLS and cryptography in general are *not able to protect availability*.

Of course, in some use cases, the availability of transmitted data is essential—for example, in domains where technical safety measures protect humans from accidents and injuries, but also in systems where downtime leads to significant financial losses, as in production or transportation. In those applications, if a message is lost, the correct functionality of a device or a whole system is at risk. These threats have to be handled by *logical or physical redundancy*.

Approaching this problem on a logical level means sending messages multiple times or adding redundancy data generated by error-detecting codes like CRC checksums or error-correcting algorithms like Hamming codes. This is useful for transmissions over noisy or unreliable channels and to handle disturbance events originating, for example, from electromagnetic interference or cosmic radiation. However, these measures don't offer adequate protection against deliberate destruction and continuous interruption of a physical communication line.

The only way to be resilient in such situations is to implement multiple physical communication channels. A common example is a *ring topology*, used in many industrial infrastructures to connect devices to one another in a ring-like structure. However, that configuration requires devices to have two network interfaces, left and right, and messages always have to be sent in both directions and can be received on two different interfaces.

This leads to engineering and component efforts on each device, and the system installation as a whole becomes more expensive. In addition, the communication delay depends on the number of devices in the ring, and the bandwidth has to be shared among all network participants. However, this physical redundancy is robust against corrupted messages, broken or cut cables, and even device replacement during system operation. The international standard IEC 62439 describes several ways to achieve high availability in industrial networks, for example, based on a ring or a mesh topology.

Summary

The IoT and its industrial counterpart are not possible without secure communication. A variety of protection goals from confidentiality to integrity to authenticity, and even availability, are demanded for modern communication channels. Besides the necessary cryptographic capabilities, devices need to support state-of-the-art protocols like TLS 1.3 to achieve a high security level. In some use cases, where the loss of messages is critical and redundant physical communication media are required, devices even have to provide multiple communication interfaces.

This chapter's case study showed an example implementation of a MQTTbroker with TLS-based communication and the necessary configuration parameters. It showed that thorough security analysis of the final result can help spot misconfigurations and weak cipher suites offered by a service.

Although TLS is one of the most common and most popular security protocols, many others exist that are meant for dedicated applications. For example, Internet Protocol security (IPsec) can be used to establish a virtual private network (VPN) on OSI layer 3, while the SSH protocol enables remote access to devices for administrators. On OSI layer 2, the idea of Time-Sensitive Networking (TSN) takes care of communication channel separation on a shared physical medium, while IEEE 802.1AE (also known as *MACsec*) aims for protected communication.

And even if you don't find any protocol that directly suits your needs, the conglomeration of modern security protocols can definitely serve as inspiration for solving your specific challenges.

PART III

ADVANCED DEVICE SECURITY CONCEPTS

Many managers and developers dream of one-shot security solutions. They believe that a secure device results from *just activating* a protection feature in the OS kernel or by *just integrating* a security component into the PCB design of the product. Clearly, that's wishful thinking. Engineering secure devices requires focus and attention from development to device production to daily operation.

The third part of this book covers concepts that can have a strong impact on device security, like system integrity, reliable update procedures, and robustness even under attack. Further, intelligent access control management and system monitoring can significantly reduce the impact of vulnerabilities. However, all of these succeed only if considered and implemented comprehensively.

8

SECURE BOOT AND
SYSTEM INTEGRITY

During the boot process of embedded systems, the initialization of basic hardware as well as the startup of an OS take place. Many of these steps involve firmware stored in flash memory since that provides device engineers with the possibility to update. However, this replaceability comes at a price: attackers are able to tamper with that data for their own advantage.

In this chapter, I'll explain the complexity of boot processes and various protection concepts. After introducing the classic secure boot chain concept, I'll discuss practical considerations like the impact of secure boot process on development and production processes. As usual, theory and practice are not one and the same, so I'll include a case study on implementing secure boot on the STM32MP157F platform.

Based on boot process integrity, you might wonder whether device integrity can be taken further, so this chapter also describes how to achieve integrity protections for filesystems and more. Finally, I'll look at a low-cost firmware integrity solution for microcontroller-based systems that don't rely on external flash memory and a complex boot process.

System Boot Complexity

Many modern microchips for embedded systems contain a variety of submodules and are therefore called *system-on-chips (SoCs)*. In addition to the availability of multiple CPU cores, GPUs, real-time cores, and similar supporting coprocessors contribute to a system's complexity. Also, SoCs that include an FPGA continue to gain popularity and add bitstream handling to the equation.

Further, some SoCs provide a *trusted execution environment (TEE)*, which is used to separate the execution of critical software logically or physically—on a dedicated processing unit—from the ordinary firmware. In ARM-based SoCs, you'll come across the terms *ARM TrustZone* and *ARM Trusted Firmware* that represent ARM's TEE. The initialization of such an environment often takes place during the boot process. And, although those features aim for higher security, it can't be denied that these technologies also lead to even more complexity—the natural enemy of intelligibility and security.

SoC devices also usually require further components on the PCB—for example, volatile double data rate (DDR) memory and nonvolatile storage, such as an embedded MultiMediaCard (eMMC) or similar flash memories. Initialization of necessary on-chip controllers and their parameters are further crucial parts of modern boot processes. Figure 8-1 gives an overview of typical software and hardware components of an SoC involved in its boot process.

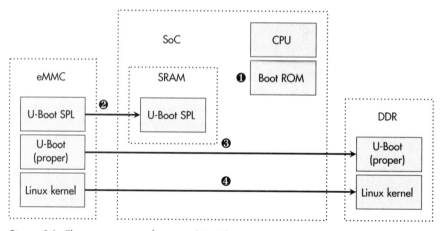

Figure 8-1: The components of a typical SoC boot process

After power up, the boot procedure is initiated in hardware based on a boot read-only memory (ROM) ❶ that initializes internal structures and loads a minimalist first-stage bootloader (FSBL) like U-Boot SPL that's copied to internal SRAM memory ❷. This piece of software initializes the external DDR memory and places a fully-fledged second-stage bootloader (SSBL) there ❸. The SSBL is able to provide several convenience features like boot medium selection, debugging, console access, and more. Afterward, the OS kernel, which in the embedded system context is often Linux, is started ❹.

At this point, the boot process is "officially" over, and the device is in its runtime state.

Figure 8-2 shows the necessary steps for booting in temporal order.

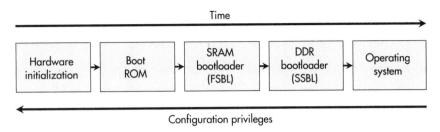

Figure 8-2: The steps of a typical boot process

There is one basic property to highlight at this point: subsequent stages in a boot process always "trust" their predecessors. That means, for example, without external monitoring measures, an OS can't tell a malicious bootloader from the original one; it just relies on every configuration set and the parameters passed to it. Therefore, optimal boot-process protection has to start at its very beginning: in hardware.

Boot Protection Concepts

From the perspective of a customer or a device user, integrity is usually a desired protection goal for a device's firmware and software. One relevant risk scenario is that cybercriminals try to persist malicious software in firmware to survive a reboot of the system—for example, to enable long-lasting backdoor access. Also, the manipulation of low-level configuration parameters and OS settings wouldn't be possible with verification routines running at boot time. Even attacks that modify a device's software during delivery, as reported to be performed by intelligence services, would render a product nonfunctional if solid integrity protection is implemented.

The authors of IEC 62443 (Part 4-2) also seem to have these scenarios in mind. The embedded device requirement (EDR) 3.14 for security level (SL) 1 or higher aims for integrity of the boot process. It requests that a device must be able to perform integrity verification of the firmware, software, and configuration data used in the device's boot and runtime processes prior to their execution. Starting at SL 2, the standard even requires authenticity of all replaceable parts of the boot process.

Device manufacturers usually agree on the importance of integrity and authenticity of firmware and software because that also prevents attackers from installing custom software for reverse-engineering purposes. However, they have another risk to consider: loss of intellectual property. Even at early boot stages, such know-how might be cast in software, like optimized algorithms, proprietary protocols, and secrets. Therefore, in some cases, vendors would like to encrypt all firmware, software, and configuration data used during the boot process in order to protect their confidentiality.

The third stakeholder in this game is the chip-manufacturing industry that provides several protection measures advertised by associated marketing terms. The following list provides an overview of typical keywords, but of course, it might not capture all future marketing creativity:

Secure boot   This generic term is the "classic" and most popular one. It usually stands for the step-by-step verification of integrity and authenticity of software components used throughout the boot process. From a cryptographic point of view, the verification is based on digital signatures and asymmetric algorithms like RSA or ECDSA. Whenever a signature verification fails, the boot process stops. Its details are explained in "Classic Secure Boot Chain" on page 145.

Verified boot   Similar to secure boot, this term stresses the cryptographic verification of the software parts executed in the boot chain. Intel uses this term, among others, as part of its Boot Guard technology, and Google utilizes it for Android and Chrome OSs.

High-assurance boot   NXP works with this label to highlight boot-process protection for i.MX devices. Among other protections, this approach also uses digital signatures to verify integrity and authenticity as described by secure boot.

Authenticated boot   This term might seem to express the authentication of firmware and other software components. However, the Trusted Computing Group (TCG) uses this term to describe a boot process that allows for reporting "an accurate record of the way that the platform booted." That means pieces of software are hashed during the boot process and written to a TPM. The startup procedure is not interrupted if manipulated software is to be executed, but the later state, be it original or altered, can be reported to an external party or used by the TPM to grant or deny access to stored secrets.

Measured boot   Microsoft uses this term in the context of TPM-based boot protection in which software is *measured*, or hashed, during the boot process. It's similar to TCG's authenticated boot.

Trusted boot   This is sometimes found in close relation to TPM-protected boot processes. However, Microsoft also uses it to describe the verification of the Windows kernel and OS components.

Encrypted boot   In contrast to all other listed forms of boot protection, this concept aims for confidentiality. In this case, firmware and related software are stored in an encrypted way, usually based on symmetric encryption algorithms. The decryption happens on the fly during boot and is usually supported by hardware.

Be careful whenever it comes to marketing terms for boot process protection. They can be misleading and sometimes implement only part of what you expect!

Classic Secure Boot Chain

For embedded devices, the most important variant of boot-process protection is the classic secure boot chain in which every component involved in the boot process verifies the next before handing over execution. Therefore, integrity and authenticity of all the software parts in a boot process can be achieved, which are often desirable requirements for several stakeholders.

Figure 8-3 shows a linear secure boot process from power up in hardware up to the point when the OS is running.

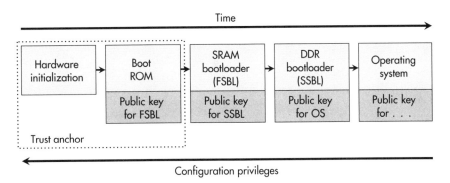

Figure 8-3: The steps in a classic secure boot process

In comparison to Figure 8-2, notice the set of additional keys at every stage. These are public keys based on asymmetric crypto like RSA or ECDSA, which means they don't carry any secret but are necessary to verify the signature of the subsequent boot stage. For example, the DDR bootloader has to carry the public key related to the signature of the OS kernel executed in the following boot step.

Although these keys aren't required to stay confidential, they have a very important protection goal to fulfill: integrity. The reason for that is simple. If an attacker is able to replace a public key, a self-generated one can be stored instead. By changing a verification key, it becomes possible to correctly verify a forged, self-generated signature of a manipulated piece of software, which would break the secure boot chain.

Figure 8-4 shows how the involved public keys are stored in various places within an SoC. Most obviously, some of them are usually stored in flash memory, which is easy for attackers to manipulate.

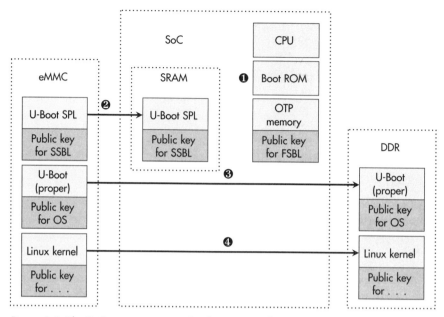

Figure 8-4: The SoC components involved in a secure boot process

The "trick" for handling this issue is that the integrity of the secure boot chain can be reduced to the integrity of the first verification key. If this initial key is stored in flash memory, the guarantees of the secure boot process hold only as long as an attacker is not able to alter this memory content.

Microchips supporting secure boot usually provide OTP memory to physically burn the first public key or its hash into the device. This key is then used during boot ROM execution ❶ to verify the FSBL. The key for SSBL verification is included in the FSBL ❷, and the SSBL carries the public key to verify the OS kernel ❸, reaching the integrity goal for the whole boot chain. This verification chain might even be extended to kernel modules or application software by integrating further public keys into the OS kernel ❹.

NOTE *Keep in mind that only a secure boot chain starting in ROM within an SoC is a robust protection against boot software manipulation, because all protection guarantees can be traced back to the beginning of the boot chain.*

Considerations for Implementing Secure Boot

Unfortunately, the implementation of secure boot is not like activating a single option in a configuration menu, which is probably why secure boot on embedded systems is still uncommon in the market. However, the following details aren't meant to scare developers away, but rather to serve as a list of tasks to keep in mind if you decide to take on secure boot.

Hardware and Software Requirements

First, it's important to understand that a consistent secure boot chain requires every part of that chain to support signature verification based on asymmetric crypto. Of course, that includes the chosen microcontroller running all software. If secure boot was not a requirement during chip purchase, integrating it afterward might not be possible.

Be sure to make secure boot a requirement during device architecture discussions. If the central microchip doesn't support it, you're forced to postpone the secure boot feature to the next device generation.

In addition, if software components don't support signature verification, as might be the case for certain bootloaders, and you can't integrate the functionality yourself, you'll need to start the possibly tedious process of finding and implementing suitable replacements.

At the far end of the boot process, verifying the operating system kernel as a final step might be enough. However, on Linux, for example, you might also want to verify integrity and authenticity of kernel modules, or even extend the verification process to filesystems and applications as discussed in "Integrity Protection Beyond the Boot Process" on page 154.

But even if all your software already supports digital signature verification, several changes are necessary to incorporate secure boot, from hardware initialization to bootloader settings and maybe even OS kernel configuration.

Development Process

On the development side, the signature generation process (for example, within a CI pipeline), has to be established. Depending on the hardware and software used within the device, integrating vendor-specific tools, such as for signing and final image generation, might be necessary. If you're lucky, the use of the openssl command line tool will be sufficient.

WARNING   *The image-signing process is crucial for secure boot implementation. However, it involves private keys that have a strong need for confidentiality protection. If they become compromised, authenticity and integrity for device software can no longer be guaranteed.*

A common obstacle to overcome during development of devices protected by secure boot is the handling of test images and devices. Various approaches exist, all valid on their own for specific situations. On the one hand, you might want to perform early testing without any secure boot restrictions on completely open devices. However, you wouldn't be able to discover issues related to secure boot. On the other hand, you might want to use one or more test signing keys on test devices to authenticate images meant for testing only. However, this bears the risk of unintentionally locking test devices with incorrect configurations or keys, which might turn them into electronic bricks.

In any case, be careful when using different key pairs for testing and production use cases. If they get mixed up, test images (with additional tools or fewer restrictions) might verify correctly and run on devices in the field.

Production and Lifetime

Another area relevant for secure boot implementations is the production of devices. Since configuration data and keys have to be burned into OTP memory, the production process has to be adapted to enable secure boot. In-production testing of secure boot can also be a reasonable extension. Just imagine if all the previous steps were taken with great care and effort, but then the devices leave production with an incorrectly activated secure boot process that can be circumvented easily in the field. At best, that would be a motivational disaster for all security engineers, probably worse.

As if the task isn't already complicated enough, secure boot implementations are also an attractive target for attackers and researchers. Therefore, the signing keys could get compromised in your development infrastructure, or vulnerabilities in hardware or firmware affecting boot process security could be found by external parties. Both cases lead to the necessity of replacing parts of the firmware with updated versions, maybe including a newly generated public verification key. A secure update functionality, as described in Chapter 9, as well as a solid key- and firmware-management process, are essential to handle these circumstances professionally.

NOTE *Implementation of secure boot requires developers, IT environment administrators, and production engineers to work together. Make sure that device security is considered a common goal for all people involved.*

Open Source Licenses vs. Secure Boot

The possibility to nail down a specific software version to hardware is valuable for device manufacturers, but this game has another player: the free and open source software community.

Around the year 2000, a company named TiVo developed a digital video recorder (DVR) that prevented the execution of modified software by users. TiVo not only was a secure boot pioneer but also attracted the attention of Richard Stallman and the Free Software Foundation (FSF). The DVR device was running software licensed under the GNU General Public License version 2 (GPLv2), like Linux, which was meant to enable users to run their own customized software. Since then, the term *tivoization* has been used to describe mechanisms that restrict or prohibit the execution of custom open source software on a device.

Following this conflict, the FSF developed GPLv3, a license that makes the implicit claims of GPLv2 explicit:

> The Corresponding Source conveyed under this section must be accompanied by the Installation Information. [. . .] Installation Information [. . .] means any methods, [. . .] authorization keys, [. . .] required to install and execute modified versions.

While the Linux kernel and the popular embedded system bootloader U-Boot are available under GPLv2, other software like the GNU Grand Unified Bootloader (GRUB) is subject to GPLv3 and might lead to legal conflicts when implemented in a secure boot scenario.

Clarifying the opposing goals of open source software licenses and secure boot protection for your individual case is absolutely necessary before going to market in order to save you quite some trouble.

It might seem not worth thinking about, but in some cases, developers seek a solution that satisfies both requirements: boot-process protection and the possibility to install modified software. One way to achieve such a compromise is to implement an unlock feature within the boot process. This feature allows the deactivation of secure boot verification in order to enable execution of custom (boot) software, but at the same time, the device has to ensure that all sensitive data, such as decryption keys, authenticators, and proprietary knowledge, are wiped from memory. This approach is already used by a variety of Android mobile phone vendors.

Case Study: Secure Boot Process on an STM32MP157F Device

In this section, I take a look at the specific boot-process protection measures of the STM32MP157F device and its corresponding software packages. However, keep in mind that this is a broad overview and not a step-by-step tutorial. A comprehensive secure boot implementation requires substantial efforts and a lot of fine-tuning.

The Boot Process

The microcontroller at hand exhibits a common boot-process complexity, as shown in Figure 8-5.

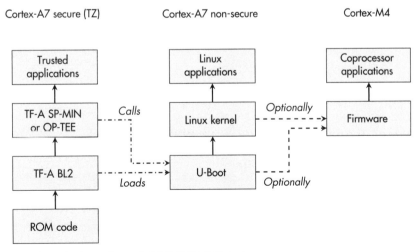

Figure 8-5: The boot chain of STM32MP157F devices

After power-up, the ROM code performs basic initialization of the platform, loads the FSBL to internal RAM, and hands over execution to the FSBL. In this case, the FSBL is the Boot Loader stage 2 (BL2) part of the Trusted Firmware-A (TF-A) provided by ARM. In a simple setup, this BL2 initializes the DDR memory of the device, loads the SSBL into it, and executes the SSBL. However, if use of ARM TrustZone is desired, the FSBL loads not only the SSBL but also the runtime software for the secure world, and then jumps to the SSBL afterward.

By default, the STM32MP157F platform uses the popular embedded system bootloader U-Boot as the SSBL. U-Boot comes with a variety of features and is commonly used to boot embedded Linux kernels. Next, Linux takes over control, launches its kernel modules, services, and user-space applications, and concludes the boot process.

Another feature of STM32MP157F devices, also increasingly seen for other microcontroller products and manufacturers, is the availability of a coprocessor. Here, an additional ARM Cortex-M4 microcontroller with dedicated RAM is integrated to allow for the robust execution of real-time tasks, as discussed in Chapter 10. Loading firmware to this additional controller might also be part of the boot process. This can be initiated either directly by an SSBL like U-Boot or later, out of the running Linux OS.

Many developers would stop here, use the platform as described, and be happy if the boot process "just works." However, until now, no protection against modification of any firmware parts has been considered.

Secure Boot Starts in Hardware

Robust secure boot concepts have to start in hardware. For this purpose, the ROM code needs to provide a verification routine that can be used to authenticate the FSBL image. Luckily, STM32MP157F devices have an integrated feature for that purpose. Figure 8-6 shows an overview of the related key generation, signing, and authentication process.

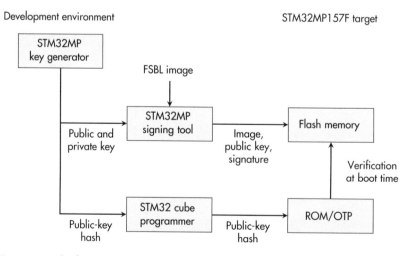

Figure 8-6: The firmware signing and provisioning process for STM32MP157F devices

The chip at hand utilizes the ECDSA algorithm to achieve integrity and authenticity of firmware images. In comparison to RSA, this enables faster signing and shorter keys, but the verification at boot time might take a bit longer. On the developers' side, the ECC key pair has to be generated by the STM32MP Key Generator tool, which results in a private key, a corresponding public key, and the SHA-256 hash of the public key. The latter is useful because it requires less OTP memory in the chip compared to storing the whole public key.

To prepare the device for secure boot, the public-key hash has to be burned into its fuse memory. This can be achieved in various ways. You can use the ST-provided STM32 Cube Programmer or the U-Boot stm32key command. Also, the secure secret provisioning (SSP) feature might be of interest to you because it establishes a protected channel between a programmer and the STM32MP157F device, making it especially useful for secure production purposes.

NOTE   *The STM32MP157F device can be locked after writing the public-key hash to its OTP memory. This is mandatory for production but should be considered with caution during development.*

After key provisioning in the device, the image has to be prepared for authenticated execution. Again, specific software, the STM32MP Signing Tool, is provided that processes the pre-generated ECDSA private key and the SHA-256 hash of the FSBL image in order to obtain the corresponding digital signature for this firmware part. The resulting image also contains the ECDSA public key and can be placed in the nonvolatile memory of the device.

At boot time, the ROM code verifies the integrity and authenticity of the presented FSBL image. First, the provided public key is verified by comparing its hash to the one stored in OTP memory. If correct, the key is used to verify the validity of the stored signature and the hash of the provided image. If successful, the FSBL payload is executed, and NOTICE: Bootrom authentication succeeded is output to the console. In any other case, the boot process halts.

Secure Boot Based on BL2 TF-A

For the FSBL, STM32MP157F devices rely on ARM's BL2 TF-A that also provides secure boot support. However, it's disabled by default and has to be activated by setting the TRUSTED_BOARD_BOOT=1 build flag. Afterward, the digital signatures of binaries loaded by BL2 are verified for integrity and authenticity based on asymmetric cryptography.

The BL2 TF-A requires a firmware image package (FIP) that can be generated with the fiptool application. It contains all binaries to be loaded and executed and the cryptographic data necessary to verify these binaries. The binaries include, for example, an SSBL and a TEE implementation like OP-TEE that runs in the ARM TrustZone. The TEE is denoted as BL32, and the SSBL is known as BL33 in the TF-A taxonomy.

Again, the first step is the generation of key pairs (X.509 certificates in this case) that can be used for signing and verification of firmware parts. For this task, ST provides the `cert_create` tool.

The TF-A requires all certificates to be part of a chain of trust (CoT). By default, the public key stored in the STM32MP157F's OTP memory is taken as the root key, so the corresponding private key is a mandatory input for the `cert_create` tool.

After all the binaries and corresponding certificates are finalized, the FIP can be generated, and the result can be deployed to the device. During the boot process, the BL2 TF-A will use Mbed TLS for certificate parsing and the STM32MP Crypto Lib for signature verification in order to use the hardware hashing module.

The order of binary loading and execution is as follows. First, BL2 loads BL32 (OP-TEE) to memory and verifies its signature. Afterward, the same happens for BL33 (U-Boot). Only after successful verification, the execution of BL32 is started, which, in turn, calls BL33 after its own completion.

U-Boot's Secure Boot Feature

After the ROM code and the BL2 TF-A, the third implementation involved in the device's secure boot is U-Boot's image-authentication procedure. In 2013, the groundwork for U-Boot's secure boot support was laid by introducing RSA-based signature verification for Flattened Image Tree (FIT) images.

To activate these features, several configuration options also have to be enabled—for example, RSA crypto functionality (`CONFIG_RSA`), FIT support (`CONFIG_FIT`), and signature handling in FIT images (`CONFIG_FIT_SIGNATURE`).

Again, key generation is a fundamental step. However, since U-Boot is an open source project, key generation is also possible with open source tools such as the `openssl` command line tool. At the time of writing, U-Boot supports digital signatures based on RSA-2048, RSA-3072, RSA-4096, and ECDSA with a 256-bit curve.

Listing 8-1 shows the two commands that generate a typical 2,048-bit RSA key and a corresponding X.509 certificate. Both are required for the later signing and image-generation process.

```
$ openssl genrsa -out keys/dev.key 2048
$ openssl req -batch -new -x509 -key keys/dev.key -out keys/dev.crt
```

Listing 8-1: The key generation for U-Boot's image verification

To generate a correctly signed FIT image, an Image Tree Source (ITS) file has to be created. Listing 8-2 shows an example.

```
/dts-v1/;
/ {
    description = "U-Boot fitImage for stm32mp157f";
    #address-cells = <1>;
```

```
images {
    kernel {
        description = "Linux kernel";
    ❶ data = /incbin/("zImage");
        type = "kernel";
        arch = "arm";
        os = "linux";
        compression = "none";
        load = <0xC0008000>;
        entry = <0xC0008000>;
        hash-1 {
            algo = "sha256";
        };
    };
    fdt-dk2 {
        description = "FDT dk2";
    ❷ data = /incbin/("stm32mp157f-dk2.dtb");
        type = "flat_dt";
        arch = "arm";
        compression = "none";
        hash-1 {
        ❸ algo = "sha256";
        };
    };
};

❹ configurations {
    default = "dk2";
    dk2 {
        description = "dk2";
        kernel = "kernel";
        fdt = "fdt-dk2";
        signature-1 {
        ❺ algo = "sha256,rsa2048";
        ❻ key-name-hint = "dev";
            sign-images = "fdt", "kernel";
        };
    };
};
};
```

Listing 8-2: An example of a FIT image source

This FIT image source example assumes the Linux kernel is available as
zImage ❶ and its device tree blob (DTB) for the STM32MP157F-DK2 board is
stored as *stm32mp157f-dk2.dtb* ❷. Both are hashed by SHA-256 ❸, but U-Boot
would also support SHA-384 and SHA-512.

Note that the kernel and DTB are combined only in the `configurations` section ❹ of the ITS file. This thwarts mix-and-match attacks that would try to boot and misuse unwanted pairs of kernels and DTBs. Using an RSA-2048 signature ❺ generated by the key *dev.key* ❻ on the configuration consisting of a specific kernel and a specific DTB grants only the execution of this explicit combination.

After processing the ITS file with the `mkimage` tool, the last firmware part is signed and ready to be stored on the STM32MP157F device's memory card. On successful verification during U-Boot's boot procedure, you'll see a message in the serial console output similar to the one shown in Listing 8-3.

```
## Loading kernel from FIT Image at c2000000 ...
   Using 'dk2' configuration
   Verifying Hash Integrity ... sha256,rsa2048:dev+ OK
```

Listing 8-3: A successful kernel and DTB verification by U-Boot

Subsequently, the execution of the verified Linux kernel is the worthy reward for your hard work.

Even if the whole verification chain "works" up to this point, you still have two important tasks to do:

Perform comprehensive testing   Confirm that every modification of a firmware part is actually detected and that the boot process is stopped accordingly. It might well be that, by mistake, a small part of the created image is not protected by a corresponding signature, which could open the door for manipulations.

Check hardware for known weaknesses   Vulnerabilities in hardware components relevant for your boot process might break the security of the whole verification chain. Just as an example, CVE-2017-7932 and CVE-2017-7936 describe such hardware issues that can't be fixed after production.

Integrity Protection Beyond the Boot Process

The classic secure boot chain usually terminates at the point where the OS takes over control. However, device architects might quite rightly want to extend integrity and authenticity protection beyond that stage.

Kernel Module Verification

Loadable Linux kernel modules enable a modular and dynamic way of extending kernel functionality. However, modification of such a loadable module paves the way for malicious code execution with kernel rights by attackers. Therefore, verifying integrity and authenticity of these modules during the loading process is desirable.

The Linux kernel already provides support for this security feature. There, RSA-based signatures of kernel modules can be verified upon loading a certain kernel module, but this functionality is disabled by default. It has to be activated in the `Enable Loadable Module Support` section of the kernel's configuration (`CONFIG_MODULE_SIG`).

By default, kernel-module signature verification runs in *permissive* mode: modules without signatures or corresponding public keys are marked as tainted but are still loaded. To enforce valid module signatures, the `CONFIG _MODULE_SIG_FORCE` option has to be enabled.

With standard settings for module signing, the kernel build process automatically generates signing keys and associated X.509 certificates at compile time by using OpenSSL. The created private keys are used to sign compiled kernel modules and might be discarded afterward. Of course, the certificates containing the public verification keys have to be integrated into the Linux kernel to enable successful verification at runtime.

Filesystem Integrity

As part of the Linux startup process, the kernel usually will mount one or more filesystems. These may contain application binaries, configuration data, trusted certificates, and public keys, all prone to tampering by adversaries. Standard filesystems like ext3 and ext4 incorporate mechanisms to deal with accidental data corruption but don't provide integrity protection from a security point of view.

When looking at integrity protection for filesystem data, it's important to distinguish between protecting data at rest (for example, in the power-off state) and protecting against data manipulation at runtime.

MAC-Based Filesystem Protection

Stacked filesystems like EncFS and gocryptfs, mentioned for confidentiality protection in Chapter 5, can additionally provide integrity protection in the form of HMACs or authenticated encryption. These mechanisms target data-at-rest protection because changing data at runtime is desired and, of course, possible. They generate cryptographic checksums whenever files are written and verify them upon reading.

Further, integrity protection can also be achieved at the block device level. The popular `dm-crypt` crypto target for the Linux device mapper infrastructure can use `dm-integrity` (`CONFIG_DM_INTEGRITY`) that generates authentication tags when writing and verifies them when data is read. Also, `dm-crypt` supports authenticated encryption ciphers like AES-GCM and ChaCha20-Poly1305. However, if only integrity protection is desired, `dm-integrity` can also be used standalone. Again, these measures aim for integrity protection against attackers modifying data in nonvolatile memory.

Read-Only Filesystems

If you're concerned about filesystem modifications at runtime, an even simpler solution exists. Read-only filesystems like CramFS and SquashFS don't implement write access for files, which means there's simply no way to alter disk data at runtime, even if a system is compromised. A further nonsecurity advantage is the compressed storage of these filesystems, decreasing the demand for nonvolatile memory. However, attackers with offline access to the mass storage media can replace the filesystem at will.

Comprehensive Integrity Protection

Finally, one solution provides integrity protection against both offline and runtime attacks: the dm-verity module (CONFIG_DM_VERITY). Originating from the Chrome OS community, it's meant as a direct extension of secure boot to filesystem integrity. Also, Android 4.4 introduced support for it in 2013, and it was strictly enforced in 2016, beginning with Android 7.0.

From a technical point of view, dm-verity uses a hash tree in which each data block in a given block device is hashed. Then, sets of hash values are hashed to obtain next-level hashes, and so on, until a single root hash remains. If this root-hash value is incorporated into the secure boot verification process, the integrity of all data within the block device can be guaranteed. At runtime, for each file access, the hash tree is verified up to the root hash. This, of course, leads to a read-only filesystem. The initialization process of such a volume is supported by the veritysetup user-space tool after filesystem image creation.

Write Protection as a Low-Cost Solution

For some microcontrollers, especially low-cost and low-performance variants, secure boot is not available. However, that's not a valid excuse for missing firmware protection.

The boot process of these platforms is usually much simpler because they use an RTOS or even just run bare-metal software. Further, their software and data are considerably smaller and often reside at least partially in *internal* flash memory. But still, the goals of integrity and authenticity can be important to protect devices from malicious modifications.

A simple yet powerful feature in this context is the activation of write protection for internal flash memory. The firmware is written to the device and the memory is "locked" afterward. Also, debugging interfaces like Joint Test Action Group (JTAG) should be deactivated. Following the principle of defense in depth, it makes sense to implement verification functions within such firmware that check whether lock-bits and other anti-debugging measures are set properly. Then, even if write-protection mechanisms are circumvented—for example, by physical attacks—an adversary still has to invest a substantial amount of reverse engineering to completely break the firmware integrity protection.

Of course, this internal, integrity-protected software might implement cryptographic signature verification and become the starting point of a verification chain that transfers the internal protection goals to data stored in external memories.

Summary

Processor hardware and its manufacturers play an important role in the implementation of secure boot processes for embedded systems. Proprietary architectures, heterogeneous multicore complexity, and a conglomeration of marketing terms contribute to the high barrier that device architects and developers have to climb when aiming for a protected boot process.

The basic principle is simple: an immutable hardware component verifies the first software component to be loaded for integrity and authenticity. If successful, execution is handed over to that software, which again might verify the next piece of software, and so on. However, in practice, as shown in this chapter's case study, every stage of the boot process is different and requires product-specific knowledge and often vendor-specific tools. In addition, a series of cryptographic keys has to be managed, and device production processes even have to be prepared for secure boot support. The promising gain of this protection measure for the overall device security exacts its toll.

A robust secure boot implementation is a strong foundation for further security measures like kernel-module verification, filesystem integrity protection, and a variety of runtime integrity measures. It even has a positive impact on reverse-engineering protection and the secure data storage approaches described in Chapter 5, because it prevents attackers from executing custom code on your product and thereby exploring its internals.

9

SECURE FIRMWARE UPDATE

Security updates are annoying, for consumers, for administrators, and especially for manufacturers. The latter constantly need to watch out for possible vulnerabilities in their products and react to corresponding notifications, while users and administrators have to apply published patches in a timely manner. Since we can regard a device's security as a volatile state that might change tomorrow, having a solid update strategy is imperative.

However, software update handling is not a trivial process. Only authorized entities should be able to supply updates to devices, and they shouldn't break device functionality or turn it into an expensive brick. In addition, safety experts are often rather reluctant to introduce patches to their certified devices, while corresponding certification bodies increasingly recognize the importance of security updates even in safety-critical areas.

This chapter walks through the options for secure update approaches and the reasoning behind them. A central consideration is the secure implementation of update verification and its reliable application on the device itself. The chapter concludes with a practical case study for firmware updates based on the popular SWUpdate framework and a Yocto-based toolchain.

The Inevitability of Updates

In some software and product development communities, a *perpetual beta* phase is common: a product never leaves its beta status, and new features are continuously added, even if the software or device is already in the field and in productive use by customers. This concept is sometimes also described as the *banana principle*, because those fruits are harvested when still green and continue to ripen on their way to customers and even after purchase. In such cases, it's blatantly obvious that the delivered product isn't completely finished and requires several software updates to develop its full potential. A secure update approach is essential.

If we look at industrial systems and critical infrastructures, the situation is very different. Although these systems usually have a long lifetime, their manufacturers and operators may not have seen a need for patch management in the past. However, the increase in connectivity and digitalization in this field, along with the continuous discovery of vulnerabilities in industrial products, forces vendors and users to act and prepare for secure update processes. This situation is especially challenging because manufacturer support for security updates and operational patch management processes for industrial components usually have to run for decades.

Even if you work in an industry that has a strong security focus and your development processes yield highly secure and robust products, you can't guarantee that your software, your firmware, and your hardware components are free of bugs. Also, you don't know whether new attack methodologies—not even invented at the time of product development—will cause security issues for your devices and may demand the replacement of crypto algorithms or the further enhancement of security features. In a nutshell: no product is perfect. Prepare it to be updatable.

Some prominent cases stress the need for secure update support in embedded and IoT devices. The vulnerability collections *Urgent/11* from 2019 and *Ripple20* from 2020 showed that fundamental software components like TCP/IP stacks and OSs may exhibit severe weaknesses. Millions, if not billions, of devices were affected, and many are assumed not to be patchable because they don't provide the necessary means. In the end, that inability forces customers to replace those devices or leaves them with insecure systems. At this scale, it might even pose a risk to society as a whole because malicious actors know how to invite those IoT products to their botnets. The bottom line is that every digital device sold in the 2020s should have a secure update mechanism.

NOTE *I'm not the only one stressing the need for secure update strategies. IEC 62443 for industrial cybersecurity, United Nations (UN) Regulation 156 for the automotive industry, and the cybersecurity part of the US FD&C Act for medical devices also agree, just to name a few.*

Security Requirements

As with every concept that has the term *secure* in its title, the obvious question is which (protection) goals are associated with it in this specific context. The following sections describe requirements you must consider for a secure firmware update.

Authenticity

It is essential that a firmware update can cryptographically prove its authenticity, which ensures that it originates from the original manufacturer of the given device. This prohibits the installation of maliciously crafted updates and should be mandatory for all secure update procedures. This goal is typically achieved by digitally signing an update package.

Confidentiality

Firmware images are regularly used by people to reverse engineer devices for the enumeration of software libraries, to identify weaknesses, or to analyze proprietary applications for intellectual property and secrets. Confidentiality protection can be achieved by the encryption of the update contents as a whole or in parts.

However, make sure you understand there is a risk because the corresponding decryption key needs to be stored on the device, so attackers might either be able to extract that key from the device or the plain firmware update after on-device decryption.

Secure Distribution Channel

The first two requirements, authenticity and confidentiality, impose requirements on the update file itself. However, the distribution channel also might be worth protecting (for example, with TLS).

A mutually authenticated and encrypted communication between a device and an update server might even be a replacement for the confidentiality protection of the update file.

Rollback Option

This one is tricky. Rolling back the software version of a device to an older state is sometimes absolutely helpful—for example, if an update introduces severe issues that haven't existed before. On the other hand, attackers might use this feature to revert a device's software to a version containing known vulnerabilities that later patches have fixed. In that case, the operation of vulnerable devices and their exploitation becomes possible, although the manufacturer provided security updates.

If you decide to implement rollback protection, you need corresponding hardware support, such as a monotonic, nonvolatile version counter within your main CPU.

Version Distribution Monitoring

Monitoring the adoption of security updates in the field can be highly valuable, because doing so gives you an overview of the situation and the corresponding threat landscape for your devices and your customers. You could implement this monitoring with a confirmation notice for each device after a new firmware version has been successfully installed.

Distribution and Deployment of Updates

A central question regarding firmware updates is, "How does the update file find its way into the device?" Answers to that question have a significant impact on usability, processes, and reaction speed for your device's patch management.

Local vs. Remote Updates

Since the 1990s, devices that implement an update mechanism offer some kind of interface to upload or to store a firmware file that was previously downloaded from the manufacturer's website. The update file might even be restricted to be loaded at a local interface, such as via USB media. While local presence for updating can be a security feature, this approach provides pretty poor scalability for IoT scenarios. Millions of devices would require millions of customers with security awareness and millions of manual update installations, which is hardly feasible and results in few updates actually being applied.

The automotive industry is an interesting example regarding firmware updates. For many years, it was common for a recall to be issued if cars had a significant software bug or vulnerability. The owners had to bring their vehicles to an auto repair shop, where mechanics installed the software update provided by the corresponding car manufacturer that received it from the suppliers of the specific control unit. Nowadays, modern cars can receive software updates through their connection to mobile networks. This approach is called an *over-the-air (OTA) update*.

OTA updates are not restricted to cars. They can be applied to all sorts of IoT devices, and even if the term suggests that updates are applied over wireless channels, update transmission over wired networks is clearly not forbidden. The main advantage of this concept is that devices have a connection to an update management backend, usually operated by the device's manufacturer, that provides information about new updates. This approach provides decent scalability because the update rollout process can be automated and scheduled by manufacturers. However, such a system exposes backend servers and devices listening for updates to remote attackers and network-based attacks.

NOTE *In some industrial scenarios, manual local update procedures are still the default. I've heard from a person who personally visits hundreds of industrial robots, plugs in a USB stick, and then waits for the update to complete before he continues his journey, which might take weeks for a single update. Crazy!*

Pull vs. Push Strategy

There's no doubt that a direct connection between devices and an update server in the backend is a reasonable solution for professional update management, but one question remains: Who is in control of the update procedure?

Usually, devices follow a *pull strategy* for update management: a client application on the device periodically checks for new updates and downloads newly available images. Afterward, depending on the owner's configuration, the device might automatically install the update (for example, within a predefined maintenance window) or prompt a user or an administrator to approve installation. After a successful update, the new software state might be reported to a manufacturer's server. In this case, operators control when and which updates are installed on their devices, which is usually the preferred solution for business scenarios, but they also take responsibility for regular update schedules.

Alternatively, manufacturers might opt for a *push strategy* that gives them more power over the update process. They might even force devices into an update mode. This method could be reasonable if the manufacturer is involved and responsible for timely device updates, maybe even by legal obligations. Further, the security of specific customer target groups like private users can benefit significantly if updates are enforced automatically and they don't have to organize the process themselves. On the other hand, some customers deliberately choose to operate devices with old firmware versions, and if they deny those devices access to the update server, manufacturers are powerless. However, if such cases are part of your challenges, it makes sense to focus on software state monitoring whenever devices connect to your online services and deny access if device firmware is too old, keeping a large portion of devices in the field in a secure state.

Strategies that mix pull and push aspects are possible in practice. You might even leave the decision to your customers by providing corresponding configuration options for your device. This enables operators to perfectly integrate your device into their specific asset and patch-management processes.

Update Granularity and Format

The terms *software update* and *firmware update* are often used interchangeably and for a broad range of update scenarios, from rewriting all memory contents within a device to the change of few configuration parameters within a single file. Therefore, for your specific device, it's absolutely necessary to define which parts of your device firmware should be replaceable and in which format you would like to distribute that data.

Firmware Parts

In the PC context, *firmware* is the software programmed to the onboard non-volatile memory of the motherboard, installed daughterboards, and further peripheral devices. OSs, software applications, and user data, usually stored on hard disks, are not regarded as firmware. In the embedded system context, however, almost everything can be regarded as firmware:

Bootloader Modern embedded devices contain at least one boot-loader, usually more.

Coprocessor firmware Recent SoCs include a heterogeneous set of processors within one package. Some of these coprocessors might require their own firmware.

Controller firmware On the PCB scale, a single embedded system might have several microcontrollers that execute dedicated firmware.

FPGA bitstream As part of an SoC or as a discrete component, FPGAs are integrated into a multitude of embedded devices. Their configuration, called the *bitstream*, might be read directly from flash memory or loaded by a bootloader or an OS application.

Bare-metal software In devices running without an OS, bare-metal software is the main application.

OS kernel If your device comes with an OS or an RTOS, the corresponding OS kernel is the central software component.

Device tree The hardware components and their parameters for a specific embedded system are often described in a device-tree file that's loaded by the OS kernel.

Root filesystem The basic filesystem on top of which all other filesystems and overlays are mounted contains data that's crucial for the correct functioning of an OS.

Application software Application software might be part of the root filesystem but could also be located in one or multiple manufacturer-specific partitions.

Some of the firmware parts on that list might share a common non-volatile memory; others might come with their own discrete memory component. Make sure you are aware of all relevant firmware components when developing a secure update concept. However, don't forget that your device probably carries unique data that must not be affected by a software update:

Unique cryptographic keys Data corresponding to your device's unique identity, probably provisioned during production, is essential for trustworthy device authentication. Additionally, secrets, like SSH keys that are generated at first boot, should survive a software update.

User-dependent system data Customers rely on additional user accounts and corresponding credentials as well as custom device configuration files.

Runtime data partitions   Your device might collect and store user-specific runtime data, like sensor-value histories for data analytics applications, but it might also log data that might be relevant for maintenance and repair cases.

Update Formats

As mentioned previously, the granularity of software components that need to be covered by updates varies greatly and doesn't directly suggest a specific format for update distribution. Several requirements should be considered before deciding:

Comprehensive coverage   The chosen format should have the ability to update as many of a device's software components as possible.

Efficiency   Since the size of firmware is constantly increasing, it should be possible to reduce a firmware update to the parts that are actually new.

Atomicity   The installation of an update should be an *indivisible* operation allowing only two final states: successfully updated firmware or, upon failure, the original firmware before the update process started.

The following list provides possible update format solutions based on the previously posed requirements:

Files   A trivial update format would be to supply a device with a set of updated files that can be written to their specific paths in a filesystem. While this would enable updates for all components available in the device's filesystem, and small, efficient update packages could be created, atomicity is complex. Every file created, written, or deleted requires its own operation that might fail or succeed. In case of an error, the firmware might end up in an unknown state.

Containers   Containerized applications have become increasingly popular in larger embedded systems. The replacement of whole container images could be effective for their update management, but relying only on container-based updates would neglect important software components like the host OS running the container management.

Images   Updating entire partition images enables updates for many software components in an embedded system and has advantages regarding atomicity. This approach might lead to larger firmware updates than other formats, but some implementations also support compressed update files or differential updates to overcome this issue.

NOTE   *Firmware parts that aren't reachable by filesystem access, such as ICs that have to be updated based on a proprietary protocol, require customized treatment. Consider the pros and cons and make a conscious decision regarding the targeted update capabilities for your device.*

Issues with Package Managers

You might wonder why Linux-based embedded devices in most cases don't rely on established package manager applications like apt-get or opkg that are used back and forth on desktop and server systems. The reason lies in the testing complexity of systems that are updated on a package basis. Such an approach requires the management of *dependencies* among all possible packages in a system, and it multiplies the possible software configurations that have to be tested.

In addition, since embedded devices often operate in critical applications or industries, comprehensive testing is a must. Therefore, many manufacturers refrain from using package managers and choose an atomic, image-based updating approach instead, restricting the interplay of software components to be tested to the specific versions in a certain software release.

If you want to go down that road, you probably need a partner that offers automated and reliable testing services that handle all the mentioned issues, for example, as provided by Canonical for their Ubuntu Core OS.

Device Partitioning Strategies

A robust update procedure is possible only if the memory partitioning of your device supports it. Depending on available memory and willingness to take risks, various approaches can be used to design a system's partition layout to support updating processes.

Update/Recovery Partition

You can enhance robustness against failed firmware updates by introducing an additional *recovery partition*. This partition contains tools to download and update the main system partition, including the OS kernel and the corresponding root filesystem, as shown in Figure 9-1.

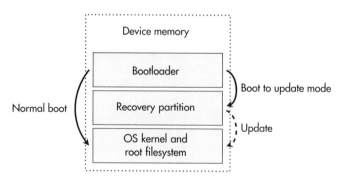

Figure 9-1: The recovery partition to perform system updates

The advantage of this approach is the low memory footprint of the extra partition, which should be feasible for many devices. However, on the downside, the device has to be rebooted to enter the update or recovery mode. If the update process fails, the main partition is corrupted and can't be booted anymore, so the recovery partition is booted again, and a fresh update process can be initiated.

A/B System Approach

For devices providing plenty of nonvolatile memory, the *A/B system* approach can be an interesting candidate. Figure 9-2 depicts the basic partition layout and update procedure.

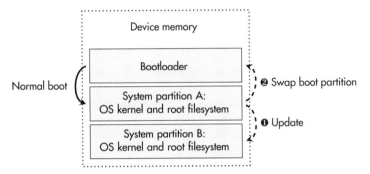

Figure 9-2: Two identical system image copies—A and B

In this layout, two copies, A and B, of the system partition exist, both holding at least the OS kernel and the root filesystem. At boot, the partition marked as "bootable" (partition A in Figure 9-2) is used to load the OS and the basic filesystem. This includes an update client that's able to receive firmware updates, verify them, and write them to the currently unused partition ❶ (B in Figure 9-2). Afterward, the bootloader is configured to swap the boot partition from A to B (or vice versa) ❷ before rebooting to the new firmware version.

In case of an update failure or partition corruption, the old version is still available in its original state and can be booted again. A significant advantage compared to using a recovery partition is that the standard device operation is not interrupted during the update download and installation. In addition, the newly downloaded firmware can be directly stored on the inactive partition instead of requiring an additional storage location for update caching. On Android devices, this concept is called *seamless system updates*, and it's increasingly implemented by phone vendors.

For devices of even higher criticality, both approaches can be combined, as shown in Figure 9-3.

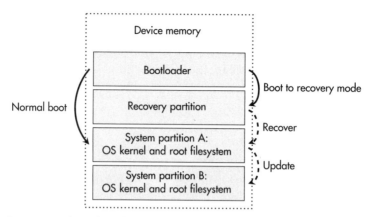

Figure 9-3: The A/B architecture with an additional recovery partition

This design aims for protection against cases in which both system partitions, A and B, are corrupted for whatever reason. For such architectures, it makes sense to store the recovery partition within a different physical memory than the system partitions. Even if the recovery partition can't successfully reinstall the system partitions, it can still report the system failure and perform diagnostics.

A Note on Updating Bootloaders

Bootloaders are used on many embedded systems. They handle basic system initialization, select a boot medium, and subsequently load an OS kernel. In many cases, these binaries are regarded as an "immutable" firmware part.

However, these days, bootloaders like U-Boot and GRUB are complex software components with a variety of features and capabilities. As a consequence, bootloaders also may exhibit bugs or even security vulnerabilities that require updates.

From a security point of view, you also might need to replace public keys or outdated cryptographic algorithms used for a secure boot process, as described in Chapter 8. On the functional side, you might come to a point when you'd like to update hardware initialization settings, kernel boot parameters, or boot configurations. All these reasons render updating bootloaders and their configuration data a valid consideration.

In most systems, however, only a single copy per bootloader is available, which means that updating it comes with the risk of breaking the device—for example, in the case of power loss or other failures during the bootloader update. Only a few SoCs and microcontrollers provide support for additional bootloader instances that can be run when the main bootloader fails. Therefore, updating a bootloader is always a critical and risky procedure that can well lead to a situation where physical access to a device is necessary for repair.

A compromise solution could be a multistage bootloader approach, splitting the functionality in two parts. The first stage is considered immutable and has minimal functionality, but provides support for multiple bootloader copies in the next stage, which carries the fully fledged bootloader. In such a system, security issues in the early stage still remain a problem and would require physical access or a risky update procedure, but the second stage can be stored redundantly, which allows for low-risk updating. However, this approach isn't standard and would require further development efforts and customizations.

The Interplay Between Development, Backend, and Device

After clarifying all the details influencing your update strategy, it's time to talk about the necessary operational processes for reliable and secure firmware updates. As described in Chapter 1, it's the manufacturer's responsibility to monitor device vulnerabilities exploited in the field and take vulnerability reports seriously.

Let's assume you have that covered already and your development team is able to provide fixes in a short time frame. An operational question still remains: Should security updates and functional enhancements be merged with firmware updates, or should each be available separately?

Some customers have to perform comprehensive testing of your device within their given infrastructure and, therefore, avoid upgrading devices with new functionalities that might require retests. However, they're probably interested in security fixes that contribute to the robustness and security of their systems. In such scenarios, a split between functional and protective updates is recommended.

In addition, imagine that a new firmware version leads to complications and customers have to downgrade to the previous version. If security updates are included in this update file, your customers would have to live with known vulnerabilities in your devices, at least until the functional issues are fixed. However, taking this separation seriously leads to more possible software configurations and more testing on the manufacturer side.

No matter the content of a firmware update, it has to be provided and packaged by the development team and corresponding build pipelines. If necessary, the firmware has to be encrypted, usually with a symmetric encryption scheme like AES. To achieve authenticity and integrity protection, the final firmware image has to be digitally signed by appropriate algorithms like RSA or ECDSA.

Both tasks include two components that have to match. On the manufacturer side, the firmware artifacts yielded by the build system have to be encrypted and signed to generate the actual firmware update files to be distributed. On the device itself, the signature verification and decryption has to be performed.

Several image-based update systems perform those tasks for you: Mender, SWUpdate, and RAUC. Mender provides the whole infrastructure, including device client software and backend server. SWUpdate and RAUC generate and apply firmware update files, but the update distribution and monitoring is typically performed by the Eclipse hawkBit backend framework. Further candidates include OSTree and swupd, which follow a "Git-like" revision-based approach for firmware updates.

Case Study: Secure Firmware Updates with SWUpdate

This case study provides an example of the necessary practical steps to bring a secure firmware update architecture to life. It's based on the Yocto toolchain delivered by ST for the STM32MP157F-DK2 board.

I've chosen SWUpdate as the central software component for this implementation. The desired outcome is an update process that verifies the authenticity of updates based on digital signatures and guarantees a reliable update procedure taking an A/B system approach.

SD Card Layout Customization

The Yocto build system compiles and packages all relevant software for my device's firmware image and provides it in formats like *.ext4* and *.tar.gz*. This is useful for further processing, such as for generating an SD card image and creating an update file, but let's take it one step at a time.

The STM32 Cube Programmer tool from ST as well as the handy shell script *create_sdcard_from_flashlayout.sh* use flash memory layout files in a Tab-Separated Values (TSV) format. Among other things, such a TSV file contains a list of partitions, their offset, and the files required to populate them. Selected columns of the default flash layout for the STM32MP157F-DK2 board are shown in Listing 9-1.

Name	Offset	Binary
fsbl-boot	0x0	arm-trusted-firmware/tf-a-stm32mp157f-dk2-usb.stm32
fip-boot	0x0	fip/fip-stm32mp157f-dk2-optee.bin
fsbl1	0x00004400	arm-trusted-firmware/tf-a-stm32mp157f-dk2-sdcard.stm32
fsbl2	0x00044400	arm-trusted-firmware/tf-a-stm32mp157f-dk2-sdcard.stm32
metadata1	0x00084400	arm-trusted-firmware/metadata.bin
metadata2	0x000C4400	arm-trusted-firmware/metadata.bin
fip-a	0x00104400	fip/fip-stm32mp157f-dk2-optee.bin
fip-b	0x00504400	none
u-boot-env	0x00904400	none
bootfs	0x00984400	st-image-bootfs-openstlinux-eglfs-stm32mp1.ext4
vendorfs	0x04984400	st-image-vendorfs-openstlinux-eglfs-stm32mp1.ext4
rootfs	0x05984400	st-image-core-openstlinux-eglfs-stm32mp1.ext4

Listing 9-1: The default flash layout for the STM32MP157F-DK2 board

The TSV file contains many lines concerning bootloaders and trusted firmware artifacts that are of minor interest at this point. The last three lines, however, reveal two important facts. First, a dedicated bootfs partition contains U-Boot configuration files, device-tree blobs, and the Linux kernel as a uImage. Second, the rootfs partition is a perfect candidate for duplication for an A/B system approach. Listing 9-2 shows the changes I made to the TSV file.

```
Name      Offset      Binary
...
bootfs    0x00984400  st-image-bootfs-openstlinux-eglfs-stm32mp1.ext4
vendorfs  0x04984400  st-image-vendorfs-openstlinux-eglfs-stm32mp1.ext4
rootfs-a  0x05984400  st-image-core-openstlinux-eglfs-stm32mp1.ext4
rootfs-b  0x35984400  st-image-core-openstlinux-eglfs-stm32mp1.ext4
userfs    0x65984400  st-image-userfs-openstlinux-eglfs-stm32mp1.ext4
```

Listing 9-2: An adjusted partition layout for the A/B update approach

The original `rootfs` partition was cloned, resulting in two new partitions: `rootfs-a` and `rootfs-b`. Also, a `userfs` partition, already available in the toolchain provided by ST, was added to store data that should "survive" an update of the root filesystem.

For SD card image generation with the new parameters, the *create_sdcard _from_flashlayout.sh* shell script also had to be adapted to correctly handle the newly introduced partitions `rootfs-a` and `rootfs-b`. The SD card image size was set to 2,048MB, while both root partitions were configured to occupy 768MB, as already indicated by the offset of `0x30000000` in the flash layout file.

An important setting in the image creation script is the allocation of individual partition UUIDs for partitions `rootfs-a` and `rootfs-b`, as shown in Listing 9-3.

```
DEFAULT_ROOTFSA_PARTUUID=e91c4e10-16e6-4c0e-bd0e-77becf4a3582
DEFAULT_ROOTFSB_PARTUUID=997046a6-c6f4-4f41-adb4-9fe614b2a92a
```

Listing 9-3: The individual UUIDs for both copies of the root filesystem

I reused the UUID of the original `rootfs` partition for `rootfs-a` and randomly created a new one for `rootfs-b`. These UUIDs are relevant because they are used in U-Boot's *extlinux.conf* configuration file located in the `bootfs` partition to determine the partition to be mounted as the root filesystem by the Linux kernel.

Afterward, the basic partition architecture for this case study is ready to support A/B system updates.

SWUpdate Installation and Configuration

SWUpdate, a feature-rich firmware update tool for embedded systems, provides the corresponding `meta-swupdate` layer for Yocto. This layer can be cloned from its Git repository and added to the STM32MP1 Yocto project.

Addition of Security Features

One of the first tasks is to create a recipe that patches the configuration of SWUpdate to enable signed and encrypted images. Listing 9-4 shows the three lines that have to be explicitly activated.

```
CONFIG_HASH_VERIFY=y
CONFIG_SIGNED_IMAGES=y
CONFIG_ENCRYPTED_IMAGES=y
```

Listing 9-4: Activating important security features of SWUpdate

The two options `CONFIG_HASH_VERIFY` and `CONFIG_SIGNED_IMAGES` add capabilities to SWUpdate that allow it to verify hashes and digital signatures of images included in a software update. The `CONFIG_ENCRYPTED_IMAGES` option enables support for AES-encrypted images, which we don't implement at the moment, but it might be a valuable option for the future.

Key Generation

As explained in Chapter 2, digital signatures are an asymmetric crypto primitive that allow for verification of integrity and authenticity of signed data. SWUpdate can generate signatures based on plain RSA keys or certificates. For this case study, I chose to use 4,096-bit RSA keys. Their generation can be split into three steps, as shown in Listing 9-5.

```
$ echo "SuperS3cr3t" > passphrase
$ openssl genrsa -aes256 -passout file:passphrase -out swu_signing_key.pem 4096
$ openssl rsa -in swu_signing_key.pem -pubout -passin file:passphrase
            -out swu_verification_key.pem
```

Listing 9-5: The RSA key generation for update signing and verification

First, the file *passphrase* is created that should contain a strong password. Afterward, the RSA key can be generated (for example, with 4,096-bit length). The resulting private key is encrypted based on the given passphrase file and stored as *swu_signing_key.pem*. Note that this is the RSA private key used for signing a firmware update after the build process. The corresponding public key is extracted and saved as *swu_verification_key.pem* in the third line of the listing. This is necessary to make that key available in the final device firmware because it's required for update signature verification.

Software Collection

Next, SWUpdate needs to know which Yocto build artifacts should be included in the firmware update. This information is stored in the *sw-description* file, which is used for update generation, but it's also included in the firmware update package itself.

Listing 9-6 shows the software collection I defined for this use case.

```
software = {
  version = "0.1.0";
❶ hardware-compatibility: ["CO2"];
  stable = {
  ❷ rootfs-a: {
      images: (
```

```
    {
❸ filename = "st-image-core-openstlinux-eglfs-stm32mp1.ext4.gz";
❹ compressed = "zlib";
❺ device = "/dev/mmcblk0p10";
❻ sha256 = "$swupdate_get_sha256(st-image-core-...-stm32mp1.ext4.gz)";
    });
  }
❼ rootfs-b: {
    images: (
    {
      filename = "st-image-core-openstlinux-eglfs-stm32mp1.ext4.gz";
      compressed = "zlib";
      device = "/dev/mmcblk0p11";
      sha256 = "$swupdate_get_sha256(st-image-core-...-stm32mp1.ext4.gz)";
    });
  }
  }
}
```

Listing 9-6: The software collection defined in the sw-description *file*

The first point you might stumble upon is the `hardware-compatibility` parameter ❶. I set it to `C02` because it's the hardware and assembly revision of my STM32MP157F-DK2 board. At runtime, this parameter has to match the data given in */etc/hwrevision* (for example, `stm32mp157f-dk2 C02` in my case).

Second, both partitions `rootfs-a` ❷ and `rootfs-b` ❼ are represented in this software collection, although only one will be used for updating at runtime. Both contain the same filename of the artifact to update ❸—in this case, the root filesystem generated by Yocto. The `compressed` parameter ❹ indicates whether the data is available in compressed form, while `sha256` ❻ integrates the SHA-256 hash value of the provided artifact into the *sw-description* file.

The two images differ in only one property: the partition indicated by the `device` parameter ❺. This determines where the SWUpdate client writes the update to. In this case, */dev/mmcblk0p10* and */dev/mmcblk0p11* are the device names under which the earlier created partitions `rootfs-a` and `rootfs-b` are available within Linux. If */dev/mmcblk0p10* is the active partition, the update has to be written to */dev/mmcblk0p11*, and vice versa.

Recipe for Update File Generation

SWUpdate's firmware update files have the *.swu* extension. The `meta-swupdate` layer comes with a class that supports SWU filegeneration by Yocto based on artifacts previously built and stored in Yocto's *deploy* directory. Listing 9-7 shows the corresponding code for a Yocto recipe that automatically generates a valid and digitally signed SWU file.

```
# Local files to be added to the SWU file
SRC_URI = "file://sw-description"
```

```
# Images to build before creating the SWU file
IMAGE_DEPENDS = "st-image-core"

# Images to include within the SWU file
SWUPDATE_IMAGES = "st-image-core-openstlinux-eglfs"

# Format of image to include
SWUPDATE_IMAGES_FSTYPES[st-image-core-openstlinux-eglfs] = ".ext4.gz"

# SWU signing parameters
SWUPDATE_SIGNING = "RSA"
SWUPDATE_PRIVATE_KEY = "path-to-signing-key/swu_signing_key.pem"
SWUPDATE_PASSWORD_FILE = "path-to-unlocking-passphrase/passphrase"
```

Listing 9-7: The recipe code that generates an SWU update file

The recipe adds the *sw-description* file created earlier and states the dependency on the st-image-core image. Within Yocto's *deploy* directory, the desired update content (the device's root filesystem) can be found in files starting with *st-image-core-openstlinux-eglfs*, while the target machine is added automatically by SWUpdate.

In contrast to SD card image creation, where the file with the *.ext4* extension is used (as shown in Listing 9-2), the firmware update should be as small as possible to optimize transfer times. Therefore, the compressed artifact with *.ext4.gz* is used for the SWU file. Finally, to enable firmware update signing, I set SWUPDATE_SIGNING to "RSA" and provided the paths to the private RSA signing key and its corresponding passphrase file.

Running this recipe ensures that the st-image-core image is built and then yields the *swupdate-swu-gen-openstlinux-eglfs-stm32mp1.swu* file within the *deploy* directory. This file is actually a copy-in-and-out (CPIO) archive that contains the *sw-description* file and its signature *sw-description.sig* file. Additionally, the compressed *st-image-core-openstlinux-eglfs-stm32mp1.ext4.gz* file is shipped within this archive, which contains the root filesystem.

NOTE *If you wonder why there isn't any signature file for the root filesystem, remember that the* sw-description *file contains the hash of this image, which would change if anyone had tampered with it. The signature of the description file also protects the authenticity and integrity of the root filesystem.*

Device-Specific Customization

Now let's turn to the device, the update client, and the necessary customizations to make SWUpdate work properly.

Update Daemon

To install SWUpdate's device client and its web server components, swupdate and swupdate-www have to be added to ST's core image. For configuration, the first consideration on the device side is which update methods it should support. In general, SWUpdate provides three typical ways:

Mongoose mode This daemon provides a simple web interface to allow for manual updates over a network.

Suricatta mode In conjunction with Eclipse's hawkBit, SWUpdate supports comprehensive OTA update setups that can be managed and controlled by a central server instance.

Local install If the SWU file is locally available (for example, on a USB flash drive), the update can be directly installed without requiring a network connection.

For this case study, I've chosen the mongoose daemon. As the system at hand uses systemd for Linux service configuration and management, a service file (*swupdate.service*) can be created as shown in Listing 9-8 and installed in the */etc/systemd/system/* directory.

```
[Unit]
Description=SWUpdate daemon

[Service]
Type=simple
ExecStart=/usr/bin/swupdate -w '-r /www -p 8080' -e 'stable,rootfs-b'

[Install]
WantedBy=multi-user.target
```

Listing 9-8: A basic service file to start swupdate in mongoose mode after boot

SWUpdate's binary is located at */usr/bin/swupdate*. It can be started in mongoose daemon mode at system boot with the -w command line parameter. The -r /www and -p 8080 arguments following in single quotes tell it to use the default web application located at */www* and to bind its web server to port 8080.

The string provided after the -e option defines which part of the expected software collection should be installed in the case of an update. In the default scenario, where rootfs-a is the active partition, the daemon should be started with -e 'stable,rootfs-b' to make sure that a potential update is written to rootfs-b, the inactive partition.

Besides setting configuration options with command line arguments, you could also provide the *swupdate.cfg* configuration file at a path matching the client's compile-time configuration—for example, */etc/swupdate/*. As shown in Listing 9-9, logging parameters, paths to keys, and post-update shell scripts are typical settings you might want to place here.

```
globals :
{
    verbose = true;
    loglevel = 5;
    syslog = true;
    postupdatecmd = "/etc/swupdate/postupdate.sh";
    public-key-file = "/etc/swupdate/swu_verification_key.pem";
};
```

Listing 9-9: An example configuration file for swupdate

However, whether you use command line arguments or a configuration file is mainly a matter of taste.

Post-Update Tasks

Every device, its architecture, and its update strategy is different. Therefore, a general tool like SWUpdate can't automatically derive what to do before and after a firmware update is written to its corresponding memory device or partition. On the command line, the -p and -P parameters allow for defining paths to *post-update* and *pre-update* commands, respectively.

In my case, only a post-update routine was necessary to prepare the device for booting the new firmware version. Listing 9-10 shows the contents of the *postupdate.sh* shell script that's executed after the update installation, as defined in *swupdate.cfg*.

```
#!/bin/sh

❶ if grep -q PARTUUID=e91c4e10-16e6-4c0e-bd0e-77becf4a3582
        /boot/mmc0_extlinux/stm32mp157f-dk2_extlinux.conf; then

    # Update swupdate service parameters
    mount PARTUUID=997046a6-c6f4-4f41-adb4-9fe614b2a92a /mnt
❷ sed -i 's/rootfs-b/rootfs-a/g' /mnt/etc/systemd/system/swupdate.service
    umount /mnt

    # Update rootfs boot parameter in extlinux.conf
❸ sed -i 's/PARTUUID=e91c4e10-16e6-4c0e-bd0e-77becf4a3582/
        PARTUUID=997046a6-c6f4-4f41-adb4-9fe614b2a92a/g'
        /boot/mmc0_extlinux/stm32mp157f-dk2_extlinux.conf

else

    # Update swupdate service parameters
    mount PARTUUID=e91c4e10-16e6-4c0e-bd0e-77becf4a3582 /mnt
    sed -i 's/rootfs-a/rootfs-b/g' /mnt/etc/systemd/system/swupdate.service
    umount /mnt
```

```
    # Update rootfs boot parameter in extlinux.conf
    sed -i 's/PARTUUID=997046a6-c6f4-4f41-adb4-9fe614b2a92a/
            PARTUUID=e91c4e10-16e6-4c0e-bd0e-77becf4a3582/g'
        /boot/mmc0_extlinux/stm32mp157f-dk2_extlinux.conf
fi

❹ reboot
```

Listing 9-10: A script to prepare a device for booting the updated firmware

The first if statement ❶ checks whether the board's U-Boot configuration file, *stm32mp157f-dk2_extlinux.conf*, located at */boot/mmc0_extlinux/*, contains the default partition UUID e91c4e10-16e6-4c0e-bd0e-77becf4a3582. If so, rootfs-a is the active partition, and the update was just written to rootfs-b. Therefore, the *swupdate.service* configuration file on the new partition has to be set to update the soon-to-be-inactive partition, rootfs-a ❷.

Afterward, the partition UUID in U-Boot's configuration file is replaced by the one representing rootfs-b ❸. This ensures that U-Boot starts the Linux kernel with the new root filesystem. If anything fails before this operation or a power loss occurs, the device will just boot into the existing firmware. But if everything goes well, the partition for the root filesystem is swapped and the device is deliberately rebooted ❹. Of course, the same procedure works the opposite way if the script detects that rootfs-b is the active partition.

Obviously, this is just one possible implementation of a post-update script that works for the specific architecture in this case study. Your device might require completely different reconfigurations before or after installing a firmware update.

Update Process Evaluation

To conclude this case study, I flashed the previously created 2GB image to a 16GB microSD card and booted my STM32MP157F-DK2 board from it. First, I checked which root filesystem partition was currently active. Listing 9-11 shows that both copies A (mmcblk0p10) and B (mmcblk0p11) are available and correctly sized. The slash at the right end of the line indicates that rootfs-a is currently mounted as the root filesystem.

```
# lsblk
NAME          MAJ:MIN RM   SIZE RO TYPE MOUNTPOINTS
mmcblk0       179:0    0  14.4G  0 disk
...
|-mmcblk0p10 179:10   0   768M  0 part /
|-mmcblk0p11 179:11   0   768M  0 part
...
```

Listing 9-11: The mmcblk0p10 partition mounted as the root filesystem

As a second step, I printed the logs of the installed swupdate daemon. Listing 9-12 shows selected lines of the output.

```
# journalctl -u swupdate.service
```
❶ Apr 28 21:34:54 stm32mp1 systemd[1]: Started SWUpdate daemon.
...
Apr 28 21:34:54 stm32mp1 swupdate[520]: [INFO] : SWUPDATE running :
    ❷ [main] : Running on stm32mp157f-dk2 Revision C02
...
Apr 28 21:34:54 stm32mp1 swupdate[520]: [INFO] : SWUPDATE running :
    ❸ [main] : software set: stable mode: rootfs-b
...
Apr 28 21:34:54 stm32mp1 swupdate[520]: [INFO] : SWUPDATE running :
    [start_mongoose] : Mongoose web server version 7.8 with pid 533
    ❹ started on [0.0.0.0:8080] with web root [/www]
...

Listing 9-12: The swupdate service logs

The result indicates that the daemon started ❶ and the board as well, as the hardware revision was read correctly ❷. Further, the configuration that a potential update should be written to rootfs-b ❸ is shown as desired. In addition, the start of the included web server with the configured port and given directory is confirmed ❹.

I used a common browser to connect to the device's IP address on port 8080, and it immediately showed the default web interface of SWUpdate. There, the SWU file created by Yocto could be uploaded to the device, and a progress bar showed the percentage of update completion. Shortly after reaching 100 percent, the device rebooted as expected, and a second look at lsblk, as shown in Listing 9-13, indicated that the swapping from copy A to copy B succeeded. The second update attempt also worked successfully and swapped the root filesystem back to mmcblk0p10.

```
# lsblk
NAME          MAJ:MIN RM   SIZE RO TYPE MOUNTPOINTS
mmcblk0       179:0    0  14.4G  0 disk
...
|-mmcblk0p10 179:10   0   768M  0 part
|-mmcblk0p11 179:11   0   768M  0 part /
...
```

Listing 9-13: The mmcblk0p11 partition mounted as the root filesystem after the update

Finally, to test digital signature verification, I also tried to maliciously modify the firmware update file by extracting the original files, changing the target partition of rootfs-a to /dev/mmcblk0p9, and combining the modified files into a valid CPIO archive again. However, when uploading over the web interface, it soon responds with the message Update failed. Looking at the log data on the device shows that the signature verification failed as expected (Listing 9-14).

```
# journalctl -u swupdate.service
...
Apr 29 04:03:57 stm32mp1 swupdate[520]: [TRACE] : SWUPDATE running :
    [swupdate_verify_file] : Verify signed image: Read 581 bytes
Apr 29 04:03:57 stm32mp1 swupdate[520]: [ERROR] : SWUPDATE failed [0] ERROR :
    EVP_DigestVerifyFinal failed, error 0x2000068 0
Apr 29 04:03:57 stm32mp1 swupdate[520]: [TRACE] : SWUPDATE running :
    [swupdate_verify_file] : Error Verifying Data
...
```

Listing 9-14: The signature verification fails for the modified firmware update.

Testing software update verification routines for their correct *rejection behavior* is not only valuable during development. It also makes absolute sense to integrate similar test cases into release or production testing, because it wouldn't be the first time that verification got switched off by accident.

Summary

Providing software and firmware updates for devices doesn't seem like a very difficult task at first glance. However, if all requirements regarding security, scalability, and reliability are considered, it becomes a complex topic that impacts development pipelines, nonvolatile memory layouts, backend services, and customer processes.

This chapter stressed the inevitable need to provide secure update mechanisms for all kinds of IoT devices because none of them is perfect, and at some point, manufacturers as well as customers will demand firmware updates that have to be distributed and applied securely and must not break the device. To achieve these requirements, manufacturers have to ensure authenticity and integrity protection, they have to discuss update formats and granularity, and the memory partitioning has to support atomic and failsafe update procedures. Also, backend servers that schedule, distribute, and monitor update deployments in the field have to be operated.

If you still think it's all too much for you to handle, and maybe your devices will never need any updates because that was the case during past decades, pull out the risk analysis for your networked device and reconsider the impact ratings in the event that you wouldn't be able to fix vulnerabilities. Also, make sure you add "update misuse" to your list of threats if you're going with an update mechanism that resembles an invitation for adversaries to install their custom software.

10

ROBUST DEVICE ARCHITECTURE

Robustness is *the* key feature for components in industries like automotive, aerospace, and industrial automation. Neither dirt and dust nor freezing or broiling temperatures should be able to do any harm to those devices. Products in this category are built to survive over a long lifetime. They're designed with the requirement of *physical robustness* as a high priority.

However, since connectivity and communication are increasing even in those rather conservative areas, a new concern has emerged: *digital robustness*. Threats like network-based DoS attacks aim for temporary service interruption that can be critical for real-time systems depending on timely system reactions. Therefore, the protection goal of *availability* rises in importance for such embedded systems.

In this chapter, I highlight the relevance of robust device architectures for connected devices facing increasing network stress. I discuss the impact on real-time systems and essential functions of embedded devices. Afterward, we'll look at strategies for coping with DoS attacks on embedded systems on the hardware, OS, and application level. This chapter's case study then takes a look at the real-time and robustness behavior of a Linux-based embedded system under various conditions.

Devices Under Network Stress

Almost every device has some kind of network interface, whether it's Wi-Fi, Ethernet, or a domain-specific networking standard like the CAN bus. Threats like cut cables and jammers blocking wireless communication channels are well known. Because they lead to the physical loss of the communication medium's availability, messages sent over affected channels will be lost and won't reach the initially connected device. While this issue affects overall system communication, the resources of the device itself are not impacted, and (even if perfectly designed) the device won't be able to help in this situation.

The threats covered in this chapter are of a slightly different nature. They're initiated over a network connection, but in contrast to targeting the communication channels, they have an impact on a device's operations and resources. This can be as simple as a wrong packet on the wrong port, causing a sloppily engineered industrial device to drop everything and jump into an undocumented update mode while bringing its control function to a halt. Overloading a device with a large number of messages, however, is more often the main threat.

Such device weaknesses can be provoked on numerous occasions that happen more frequently with rising network complexity, the introduction of security management processes by operators, and an increased attack surface. Let's consider some typical cases.

Malfunctioning Neighbor Devices

The more complex and heterogeneous a system, the higher the probability that a device goes wild someday and broadcasts tons of messages to all participants in the same network. The constant and eventually high-volume traffic is able to unintentionally reveal the unreliability of connected devices in this domain.

Protocol Fuzzing

Fuzzing is a security testing technique that repeatedly generates randomly mutated, malformed inputs and feeds them to a device with the goal of exhibiting unconsidered corner cases. Developers often apply fuzzing to test their own devices. Systems integrators, operators, and researchers also use fuzzing to analyze the robustness and security of devices, and to uncover undesired behavior.

Network and Vulnerability Scanning

IT environments are used to being scanned regularly for open network ports, vulnerable client machines, and misconfigured server instances. Environments like industrial production sites are much less likely to be subject to such IT security methods, but they will be in the future. Components should be able to handle such scans and not show unexpected behavior, such as temporary deviations in processing speeds or even complete device failure.

Flooding Attacks

As soon as an attacker has access to a network, they're able to send packets to connected devices. Certain tools can initiate network-based DoS attacks with a one-liner that even script kiddies can easily perform. Truly robust devices shouldn't be affected by such attacks and should continue operating properly.

Robust Architectures

Many cases of low robustness against unusual network communication are due to bugs that should be discovered during functional and security testing, which is a mandatory part of the secure development process described in Chapter 1. However, some devices' DoS vulnerabilities arise from the architectural decisions you may have made for your device.

If you're part of an engineering team that's proud of its ruggedized products, take a step forward and also make digital robustness a high-priority feature. The following sections provide advice for engineering digital robustness.

Essential Device Functions

It's easy to say that a flooding attack shouldn't impact a device's functionality, but the practical implementation of protection measures requires more detailed considerations than you might expect. It's clear that communication capabilities might suffer from high message load and might be reduced or even completely lost, which influences every device feature that depends on data received from other entities and possibly operations that need to transfer data from your device to other network participants. These impacts are inevitable from a device's perspective and require corresponding mitigation measures.

Part 4-2 of the industrial standard IEC 62443 covers technical security requirements for industrial components, and it includes the specific requirement CR 7.1 that deals with DoS protection on embedded systems. Its central demand is that a device should maintain its *essential functions* even under a DoS attack and while operating in a *degraded mode*. If you want to fulfill this requirement, the obvious question you have to pose first is, "What actually are my device's essential functions?"

Let's consider three generic types of devices and their possible essential functions.

Sensors

Sensors measure environment parameters. No matter whether it's tracking temperature, distance, pH value, or fill level, the sensor's task is to capture the current situation and communicate it to a control or monitoring system. However, if the communication channel and/or corresponding device resources can be overloaded and communication capabilities are lost, the sensor should still be able to collect its data.

In this case, the essential function could be the correct sensing and storage of the acquired values. From a product engineering perspective, this could lead to a new requirement—namely, a sufficiently large data buffer and recovery procedure for when communication is working again.

Actuators

Actuators like drives, valves, engines, or even lasers influence the physical world. They're usually parameterized by a central controller instance, which communicates with the actuator—for example, over an Ethernet network.

Let's assume a drive is operating at 1,000 revolutions per minute when suddenly a DoS attack on its network interface starts. Should the essential function (turning the drive at a certain speed) keep operating? From a security and an availability perspective, that could make sense. However, safety experts might argue that the system isn't in a safe state anymore and should react with a shutdown to avoid unsafe behavior.

Controllers

Control devices for automotive, industrial automation, or critical infrastructures usually follow the simple principles illustrated in Figure 10-1: receive inputs, process them by a given program, maybe do some communication, and then set the new output signals.

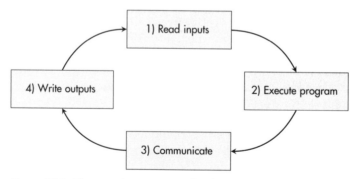

Figure 10-1: The typical execution cycle of a control device

Afterward, the cycle begins anew. However, in case of network stress, the communication slot could consume too much time and resources. Again, you need to define your strategy: it might be reasonable to say that cycle execution (except for communication) is the essential function that should keep running, even if the device is stressed over the network interface. If network communication itself is essential, the question would be whether it's absolutely required for every single cycle or whether at least once within 10 cycles would be acceptable, for example.

If the defined requirements can't be fulfilled at runtime, the system should probably come to a stop. A good example of such devices might be automotive components that read pedal sensor values and control the engine accordingly. Architects and developers of these control units have to specify the devices' essential functions in order to prepare them for the case that the sensor communication or its corresponding task fails—for whatever reason.

NOTE *Defining a device's essential functions is a fundamental design decision that can have significant influences on the device's software and hardware architecture. Be sure to consider this topic early and seriously.*

Real-Time Systems

Digital robustness is relevant for almost every product, as device failures often lead to financial losses for operators. However, it's especially desirable for *real-time embedded systems*. These devices are not only required to maintain the availability of their services but also have to make sure that, upon an initial event, the results of the device operation are *available before a given deadline*.

Although high-performance processors and super-fast reaction times can be the results of such a requirement, those features aren't mandatory. The only important constraint is that a system's response is provided *before the time limit is over*, be it a microsecond or half a minute.

Real-time systems have three categories that differ in terms of the impact of missed deadlines: soft, firm, and hard real-time systems.

Soft Real-Time Systems

Soft real-time systems can tolerate missing deadlines even frequently. However, the usefulness and value of delayed results are continuously decreasing. If the deadline is missed significantly, the results might turn out to be worthless. Application examples include weather stations, live audio transmission, and video gaming.

Firm Real-Time Systems

A missed deadline in a *firm real-time system* leads to a defect or a degraded quality of service. However, misses that happen only infrequently might be tolerable. An example of such a system could be a pick-and-place robot. If its controller misses a deadline, the currently processed component might be broken or placed the wrong way, but after handling this single failure, the device is able to continue normal operation.

Hard Real-Time Systems

Hard real-time systems have to satisfy the highest requirements. For these systems, any missed deadline is critical. Depending on the application, it might even lead to catastrophic consequences. Typical examples are engine control units in planes or trains, high-quality manufacturing processes, and medical devices like pacemakers.

Impact of DoS Attacks

If your device falls into one of these real-time groups, you have to consider the potential corresponding impacts of DoS attacks, or even accidentally occurring network stress, during your threat and risk assessment and mitigate the resulting weaknesses accordingly.

Resource Exhaustion and Prevention Strategies

Network-based DoS attacks, like flooding, aim for *temporary resource exhaustion* on the target device. In a simple scenario, an attacker can achieve this by utilizing most of the available network bandwidth to send packets to a target device. The victim device receives all the packets and has to process them. The required processing power depends on the type and content of the network packets.

However, if the accumulation of network packets reaches a level that fills all internal buffers and the device is not able to process the packets faster than they arrive at its network interface, CPU resource exhaustion occurs. The device isn't able to perform its queuing tasks anymore, including its essential functions.

WARNING *The cause of resource exhaustion doesn't have to be a deliberate attack. A careless network scan with nmap might be enough to temporarily provoke resource exhaustion on your device, as shown in this chapter's case study.*

Overall prevention of resource exhaustion isn't always possible in practice and depends on specific device parameters and attacker capabilities. However, a strong separation between essential functions and secondary operations is a solid architecture that can keep operating in a degraded mode, even under significant network stress. A given set of device resources can be distributed among critical and rather less critical operations by using two basic strategies:

Fixed resource allocation   A static allocation of resources to tasks has the advantage of providing a transparent and clear segregation of duties. However, fixed limits lead to inefficiencies at runtime, when a resource isn't consumed by its allocated task and another task would benefit from using that resource but isn't allowed to.

Dynamic resource allocation   To foster efficient resource use, resources can be allocated to specific tasks at runtime, based on task attributes that are used to derive a priority metric.

These approaches should be considered during the design of your device's hardware architecture and the selection of the main processing units.

Moreover, the choice and configuration of your OS can have significant impacts on your device's robustness.

Hardware-Level Implementation Options

A device's hardware architecture defines its basic computing resource conditions. During its development, ICs for various purposes are selected, including microcontrollers, multicore SoCs, and FPGAs, but also dedicated chips like Ethernet PHYs that handle network communication on the physical layer.

If robustness against network flooding is one of your main concerns and you take that into account at an early stage of your development process, you can design your device's hardware architecture in a way that significantly reduces the risk of network-based DoS attacks.

Dedicated Preprocessing Unit

Figure 10-2 shows the basic concept when introducing a dedicated preprocessing unit for network traffic. The main idea behind this architecture is the physical separation of the main application's processor and the network processing, or at least parts of it.

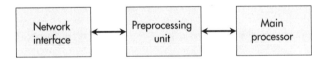

Figure 10-2: An architecture with network traffic preprocessing

One specific example of such an architecture is a *communication preprocessor* that implements a TCP/IP stack and takes care of processing network packets and their payload. The communication of relevant data between the main processor and the preprocessing unit is carried out over a preferably simple interface. In case of a flooding attack or just very high network load for unknown reasons, the communication unit is likely to run into resource exhaustion, but the application processor behind it will not be impacted and will be able to perform the device's essential functions.

The use of a *hardware packet filtering unit* is a second example of this approach. Here, the network stack remains on the main processing unit, and the preprocessor is used only to filter the stream of network packets arriving at the device's network interface. Rules for filtering might, for example, include rate limits to guarantee that your application processor receives only the number of packets it's able to handle.

Such an architecture could be implemented by specific networking ICs that provide this functionality, but, at the time of writing, these are rather uncommon in embedded systems. For devices hosting an FPGA, the MAC controller could be implemented in digital logic followed by a custom packet-filtering core before handing network data to the main CPU.

Be careful when designing the communication between a main processor and a pre-processing unit. If the former shows a heavy dependency on the latter, the device might fail despite the solid architecture.

Multicore Architectures

If digital robustness appears too late on the list of requirements and the hardware design is already fixed, you might be lucky if you've opted for a multicore SoC as the main processing unit in your device. Admittedly, individual cores in multicore chips are not completely separated and independent of one another; they share resources like buses, cache memories, and the like. However, a well-considered distribution of tasks among cores, as shown in Figure 10-3, can reduce the probability of a DoS event.

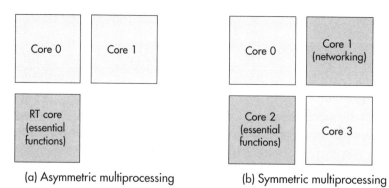

(a) Asymmetric multiprocessing   (b) Symmetric multiprocessing

Figure 10-3: Using multicore architectures for robustness

An increasing number of SoCs for embedded systems implement *asymmetric multiprocessing (AMP)*. They include one or more high-performance cores that are meant to run feature-rich OSs, such as Linux, and one or more smaller cores that, for example, excel at real-time applications. One approach toward increased robustness could be the allocation of essential functions like control tasks to the dedicated real-time core, as indicated by Figure 10-3a. Similar structures are possible on SoCs that combine hard processors with soft cores that reside within an FPGA fabric.

If your device runs on a *symmetric multiprocessing (SMP)* SoC—which means it has two, four, eight, or even more cores of the same type—you still have options to improve robustness. The architecture in Figure 10-3b is meant to separate networking tasks from essential functions by binding their processes to dedicated cores. This concept is known as *core pinning*, or *processor affinity*, and has to be supported by your OS.

Again, (communication) dependencies between processes on different cores might break the intended separation and should be conceptualized with care.

Operating System Capabilities

A central duty of an OS is the management of CPU cores, memory regions, and a diverse set of hardware interfaces. The component handling the difficult task of allocating processing time during runtime is called the *scheduler*. It's absolutely reasonable to consider capabilities and responsibilities of OSs and schedulers when talking about preventing resource exhaustion.

Operating System Options

When it comes to selecting an OS, device engineers have basically four options: bare-metal software without an OS, a real-time OS, a fully fledged OS, or a hypervisor-based OS combination.

Bare-Metal Software Without an OS

In simple devices and applications, an OS might not even be necessary. Events and corresponding resource allocation can be handled by polling loops or interrupt service routines.

Real-Time OS

An RTOS is a rather low-complexity OS that is specifically meant for real-time applications that have a high interest in reliability. Its scheduler manages resources based on task priorities: tasks with a higher priority can interrupt currently running ones that have a lower priority.

In such a system, it's important not to configure networking-related tasks as the top priority, because doing so could lead to network-induced DoS situations. In practice, you can find a variety of RTOSs in the field, including commercial ones like QNX or VxWorks, but also open source variants such as FreeRTOS, RIOT, or Zephyr.

Fully Fledged OS

Many modern, feature-rich devices rely on open source libraries and tools that handle, for example, network communication, presentation of user interfaces, or data-processing tasks. Those devices are usually based on a fully fledged OS like Linux. However, such complex and not fully deterministic OSs share a disadvantage: the lack of proper real-time capabilities. In the next section, I'll discuss a possibility that makes Linux more real-time capable.

Hypervisor-Based OS Combination

Some manufacturers want to combine the real-time advantages of RTOSs with the many libraries and capabilities of Linux. In these cases, a further abstraction layer is introduced below those OSs: a *hypervisor* takes over the task of hardware resource allocation and thereby plays an important role in separating essential functions (probably running on top of an RTOS) from the supporting functionalities implemented within Linux. These setups further increase the complexity of your product's software architecture.

Linux with a Real-Time Patch

In its typical configuration for desktop and server systems, Linux doesn't offer reliable real-time capabilities. However, for several years, the real-time community has maintained a kernel patch known as PREEMPT_RT. It includes a variety of changes to the Linux kernel that share the common goal of enabling *preemption* of kernel threads and in-kernel primitives, which means that nondeterminism in task scheduling is reduced and computing resource allocation comes closer to a purely priority-based system. In current Linux kernel versions, you can activate real-time support with the CONFIG_PREEMPT_RT configuration option.

Thread scheduling in Linux happens based on a scheduling policy and a static scheduling priority. "Normal" threads are scheduled with policies like SCHED_OTHER, SCHED_IDLE, or SCHED_BATCH and a priority of 0. Threads that have to fulfill real-time requirements are scheduled with one of the following policies:

SCHED_FIFO   This scheduler follows the *first-in first-out (FIFO) principle*, which means that a running thread is executed until it is preempted by a thread with a higher static priority.

SCHED_RR   The classic *round-robin (RR)* scheduling approach is similar to SCHED_FIFO except that threads are allowed to run for only a defined maximum amount of time. Afterward, the thread is interrupted and added to the end of the queue for threads with the same priority. Threads with higher priority may preempt those with lower priority.

SCHED_DEADLINE   In contrast to the other schedulers, this one is based on *global earliest deadline first (GEDF)*. It doesn't rely on static priorities but assigns them dynamically. Its decisions are based on a thread's absolute deadline and its total computation time.

NOTE   *Although PREEMPT_RT makes Linux behave more like a real-time OS, it's still a complex piece of software that's not suitable for many hard real-time requirements.*

Application and Protocol Considerations

While this chapter is primarily concerned with the robust device architecture on the hardware and OS level, I don't want to ignore the application and communication levels. Many DoS situations in the real world arise from sloppy software and protocol design.

Such issues can be introduced in various phases of the development process. A protocol specification might already lack a solid definition of correct behavior in corner cases—for example, minimum or maximum values of message parameters. Further, even simple bugs in software, such as missing bounds checking, can lead to undesired side effects like endless loops or deadlocks under certain circumstances. Then, if security testing is performed only superficially, devices leave production with firmware that gives attackers the opportunity to trigger a DoS event with as little effort as a single network packet.

The following sections provide practical suggestions for tackling this complex issue. The important possibility you should be looking for is an attacker's ability to *force a state transition* within your device that results in a DoS.

Identify Logical Flaws

Protocol design is a complex task, but many companies take this path and develop their own, proprietary message and communication format. If you find yourself in such a situation, be sure to do your best to eliminate logical flaws in your protocol.

First, you can do that on the concept level by asking questions like these: What is the range of validity for each value in our messages? Is a network participant able to force our device into an undefined state? Are the validity and plausibility of message values verified before they're used? Second, testing your protocol implementation with messages that only partially fulfill the specification or even try to manipulate your device's state on purpose can be helpful for discovering vulnerabilities.

Implement Input and Sender Validation

In many embedded system scenarios, an adversary is able to communicate directly with a device—for example, over the network. Even if official client software *should* be used for interacting with your device, attackers might simply craft their own manipulated messages, so devices shouldn't trust any packet arriving at their network interface.

Critical commands, such as switching into update mode and halting all operations, should be allowed only after the authenticity of the sender has been verified successfully. Therefore, a developer's default attitude should be to *expect* malicious input and implement suitable input validation and filtering mechanisms accordingly, whether on the firewall level or within the application that processes a message's payload.

Analyze Active Protection Measures

Sometimes attackers can misuse active protection measures to force a device into a DoS state. For example, your login process might be hardened to prohibit brute-force attacks by allowing only 10 login attempts. After reaching that limit, the device changes into a locked mode from which it can be reactivated only by a recovery procedure. While this might be an absolutely reasonable security measure, it also allows attackers to force a DoS situation, even for legitimate users, by entering the wrong user credentials 10 times.

Firewall configurations that block IPs based on their amount of traffic have similar mechanisms. In that case, attackers might spoof sender IP addresses of valid devices and trigger the protection feature by sending a large number of packets. As a result, the communication attempts of legitimate devices will be blocked afterward.

Introduce Chaos Engineering and Fuzzing

The human imagination is limited. It's unrealistic to assume that developers will anticipate all potential issues that might lead to a DoS event on your device. Two testing methods push the limits in this regard, however.

Chaos engineering is a kind of reliability and resilience testing for IT systems that introduces "chaos" into an IT infrastructure in the form of random failures of services or applications. In the area of embedded system testing, this "chaos" can be crashed processes or the loss of communication channels in order to analyze the device's behavior under adverse circumstances.

The discipline of *fuzzing* might be applied to communication protocols, but also on input data like the configuration files or certificates that a device processes. It can be used to create a large number of test messages or test files by cleverly mutating input data many times. In this way, you can discover cases that lead to a DoS state that would have been very hard to find by manual, human analysis.

NOTE *All that said, keep in mind that your product development team's mindset and awareness can be decisive factors in detecting DoS vulnerabilities early in your development process.*

Case Study: Robustness Options on an STM32MP157F Device

In this case study, I'll analyze the real-time and robustness capabilities of an STM32MP157F device. I'll shed light on corresponding measurement methods and tools used to simulate CPU and network stress on a device.

Basic System Properties

Regarding hardware-level options, the STM32MP157F device at hand provides two Cortex-A7 cores running at 800 MHz and a dedicated Cortex-M4 core at 209 MHz for real-time applications. This basic information allows us to conclude that both pinning tasks to one of the A7 cores and moving essential software applications to the separated M4 core would be possible. In principle, using the M4 core as a preprocessing unit for Ethernet traffic might even be an option, but that's probably not the first solution I would pursue, and it would require further feasibility analysis based on the SoC's architecture.

The MAC unit included in the STM32MP157F's Ethernet peripheral supports data transfer rates of 10, 100, and 1,000Mbps. After looking into ST's *Reference Manual RM0436* for STM32MP157F devices, it becomes clear that this module even comes with hardware-assisted packet filtering. Received packets can be filtered based on their source and destination MAC addresses, the virtual local area network (VLAN) tag in the Ethernet frame of a packet, the source and destination IP address, and the source and destination port of TCP and UDP messages. Unfortunately, the module doesn't have any kind of rate-limiting feature, which would be useful for DoS protection.

The third part of this initial analysis concerns the Linux OS running on my STM32MP157F device. As previously described, Linux can be patched or configured to behave similarly to a real-time system. With the command and output shown in Listing 10-1, I checked whether my Linux system, which was created by Yocto based on ST's `st-image-core` image, comes with real-time scheduling capabilities.

```
# uname -a
Linux stm32mp1 5.15.67 #1 SMP PREEMPT ...
```

Listing 10-1: The Linux kernel properties of my system

The string `SMP` points out that the Linux system at hand was configured at compile time to support symmetric multicore architectures like the A7 dual core of the STM32MP157F, while `PREEMPT` indicates that the Linux kernel was compiled with the `CONFIG_PREEMPT` option. The system runs a *low-latency kernel*, which means that kernel code not executed in a critical section can be interrupted by higher-priority tasks. However, this configuration shouldn't be confused with the `PREEMPT_RT` indicator, which represents a fully preemptible Linux kernel enabled by `CONFIG_PREEMPT_RT`.

Measurements on a Low-Latency Kernel

You can measure a device's latency behavior in two ways. If you have internal access to the device's Linux system, you can run software that analyzes the scheduling behavior of that Linux system. On the other hand, for example, if you analyze a third-party component, you might be forced to regard the device under testing as a black box. In such a case, you can observe the device's latency behavior only with respect to input and output signals—for example, with an oscilloscope or a logic analyzer. While the former approach is more suitable for showing the principle capabilities of a device, the latter can yield results that are much closer to a specific use case.

In this case study, I use the `cyclictest` tool to analyze the system's real-time capabilities because I have access to the device's Linux console and I don't yet have a specific application in mind. This tool measures the latency between the programmed and the actual execution of a real-time task scheduled with `SCHED_FIFO`. Listing 10-2 shows a sample test and its results.

```
# cyclictest --mlockall --smp --interval=200 --distance=0 --priority=80
    --loops=40000
...

T: 0 (  874) P:80 I:200 C:  38735 Min:    15 Act:    47 Avg:    36 Max:  158
T: 1 (  875) P:80 I:200 C:  38596 Min:    15 Act:    42 Avg:    35 Max:  165
```

Listing 10-2: The task latency in idle mode

The `--mlockall` parameter is used to reduce overhead and influences from the tool itself, while `--smp` is necessary for testing on a multicore system. The measuring thread is executed every 200 μs as set by the `--interval` option, and there's no difference between the measuring periods of the various threads, as denoted by --distance=0. The measuring tasks are executed 40,000 times (--loops=40000) with a task priority of 80 (--priority=80).

The result output shows two lines, one for each CPU core. The letters P, I, and C stand for the priority setting, measuring interval, and count of performed measurements, respectively. The values on the right show the minimal, actual, average, and maximum observed latency. The rightmost number is the most important one because it indicates worst-case latencies for scheduled tasks that may or may not be tolerable for you.

In the current state, the given Linux system with a PREEMPT low-latency kernel shows maximum latencies of 158 and 165 μs. However, if I use a second device on the same network to apply a SYN flooding attack—for example, by running hping3 --syn --flood *device-ip*, the maximum latency is affected significantly, as shown in Listing 10-3.

```
# cyclictest --mlockall --smp --interval=200 --distance=0 --priority=80
    --loops=40000
...

T: 0 (  902) P:80 I:200 C:  14253 Min:   15 Act: 2406 Avg:  409 Max: 5475
T: 1 (  903) P:80 I:200 C:  40000 Min:   15 Act:   15 Avg:   23 Max:  185
```

Listing 10-3: The effect of SYN flooding on task latency

In such a situation, even with a low-latency kernel, task latency might rise to over 5 ms, a multiple of the actual task interval. Clearly, this could be critical if your application has to fulfill real-time requirements. Listing 10-4 shows a sample measurement result while a simple port scan was performed with nmap *device-ip*.

```
# cyclictest --mlockall --smp --interval=200 --distance=0 --priority=80
    --loops=40000
...

T: 0 (  932) P:80 I:200 C:  37581 Min:   14 Act:   41 Avg:   46 Max: 6573
T: 1 (  933) P:80 I:200 C:  39086 Min:   15 Act:   46 Avg:   34 Max:  199
```

Listing 10-4: The effect of a SYN scan with nmap on task latency

In conclusion, we can see that the low-latency kernel of the standard Linux distribution for the STM32MP157F device isn't able to provide strong real-time features. Even short periods of intense network traffic can affect the system's reaction times.

Measurements on a Real-Time Kernel

If robustness is one of your top requirements, you might want to look for a Linux distribution that implements a fully preemptible kernel to fulfill real-time constraints. Luckily, ST provides the Yocto layer meta-st-x-linux-rt for the STM32MP157F device. After adding it to my build system, I only have to set `MACHINE=stm32mp15-rt` and re-create the build environment before I can use bitbake to generate the `st-image-core` image and a Linux kernel with `CONFIG_PREEMPT_RT` enabled.

After booting the new image, I double-checked that the kernel actually provides real-time capabilities. The output in Listing 10-5 shows the typical `PREEMPT_RT` feature as desired.

```
# uname -a
Linux stm32mp15-rt 5.15.67-rt49 #1 SMP PREEMPT_RT ...
```

Listing 10-5: The Linux kernel features including real-time capabilities

Again, you can test the system's real-time behavior with cyclictest as in the previous section. Listing 10-6 shows the positive effects of the real-time kernel.

```
# cyclictest --mlockall --smp --interval=200 --distance=0 --priority=80
    --loops=40000
...

T: 0 ( 1195) P:80 I:200 C:  40000 Min:    15 Act:    17 Avg:    19 Max:    64
T: 1 ( 1196) P:80 I:200 C:  39838 Min:    16 Act:    25 Avg:    18 Max:    72
```

Listing 10-6: The task latency of the real-time kernel in idle mode

In comparison to the low-latency kernel's values in Listing 10-2, 158 and 165 μs, the maximum latency was significantly reduced to 64 and 72 μs, respectively. The results shown in Listing 10-7 indicate even better behavior.

```
# cyclictest --mlockall --smp --interval=200 --distance=0 --priority=80
    --loops=40000
...

T: 0 ( 1186) P:80 I:200 C:  40000 Min:    15 Act:    29 Avg:    24 Max:    91
T: 1 ( 1187) P:80 I:200 C:  39800 Min:    16 Act:    34 Avg:    19 Max:    77
```

Listing 10-7: The effect of SYN flooding on the real-time kernel's latency

The maximum latency of the Linux system doesn't exceed 100 μs, even in the face of a SYN flooding attack performed with hping3.

You can observe a similar effect in Listing 10-8, which was captured while running network scans on the device under test.

```
# cyclictest --mlockall --smp --interval=200 --distance=0 --priority=80
    --loops=40000
...

T: 0 ( 1189) P:80 I:200 C:  40000 Min:    15 Act:    17 Avg:    20 Max:    78
T: 1 ( 1190) P:80 I:200 C:  39837 Min:    16 Act:    23 Avg:    19 Max:    73
```

Listing 10-8: The effect of a SYN scan with nmap on the real-time kernel's latency

While common nmap commands provoked worst-case latencies of more than 6 ms for the standard image with its low-latency kernel, the real-time kernel analyzed in this section can be incited to raise maximum latencies by only less than 15 μs compared to the idle state.

What all this amounts to is that a low-latency Linux kernel doesn't guarantee any robustness, and even a fully preemptible Linux kernel comes only close to real-time behavior. If this is a viable option for you, make sure to understand that you trade performance for determinism when switching to the real-time Linux kernel. Further, features like the SoC's dynamic power management and frequency scaling might be deactivated to reach real-time behavior.

NOTE   *All the presented measurements of maximum latency have to be regarded as only rough estimations. Your device could run into an even worse condition that leads to even higher maximum reaction times.*

Real-Time Coprocessor

If you're aiming to fulfill hard real-time requirements, Linux is likely not your best choice. However, the STM32MP157F provides an additional Cortex-M4 core for exactly that purpose. The development and build process of dedicated M4 firmware is beyond the scope of this case study, but you can use ST's STM32CubeIDE or your favorite customized makefile for that purpose.

Let's assume you've created a firmware file *m4_fw.elf* that contains your real-time application. Typically, you would place that file in the */lib/firmware/* directory, as it's firmware for a coprocessor. Listing 10-9 shows the basic initialization of Linux's remoteproc framework to prepare M4 firmware execution.

```
# echo -n "/lib/firmware/" > /sys/module/firmware_class/parameters/path
# echo -n "m4_fw.elf" > /sys/class/remoteproc/remoteproc0/firmware
```

Listing 10-9: Initializing M4 firmware using the remoteproc framework

In the first step, the firmware path */lib/firmware/* is written to the corresponding sysfs node. Afterward, the name of the specific firmware file, *m4_fw.elf* in this case, is passed to the remote processor instance remoteproc0, representing the M4 real-time core.

At this point, nothing runs. The output in Listing 10-10 confirms that the M4 is still offline. To start the provided firmware, the start keyword has to be written to remoteproc0/state.

```
# cat /sys/class/remoteproc/remoteproc0/state
offline
# echo start > /sys/class/remoteproc/remoteproc0/state
... remoteproc remoteproc0: powering up m4
... remoteproc remoteproc0: Booting fw image m4_fw.elf, size 456520
...   remoteproc0#vdev0buffer: assigned reserved memory node ...
... virtio_rpmsg_bus virtio0: rpmsg host is online
...   remoteproc0#vdev0buffer: registered virtio0 (type 7)
```

```
... remoteproc remoteproc0: remote processor m4 is now up
# cat /sys/class/remoteproc/remoteproc0/state
running
```

Listing 10-10: Starting M4 firmware using the remoteproc framework

Subsequently, the core is powered up, and execution of the real-time application begins. Now, even if the Linux system suffers from high network load and is running out of resources, the real-time firmware will continue operating at its CPU's clock frequency of 209 MHz unperturbed. Also, the state of remoteproc0 has changed to running, accordingly.

As shown in Listing 10-11, the Linux system is able to stop the firmware execution by writing stop to remoteproc0/state.

```
# echo stop > /sys/class/remoteproc/remoteproc0/state
... remoteproc remoteproc0: warning: remote FW shutdown without ack
... remoteproc remoteproc0: stopped remote processor m4
```

Listing 10-11: Stopping M4 firmware using the remoteproc framework

If necessary for your application, Linux's remote processor messaging (RPMsg) framework enables the exchange of information between the main CPUs and the coprocessor. However, make sure to avoid strong dependencies of the real-time application on the Linux system as this might cause your whole device to stumble, again.

Summary

Many industries regard robustness as a fundamental feature for all their devices. However, when it comes to highly interconnected and automated systems, both customers and manufacturers typically have difficulty specifying their understanding of digital robustness.

This chapter bridged the gap between the real-time world of embedded systems and the security protection goal of availability. The most important takeaways for device engineers and architects should be that they must consider potential digital stress on the network and other interfaces, essential functions of their devices that should work properly even under attack, and architecture decisions that support true real-time behavior.

Options for achieving a robust device architecture range from the integration of dedicated hardware resources to the separation of duties within multicore SoCs to the careful selection and configuration of a device's OS. But, again, as shown in this chapter's case study, nothing replaces the practical evaluation of your device's behavior during idle and potential situations of stress.

11

ACCESS CONTROL AND MANAGEMENT

In IT systems, the management of users and permissions has a long tradition because humans have played a central role from the beginning. By contrast, embedded systems were not meant for interaction in the past and often come with only a few users or even just a single system user.

Today, with the increasing complexity of IoT business models and application scenarios, many players are involved in the life-cycle processes of IoT devices—from developers to maintenance personnel to third-party service providers to the end users themselves. Devices must be able to *handle* all these roles and to *separate* them from one another. Further, internal processes and applications running on your device will also require various permissions to fulfill their purposes. Restricting them according to the principle of least privilege can save your device from severe damage.

This chapter starts with a look at a variety of situations where access control can make an important contribution to device security. Afterward, I explain common concepts you can use to implement access restrictions on devices running Linux. The case study at the end of the chapter teases the practical possibilities of process restrictions with the AppArmor tool.

Everyday Threats

Database leaks and breaches happen nearly every day. Often, the data published or sold by criminals contains long lists of usernames and passwords. Credentials for your IoT devices could be among those secrets, enabling adversaries to log into your products. You might jump to the conclusion that these are your customers' risks and that you don't have any responsibility in case of credential theft, but that's not completely true.

You have to ask yourself at least two questions: "Did we separate end-user accounts from manufacturer accounts?" and "Did we restrict those end-user accounts as far as possible in order to contain the damage in case of leaked credentials?" If you don't consider these topics, they might boomerang and negatively affect your product's reputation, at the very least.

On a regular basis, penetration testers, security researchers, or even customers identify unknown vulnerabilities in products. And the probability of security issues increases with device and software complexity and the number of services exposed on network interfaces. Even though you might have established a solid vulnerability-management process, as described in Chapter 1, and are even prepared to roll out updates securely, as explained in Chapter 9, your product could still be vulnerable during a certain time frame. If such a case leads to attacks in the field that significantly affect your devices, the obvious question experts will pose is, "Why was the vulnerable application able to cause impacts on all of the system's parts when it has a rather constrained purpose?"

Currently, a common topic among manufacturers in multiple industries is the transformation of their devices into *platforms* that can install and run apps from a corresponding marketplace that is, in turn, fed by app developers all around the world. Again, it might seem obvious that those developers are in charge of their apps' security. However, if an actual vulnerability is exploited in an app, it's the responsibility of the platform's designers to protect system processes and configurations as well as other apps from the one causing trouble.

Sometimes access control is considered only on a software or OS level. However, an additional threat has significant relevance for embedded systems: physical access. Attackers as well as penetration testers and researchers can analyze a device physically by interacting with local (debug) interfaces like JTAG, Universal Asynchronous Receiver-Transmitter (UART), or the Inter-Integrated Circuit (I^2C) bus.

Mitigating this threat by stating that "no one will open up our device" and, even if so, "the internals are so complex that even our engineers don't know all the details" is common, but it's rarely reasonable. Interested attackers will definitely remove the product housing and look for local interfaces, and if they have a certain motivation, they'll also be willing to spend time on manually reverse engineering the device until they reach their goal.

Access Control and Damage Containment

In many cases, solid access-control management can reduce or even prevent an attack's impact. It's a perfect example of how engineers and developers can take seriously the principle of defense in depth. If one security layer, like the confidentiality of user credentials, fails or an unknown software vulnerability is discovered, the access-control layer steps in and prevents the worst consequences.

However, this works only if you have a sound basis for deciding whether access should be granted and, if so, how much access is actually necessary. You should take several properties into account when granting a user access to an object like a file or hardware resource.

Permissions can be granted and denied on the basis of the user's identity, sometimes known as *identity-based access control (IBAC)*. However, managing every single user or human independently might be too complicated. Therefore, *role-based access control (RBAC)*, which sets permissions according to the user's role, has gained popularity. This not only eases permission management but also requires you to explicitly assign roles to every user, which increases transparency.

Yet another access-control approach relies on the attributes of subjects, objects, and maybe even their environments. Known as *attribute-based access control (ABAC)*, it allows for more dynamic access decisions than IBAC or RBAC.

A common strategy for optimizing access control in terms of security is to reduce permissions to the minimum required by a given user or application. However, that's the crux of the matter, because those minimum requirements are often not explicitly known.

Thus, developers often tend to set permissions generously, leaving space for malicious activities or compromise. Their reasoning is understandable because restricting users and applications too much might render the device inoperable. And, to make the situation worse, the duties of a user and the access privileges of an application might change over time. Therefore, it's important to consider access-control management early and comprehensively over the whole device life cycle.

Design and Development Phase

During hardware design, discussions about physical access to IC pins, pads, and traces on a PCB should already be on the agenda. Obfuscation of debug ports or the application of epoxy resin on critical parts might be solutions to think about. The impact of physical access also might be reduced by contact switches or springs that indicate to the main processor that the product casing was opened.

For higher security, there's even the possibility of integrating a conducting mesh structure into a plastic case, which continuously runs signals on its lines to detect any tampering with the housing. Such mechanisms are already used in payment terminals.

An important part of firmware development is the specification of system users, their roles, directories, initial files, and corresponding permissions. Even if this sounds trivial at first, make sure to take the whole range of your device's intended use cases into account. The results have to be implemented in the build system of your choice (for example, Yocto or Buildroot) and should be monitored for correctness throughout the whole development process.

Next, you must analyze all the device's software applications and services. On the one hand, you must specify in which user context each application should be run. This defines the rights a process has at runtime, which becomes especially important when it's taken over by a malicious actor. Consider carefully whether root is always your best choice.

On the other hand, applications can also play an active role in access-control management. Let's take a web server as an example. This common type of application has control over the web pages it serves to connected clients. Some parts of the web interface, like the page for device administration, might be more critical than others. Based on OS users or the web server's own user management, the server has to be configured appropriately to grant admin access only to legitimate users.

Of course, the application might have several "admin" users: a `webadmin` for administration tasks carried out by the web application, a `sysadmin` for Linux system administration, and maybe a `superadmin` used for manufacturer access. And all of them have different permissions.

Production Considerations

Device production is usually not considered an important step in access-control management, but more and more standards—for example, the European ETSI EN 303 645 for consumer electronics—require devices to refrain from implementing global default passwords. Since a device's firmware is usually a static global artifact, a device-individual password has to be generated and set during production.

And it's not only the firmware that has to be individualized. A piece of paper, a sticker, or a part of the product packaging also has to be labeled with the individual password. This process depends heavily on your device's firmware structure and your production processes.

An alternative to in-production password generation is to force end users to set a new, custom password at first login. The advantage of this approach is that you can use a single, global firmware image, which is much easier to handle during production. However, your product is also left with a universal default password that can be used at least once during initialization—by users and adversaries.

Customer Activities and Decommissioning

In the field, customers might want to create additional users themselves or change the permission of given accounts. You have to decide whether that should be possible and, if so, within what limits. Allowing a customer to choose freely which permissions to grant could lead to an *elevation of privilege*, resulting in the end user receiving more rights than implicitly intended.

Manually changing passwords on hundreds of devices is absolutely tedious and also error-prone. Therefore, modern IoT infrastructures require a central management of assets and configurations—including users, roles, and permissions—in order to stay manageable at all. For device manufacturers, preparing devices to support Lightweight Directory Access Protocol (LDAP) integration or something similar might be reasonable to ease central management. However, make sure to consider the potential threats when you trust a remote server to handle users, credentials, and permissions for your device.

As mentioned before, applications should be restricted to the minimum permissions necessary to function correctly. However, with every firmware update, the features and behavior of a device's software components might change. New functionality might require further permissions, and strict security could be a showstopper. Also, security updates might remove software routines that required specific permissions, and those permissions wouldn't be needed anymore afterward. In general, if you work with tools that restrict software applications and you update that software, you always have to double-check that the related permissions match the new version.

Last but not least, you have to consider that your device might be resold and used by another customer. That customer should still be able to initialize the device and to reset users and permissions, but shouldn't have access to data created by the previous owner. The same applies for final decommissioning when curious dumpster divers or scrap dealers might want to get hold of access-restricted data. The original customer should be provided with a "clear all private data" button that actually does what it says, and newly added users shouldn't be able to access others' data even if it isn't cleared.

Discretionary Access Control

Discretionary access control (DAC) is a fundamental approach to managing access rights of subjects and groups to objects within a system. The subjects in our case are users in a Linux OS, while objects might be files, directories, memory locations, interprocess communication, and all sorts of system devices and interfaces. This methodology is *discretionary* because permissions for a certain object are granted *at the discretion* of a user owning this specific object; *owners* can pass on permissions to other users and groups.

In Linux systems, the root user is omnipotent. It's able to override permissions set by owners. Therefore, "becoming root" is one of the most attractive goals for attackers. For developers, this means processes that could potentially be compromised, such as all applications listening on network ports, should never run as root!

Linux Filesystem Permissions

Every single file in a Linux filesystem has a permission string associated with it. As shown in Listing 11-1, the ls tool can print the string always at the beginning of each line.

```
# ls -l
-rw-r--r-- 1 root root     23 Apr 30 13:13 README
lrwxrwxrwx 1 root root     17 Apr 30 14:15 current_logfile -> logs/73944561.log
drwxr-xr-x 2 root root   1024 Apr 30 14:14 logs
-rw-r--r-- 1 bob  guest    12 Apr 30 17:15 my_notes.md
# ls -l logs/73944561.log
-rw-r--r-- 1 root root      9 Apr 30 12:20 73944561.log
```

Listing 11-1: A file permission listing on Linux

The prominent strings root root show that all files are owned by the root user from the root group, except for the *my_notes.md* file, which is owned by *bob* of the *guest* group. Further, the very first character of each line specifies whether it's a regular file (-), a directory (d), or a symbolic link (l). Block devices (b) and character devices (c) would also be indicated there. The following nine characters represent the permissions granted for each file. They're separated in three groups of three characters each, concerning read (r), write (w), and execute (x) permissions of the owner, a corresponding group, and anybody else, respectively.

For example, the *README* file in Listing 11-1 can be read and written by the root user, but other users in the root group may only read. Read permission is also granted to any other user, no matter in which group, as indicated by the trailing r--.

Whenever you read tutorials or third-party source code for Linux access-control management, you'll likely stumble over an efficient, three-digit notation of access permissions. The 9-bit permission strings can be written efficiently as three octal numbers: one for owner permissions, one for group member permissions, and the last one stands for all others.

For example, 777 means that everybody may read, write, and execute a given object. In contrast, 740 says that the owner may read, write, and execute; group members are allowed only to read; and anybody else has no access rights at all. Table 11-1 details the conversion of permissions to octal numbers, and vice versa.

Table 11-1: Octal Representation of Linux File Permissions

Octal	Binary	Permissions
0	000	---
1	001	--x
2	010	-w-
3	011	-wx
4	100	r--
5	101	r-x
6	110	rw-
7	111	rwx

Understanding file permissions is straightforward, but directories behave a little bit differently. There, read permission enables the enumeration of items within a directory. Write permission grants the right to add, delete, or rename directory items. Execute permission allows users to navigate to the directory, such as with the cd command, and access files or subdirectories.

Linux User and Group Management

In Linux, several tools exist for managing users and groups. The most basic commands, available in all distributions, even on embedded systems, are the following:

useradd	Create a new user
usermod	Modify properties of an existing user
userdel	Delete a user
groupadd	Create a new group
groupmod	Modify properties of an existing group
groupdel	Delete a group

When engineering secure devices, the most important commands are useradd and groupadd, because they can be used at image-creation time to implement users and roles defined in an associated access-control concept.

For user creation, of course, the new user's name has to be provided. Further options you might want to specify are its *user identifier*—or *UID* (--uid)—its home directory (--home), and whether this directory should be created automatically (--create-home). In addition, you can define whether a user group with the same name should be created (--user-group) and which groups the user should belong to (--groups). The --shell option allows for specifying the shell used after login, but it can also be used with false and nologin to disable user login. Finally, you can set the user's password (in hashed form) with the --password option.

The main parameters to specify for creating a group with `groupadd` are the group's name and, if desired, a corresponding *group identifier (GID)* (`--gid`) that you can use to refer to the specific group at a later time.

Users as well as groups might be flagged as belonging to the system (`--system`), in contrast to being external, probably human users. Such system accounts receive a UID/GID from a reserved system range. In addition, system users don't expire and don't get a home directory created.

NOTE *The tools useradd and adduser as well as groupadd and addgroup get mixed up easily. The ones presented in this section are the basic, portable versions, while the others might be more user-friendly in an interactive session.*

Linux Permission Management

To configure owners, groups, and permissions of files and directories, we need three common tools on Linux systems:

chown Allows you to change the owner of a file or directory to another owner. For example, the owner of the *web.conf* file can be set to *bob* with `chown bob web.conf`.

chgrp Specifies a new group for a given file or directory. The group of the *manuals* directory might be changed to *guest* with `chgrp guest manuals`, for example.

chmod Manipulates permissions for files and directories. The call `chmod +x script.sh` adds execution permission to the *script.sh* file, while `chmod -wx script.sh` removes permissions for writing and execution. Both affect only the owner's permissions. By prepending g for group, o for others, u for users/owners, and a for all, you can also specify which part of the permission string should be affected. For example, `chmod go-rwx private.key` removes all access rights of the *private.key* file for all group members and anybody else except the owner.

Access-Control Lists

In principle, users and groups enable us to represent any desired access-control settings. However, in some cases, the limitation that a file or directory can have only a single owner and a single associated group makes efficient access-control management difficult.

Let me provide an example because the usefulness might not be obvious. Imagine you have a directory called *internal_logs* for storing logs and runtime data. Files in this directory are created by five users, all belonging to the *service* group. Two years after market release, you introduce a new predictive maintenance feature and an associated `predmain` user who needs read access only to the *internal_logs/freqtrack.dat* file, and the user shouldn't be able to write anything—to contain damage in case of compromise. You can't add *predmain* to the *service* group because then it would have too many permissions, and you can't make *predmain* the owner of *freqtrack.dat* because, again, compromise would leave an attacker with too much control.

One solution is to use access-control lists (ACLs) that are implemented based on the extended file attributes (xattr) of a Linux filesystem. Depending on your system, ACL support has to be installed, and the filesystem has to be mounted with the acl option before you can use the getfacl and setfacl command line tools to view and change permissions on a fine-grained level, respectively.

Case Study: Access Control for STM32MP157F-DK2 Firmware

In this case study, I first demonstrate a user- and file-initialization process with Yocto. Next, I explore the default permissions set by Linux for certain system files and the reasoning behind them. Finally, as an example of application-level access control, I take a look at the configuration of the SSH daemon Dropbear.

User Creation and File Provisioning in Yocto

The first question regarding access control you have to clarify on any Linux platform is the way you want to handle the root user. Especially during development, the root user might be used regularly and often, even without a password. Make sure to remove debug settings for production images. In my case, I removed the debug-tweaks feature from ST's st-image-core image, as shown in Listing 11-2.

```
EXTRA_IMAGE_FEATURES:remove = "debug-tweaks"
inherit extrausers
ROOT_PASSWORD_HASH = "\$6\$ZsFPzdUpnha4s1lG\$8Zxzo4UhZBomryn/SJSlVq97TLy..."
EXTRA_USERS_PARAMS:append = "usermod --password '${ROOT_PASSWORD_HASH}' root;"
```

Listing 11-2: Preparing the root user for production

I inherited the extrausers class, which allows the modification of the existing root user (for example, to protect it with a strong password). The cryptic-looking string behind ROOT_PASSWORD_HASH is the user password hash format expected by Linux. It was obtained by calling openssl passwd -6 *password*, where the -6 parameter indicates that a salted hash based on SHA-512 is used. Also note that the $ symbols act as separators in this format and that they need to be escaped within Yocto recipes.

NOTE *In many cases, completely disabling root login makes sense, unless you have convincing reasons not to, in order to rule out misuse of this powerful user.*

Yocto additionally provides the useradd class to further provision users and groups from within a custom recipe. Listing 11-3 shows the creation of two system users, *rservice* and *lservice*, as well as the end users *admin* and *guest*. Also, two corresponding groups are created, and the users are added to these groups.

```
inherit useradd
USERADD_PACKAGES = "${PN}"

USERADD_PARAM:${PN} = "--password '\$6\$fu47IexZgSH/T6d0\$9a.LjAlOsLOK...' \
                       --home /home/rservice --system rservice; \
                       --password '\$6\$tSsINjOvlFOaVrky\$9VIgdb7.LIVG...' \
                       --home /home/lservice --system lservice; \
                       --password '\$6\$VOPFagOJM.H.ZWIh\$8lELUZpkIogC...' \
                       --uid 1300 --home /home/admin admin; \
                       --password '\$6\$CPaAzKAYqkSKW42x\$KgivNUKDqsJT...' \
                       --uid 1301 --home /home/guest guest"

GROUPADD_PARAM:${PN} = "--system service; \
                        --gid 890 endusers"

GROUPMEMS_PARAM:${PN} = "--add rservice --group service; \
                         --add lservice --group service; \
                         --add admin --group endusers; \
                         --add guest --group endusers"
```

Listing 11-3: Creating users and groups for the image

All users are initialized with a password in the USERADD_PARAM variable. Specific UIDs are used only for end-user accounts. The GROUPADD_PARAM variable allows you to create new groups, while GROUPMEMS_PARAM enrolls the created users in those groups.

In some cases, you also might want to create directories for users and place initial files in them. In Listing 11-4, a snippet from a custom recipe is shown that may serve as a simple example of file provisioning for created users, including necessary commands to set owners and groups accordingly.

```
do_install () {
        install -d -m 770 ${D}/home/rservice
        install -d -m 740 ${D}/home/lservice
        install -d -m 500 ${D}/home/admin
        install -d -m 550 ${D}/home/guest

        install -p -m 400 administration.md ${D}/home/admin/
        install -p -m 440 README ${D}/home/guest/

        chown -R rservice ${D}/home/rservice
        chown -R lservice ${D}/home/lservice
        chown -R admin ${D}/home/admin
        chown -R guest ${D}/home/guest

        chgrp -R service ${D}/home/rservice
        chgrp -R service ${D}/home/lservice
```

```
        chgrp -R endusers ${D}/home/admin
        chgrp -R endusers ${D}/home/guest
}
```

Listing 11-4: The basic file provisioning for created users

First, home directories for all users are created with corresponding permissions. For example, end users should be able to read only provided data,
but not to store their own code to the device or even execute it. Further, administration information should not be accessible for the guest user.

Service users, on the other hand, have higher permissions. They may
load custom data to their directories, while the lservice local service user has
the highest rights because it might even read and write to the remote service
user's directory.

With these basic steps, you can lay the foundation for your device's
access-control management.

Exploration of System Files and Predefined Users

Luckily, Linux and its distributions already take care of permission settings
for a variety of system files. Let's look at some specific examples within the
firmware of my STM32MP157F device.

The user and password management on Linux is implemented by the
/etc/passwd and */etc/shadow* files. As shown in Listing 11-5, the first file is
marked readable for everybody because there might be various good reasons to read the list of users on a system. However, the actual password hash
of each user is not included in the *passwd* file. It resides in the *shadow* file,
which is readable only by root for login verification purposes.

```
# ls -l /etc/passwd /etc/shadow
-rw-r--r-- 1 root root 1404 ... /etc/passwd
-r-------- 1 root root  884 ... /etc/shadow
```

Listing 11-5: The access rights to password files on Linux

Shadowing password storage has been done for decades. The main idea
is to restrict the access of unprivileged users to password hashes, because if
a user uses a weak password, an adversary with access to the corresponding
password hash would be able to launch a brute-force attack against it.

NOTE   *If you wonder how passwords could be changed if /etc/shadow is only readable,
even for root: the superuser root has similar powers to Chuck Norris; it can even
write to read-only files.*

Listing 11-6 shows the permission strings for my device's microSD card
(*/dev/mmcblk0*), the Linux RNG device (*/dev/urandom*), and the hardware
RNG device of the STM32MP157F (*/dev/hwrng*).

```
# ls -l /dev/mmcblk0
brw-rw---- 1 root disk 179, 0 Apr 28 17:42 /dev/mmcblk0
```

```
# ls -l /dev/urandom /dev/hwrng
crw------- 1 root root 10, 183 Apr 28 17:42 /dev/hwrng
crw-rw-rw- 1 root root  1,   9 Apr 28 17:42 /dev/urandom
```

Listing 11-6: The permissions for a microSD card and RNG devices

You can see that, for device files, the permission string indicates whether it's a block device (b) or a character device (c). The results also show that the microSD card can be read only by root or members of the *disk* group. For RNGs, the system differentiates between the OS-provided RNG urandom, which can be read and written be everyone, and the hardware RNG device hwrng, which only root may access.

Let's shift the focus from files to processes. Listing 11-7 shows typical applications like the web server httpd or the MQTT broker mosquitto and the corresponding users executing these processes.

```
# ps | grep -E 'PID|httpd|mosquitto'
  PID USER       VSZ STAT COMMAND
 1138 root      5680 S    /usr/sbin/httpd -DFOREGROUND -D SSL -D PHP5 -k start
 1148 daemon    224m S    /usr/sbin/httpd -DFOREGROUND -D SSL -D PHP5 -k start
 1149 daemon    224m S    /usr/sbin/httpd -DFOREGROUND -D SSL -D PHP5 -k start
 1150 daemon    224m S    /usr/sbin/httpd -DFOREGROUND -D SSL -D PHP5 -k start
 1235 mosquitt  6792 S    /usr/sbin/mosquitto -c /etc/mosquitto/mosquitto.conf
 2507 daemon    224m S    /usr/sbin/httpd -DFOREGROUND -D SSL -D PHP5 -k start
 2610 root      2320 S    grep -E PID|httpd|mosquitto
```

Listing 11-7: The user context of typical network daemons

The web server httpd exhibits a common strategy to limit the attack surface in case a vulnerability could be exploited remotely. It starts under the root user, binds to its designated port (for example, 80), and then deliberately drops its high privileges by altering its GID and UID by calls to setgid() and setuid(), respectively. Therefore, in my case, the four "worker threads" of httpd run under the low-privilege user *daemon*.

The same is true for the Mosquitto broker. You can infer from its documentation that, even if started as the root user, Mosquitto immediately drops privileges after reading its configuration file and continues running in the context of a more limited user, called mosquitto in my case.

The output of usernames by ps is limited to eight characters. Therefore, mosquitto becomes mosquitt.

SSH Daemon Access-Control Configuration

Dropbear is a lightweight SSH daemon that's especially popular on embedded systems. It enables secure remote access to a device, which makes it perfectly useful but also absolutely critical. Applications like that deserve dedicated consideration regarding access-control settings, because if they implement an "open door policy," it's literally an invitation for attackers.

Listing 11-8 shows a part of the command line arguments for the dropbear daemon that are interesting from an access-control point of view.

```
# dropbear --help
...
-w  Disallow root logins
-G  Restrict logins to members of specified group
-s  Disable password logins
-g  Disable password logins for root
-B  Allow blank password logins
-T  Maximum authentication tries (default 10)
...
```

Listing 11-8: Some access-control options for dropbear

Disabling root access over SSH (-w) is a good idea in most instances. For this case study, it might also be reasonable to restrict SSH access to users from the *service* group (-G), because it shouldn't be a feature for end users. Disabling password logins completely and allowing only public-key authentication would be perfect, but if your PKI is not yet prepared for this step, the -s option isn't possible. Since we completely disabled root access, using -g would be redundant. The -B argument should be used only during development; you probably don't want to find this in a production firmware image. Lastly, you can restrict the maximum number of login tries—for example, to three (-T 3).

NOTE *You can also change the port of the dropbear SSH daemon from 22 to a custom one with the -p option. That's just obscurity, but it might save your internet-connected device from being discovered by automated SSH scans.*

To store your dropbear settings persistently, you have to change the */etc/dropbear/default* file in your firmware image. The important line that it should contain to implement the discussed access-control restrictions is DROPBEAR_EXTRA_ARGS="-w -T 3 -G service".

Mandatory Access Control

While DAC concepts are usually known among embedded system developers, *mandatory access control (MAC)* is often uncharted territory. However, MAC implementations can contribute significantly to a device's security and to the containment of damage in case of compromise.

The basic idea of MAC systems for embedded devices is that permissions and policies regarding the way users and processes may interact with files and other resources are managed by the manufacturer and enforced by the OS. In contrast to the user-centric approach of DAC, users can't override the rules defined by MAC.

MAC implementations are powerful tools, but with power comes responsibility. *Whitelisting* is a popular access-control strategy in which access is denied by default and granted only if explicitly allowed. This approach can also be used for MAC systems to permit only defined access of subjects to objects. However, if you omit specifying a legitimate access as "allowed," maybe because it's used infrequently, an application that requires it might crash during runtime whenever the access occurs.

If you choose a *blacklisting* approach—defining only dangerous cases for which access should be denied, like malware detected by virus scanners—the probability of breaking functionality is reduced. However, you have to ensure that corresponding rules for newly discovered malicious behavior find their way into your devices in a timely manner.

Linux Security Modules

Since the Linux community was not able to agree on one specific security module, Linux introduced the *Linux Security Module (LSM)* framework. It enables the implementation of various MAC systems for Linux.

These LSMs are compiled into the Linux kernel and take action if specific hook functions are called within the kernel code. These hooks are integrated in all procedures relevant for access control within the OS, from file access to task spawning to interprocess communication. If reached, the kernel hands over control to the LSM, which is able to at least log the performed action or directly decide whether access should be granted or denied based on its specific rule set.

LSM implementations differ significantly in terms of their concepts, their way of configuring rule sets, and their supporting community. However, they also share a common property: all have a negative impact on system performance. The following sections introduce popular LSM implementations.

SELinux

In 2000, the NSA published its idea of a MAC system for Linux to the open source community: *Security-Enhanced Linux (SELinux)*. Supported by other stakeholders in this field, the project flourished and was finally integrated into version 2.6 of the mainline Linux kernel in 2003. Since version 4.3, it's the default LSM in Android, and many Linux distributions for desktop and server applications support it.

SELinux relies on security policies that define which objects might be accessed by which subjects. For this purpose, objects and subjects must be registered in SELinux with corresponding *labels* containing a user, a role, and an associated type. These labels define a kind of context or domain for subjects and objects. The actual access control is implemented by *type enforcement*, which defines whether a subject with a specific type can access an object with a specific type.

Many Linux distributions provide their own set of predefined SELinux policies to restrict a variety of common applications and services. Further, there is a database of reference policies that you can use for your purposes. However, creating custom policies for your applications requires deep know-how about their functionalities and a detailed understanding of the SELinux concepts and structures. You should not underestimate the necessary characterization efforts, even if tools are available to support you.

At runtime, SELinux can be operated in three ways. The *enforcing* mode is meant for productive use, because it strictly applies all given policies and logs corresponding activities. However, during development or in a test phase, the *permissive* mode is more suitable. It processes all policies, but only generates warnings and log data without enforcing the defined rules. This can be enormously helpful for fine-tuning custom policies and troubleshooting. If *disabled*, SELinux is turned off completely and doesn't protect or restrict anything.

Although (or perhaps precisely because) SELinux provides a vast number of capabilities, it's a pretty complex tool that many embedded system engineers refrain from using. This is probably the main reason other LSM implementations emerged and became popular alternatives, as described in the following sections.

AppArmor

AppArmor is the second LSM implementation to gain significant popularity among Linux distributions. It became part of the Linux kernel 2.6.36 in 2010 and is currently the default MAC system for Ubuntu and SUSE Linux. Its development has been funded by Canonical since 2009.

Access control is managed on the basis of individual profiles per application. In contrast to SELinux, AppArmor uses filesystem paths to identify subjects and file objects, so the syntax offers better readability. Further, it allows a hybrid approach of whitelisting and blacklisting rules that control the resource access of a process. The created profiles can restrict network access and various sorts of Linux capabilities, but also permissions to read, write, and execute files.

AppArmor comes with a list of predefined profiles, and additional profiles for common applications are maintained by the Ubuntu community. Additionally, AppArmor provides several tools that support developers in profiling custom applications and generating corresponding profiles.

Generally speaking, there are two ways of characterizing access requirements. First, targeted profiling allows you to capture access events of a single application and to automatically generate a profile from it. Second, AppArmor can apply a systemic monitoring approach that logs access operations of a defined set of applications for days or even weeks and spanning multiple reboots. The collected log information can then be turned into a series of profiles restricting the analyzed applications in a preferably optimal way.

Each AppArmor profile available on a device can be put into one of three modes at runtime: enforce, complain, or audit. In *enforcement mode*, the rules set by the profile are enforced, and violation attempts are logged. The *complain mode* allows for monitoring an application's behavior under a defined profile, and operations that violate the policy are logged. This mode is also used in the automated profile creation mentioned previously and is therefore sometimes called AppArmor's *learning mode*. To log all access, whether successful or not, while enforcing a given policy, the *audit mode* has to be selected.

AppArmor is a worthy alternative to SELinux that succeeds in reducing configuration and profiling complexity. From a security point of view, it's sometimes more lax than its competitor and leaves space to circumvent access control in specific cases. For embedded systems, however, it might be a perfect compromise to introduce MAC mechanisms.

Other LSMs and Non-LSM MACs

Besides the two popular LSM implementations, SELinux and AppArmor, you might want to consider further options.

As the name suggests, the *Simplified Mandatory Access Control Kernel (SMACK)* system was developed with a focus on simplicity, in contrast to the complexity of SELinux. It has been part of the Linux mainline kernel since 2008 and was always meant for use in embedded systems. Two larger OS projects rely on its protection mechanisms: the mobile OS Tizen used in Samsung's smart TVs, and the automotive-grade Linux distribution meant as an open source platform for connected cars. However, looking at SMACK's website and its Git repositories, it seems that it's no longer actively maintained.

A further MAC system based on the LSM framework is called *TOMOYO*. The project was started in 2003 and merged into the Linux kernel 2.6.30 in 2009. Again, the motivation was simpler usage and higher usability—for example, as implemented by an automatic policy generation, which is also necessary because this MAC system doesn't come with a comprehensive set of rules for common services. In addition, TOMOYO not only serves as a MAC implementation but also facilitates system behavior analysis. It comes in three versions: 1.*x*, 2.*x*, and AKARI. The first one requires specific kernel patching and is, therefore, usually not your first choice. AKARI and TOMOYO 2.*x* use the LSM framework. At the time of writing, AKARI provides a few more features, but TOMOYO 2.*x* is catching up.

Although the LSM framework provides a multitude of possibilities for integrating custom security modules, not everybody in the community is satisfied with its implementation, especially considering the performance overhead it generates. Therefore, non-LSM MAC systems also exist that aim for higher performance or enhanced security module features. However, since those implementations are not part of the mainline kernel and have to be integrated by applying a custom set of patches, they might be an option only if you really can't reach your requirements with the popular LSM implementations.

Case Study: Application Confinement with AppArmor

In this case study, I shed light on the installation of AppArmor with the Yocto toolchain of my STM32MP157F-DK2 device and walk through its basic usage to restrict an application.

Installation

AppArmor is not included in the default installation of ST's OpenSTLinux distribution. Luckily, the Yocto `meta-security` layer maintained by Armin Kuster provides an AppArmor recipe under *meta-security/recipes-mac/AppArmor*.

After cloning the corresponding Git repository, the Linux kernel can be configured for AppArmor usage with the settings shown in Listing 11-9.

```
CONFIG_SECURITY=y
CONFIG_SECURITY_APPARMOR=y
CONFIG_DEFAULT_SECURITY="apparmor"
CONFIG_SECURITY_APPARMOR_BOOTPARAM_VALUE=1
```

Listing 11-9: The Linux kernel configuration to enable AppArmor

The first two lines enable AppArmor, and the last two lines set it as the default LSM to be used. However, I also had to add `security=apparmor` to the kernel's boot arguments in U-Boot's *extlinux.conf* files to select AppArmor at boot time.

To compile and install the AppArmor user-space tools, add the line `IMAGE_INSTALL += "apparmor"` to the image's recipe. I also had to add several distro features to the provided OpenSTLinux, as shown in Listing 11-10, in order to make Yocto successfully complete the building process.

```
DISTRO_FEATURES += "security"
DISTRO_FEATURES += "apparmor"
DISTRO_FEATURES += "tpm"
```

Listing 11-10: The distro features for AppArmor from meta-security

After booting the device, you can check whether AppArmor is actually enabled with the command shown in Listing 11-11. If it returns a Y, it was activated properly.

```
# cat /sys/module/apparmor/parameters/enabled
Y
```

Listing 11-11: Checking whether AppArmor was enabled correctly

AppArmor comes with the aa-status tool, which lists a variety of details regarding AppArmor's current status, as shown in Listing 11-12.

```
# aa-status
apparmor module is loaded.
50 profiles are loaded.
50 profiles are in enforce mode.
   ...
   apache2
   ...
   avahi-daemon
   ...
```

```
    ping
    ...
    syslogd
    traceroute
    ...
0 profiles are in complain mode.
...
2 processes are in enforce mode.
   /usr/sbin/avahi-daemon (665) avahi-daemon
   /usr/sbin/avahi-daemon (667) avahi-daemon
0 processes are in complain mode.
...
```

Listing 11-12: The initial output of aa-status

You can see that the AppArmor recipe from the `meta-security` layer also installs a set of 50 standard profiles that are loaded in enforce mode on my device. However, the first thing I noticed is that although there are profiles loaded for `apache2` and `syslogd`, the corresponding, currently running processes are not confined. Only the `avahi-daemon` processes are restricted according to their profile.

To investigate this issue, we have to take a look at the default AppArmor profiles stored in */etc/apparmor.d/*. For `apache2`, the file containing the provided profile is called *usr.sbin.apache2*. The filename is already a hint for the path of the executable it confines: */usr/sbin/apache2*, in this case. Looking at the content of the file, you can see a line stating `profile apache2 /usr/\{bin, sbin\}/apache2`, which means that the profile at hand is named `apache2` and targets the executable *apache2* located at */usr/bin/* or */usr/sbin/*.

Unfortunately, this file doesn't exist in my installation. Instead, it's called *httpd*. Therefore, I created a copy of the initial file named *usr.sbin.httpd*. I also changed the profile name to `httpd` and the path for the executable to `/usr/\{bin,sbin\}/httpd`. Afterward, I loaded the profile in enforce mode as shown in Listing 11-13 and restarted the web server.

```
# aa-enforce /etc/apparmor.d/usr.sbin.httpd
Setting /etc/apparmor.d/usr.sbin.httpd to enforce mode.
# systemctl restart apache2
# aa-disable /etc/apparmor.d/usr.sbin.apache2
Disabling /etc/apparmor.d/usr.sbin.apache2.
```

Listing 11-13: Loading and disabling profiles

I also disabled the original profile with the help of `aa-disable` in order to clean up.

Listing 11-14 presents the output of another call to `aa-status`, showing that the `httpd` profile was loaded correctly and that all four corresponding process instances are running in enforce mode as desired.

```
# aa-status
...
50 profiles are loaded.
50 profiles are in enforce mode.
...
   httpd
   httpd//DEFAULT_URI
   httpd//HANDLING_UNTRUSTED_INPUT
   httpd//phpsysinfo
...
6 processes are in enforce mode.
   /usr/sbin/avahi-daemon (669) avahi-daemon
   /usr/sbin/avahi-daemon (672) avahi-daemon
   /usr/sbin/httpd (668) httpd
   /usr/sbin/httpd (678) httpd
   /usr/sbin/httpd (679) httpd
   /usr/sbin/httpd (681) httpd
...
```

Listing 11-14: The output of aa-status after profile changes

Although we succeeded in activating the predefined profile, we have no idea whether the profile actually restricts the web server application in a secure way. A comment in the given profile says that "this profile is completely permissive," which means that you still have to customize it according to your application and requirements.

A quick look at the profile *sbin.syslogd* associated with the syslogd tool, the second example binary identified at the beginning of this subsection, reveals that the configured path, */sbin/syslogd*, matches the path of the corresponding executable, but the process is still not running in enforce mode. The properties of the binary, as shown in Listing 11-15, reveal that the executable is actually a symbolic link to another executable—namely, */bin/busybox.nosuid*.

```
# ls -l /sbin/syslogd
lrwxrwxrwx 1 root root 19 ... /sbin/syslogd -> /bin/busybox.nosuid
```

Listing 11-15: A symbolic link to another executable

This makes the situation somewhat complicated because BusyBox unites a variety of tools in one binary. Simply changing the syslogd profile's path doesn't solve this issue but rather causes further problems with other Busy-Box functionalities. In such cases, you have several options. You could just spare the syslogd profile, you could search for or create a comprehensive busybox profile, or you could install and use the original syslogd application after all.

Application Profiling

For your own applications or third-party tools that don't come with a pre-defined AppArmor profile, you have to create one yourself if you want to confine them with MAC mechanisms at runtime.

Let's look at a very simple Python application that was reduced to the minimum. Listing 11-16 shows the code.

```
#!/usr/bin/python3

import sys

if len(sys.argv) == 2:
    file_path = sys.argv[1]
    with open(file_path, 'r') as f:
        print(f.read())
else:
    print('Usage:', sys.argv[0], '<filename>')
```

Listing 11-16: A simple file-printing application in Python

This application's sole purpose is to print the content of a text file given as a command line argument. The application's filename is *printfile.py*, it's located in */home/root/*, and it's marked as executable.

Let's assume that this tool is an essential part of your web interface and needs to run with superuser privileges because it has to print the content of the *testfile* and *logfile* files, which are accessible only by root. However, during your threat and risk analysis, you discover that adversaries might be able to inject other filepaths than the two intended ones, which could lead to the exposure of sensitive information and should be prevented—for example, by using a custom-tailored AppArmor profile.

Listing 11-17 shows the basic initial profile I created at */etc/apparmor.d/ home.root.printfile.py* as a starting point for profiling this application. It includes read access (r) for the two previously mentioned files and denies any other file access.

```
/home/root/printfile.py {
    /home/root/testfile     r,
    /home/root/logfile      r,
}
```

Listing 11-17: The initial AppArmor profile for printfile.py

In the second step, I loaded the newly created profile in complain mode, as shown in Listing 11-18.

```
# aa-complain /etc/apparmor.d/home.root.printfile.py
Setting /etc/apparmor.d/home.root.printfile.py to complain mode.
```

Listing 11-18: Loading a profile in complain mode

If you now execute `./printfile.py testfile` in *home/root/*, the application will work without issues but will create log entries for all profile violations.

Listing 11-19 shows a pruned set of AppArmor kernel messages corresponding to *printfile.py*.

```
# dmesg | grep printfile.py
... audit: type=1400 audit(1652997509.490:132): apparmor="STATUS"
           operation="profile_load" profile="unconfined"
           name="/home/root/printfile.py" pid=1557 comm="apparmor_parser"
... audit: type=1400 audit(1652997771.210:133): apparmor="ALLOWED"
           operation="open" profile="/home/root/printfile.py"
           name="/etc/ld.so.cache" pid=1560 comm="printfile.py"
           requested_mask="r" denied_mask="r" fsuid=0 ouid=0
... audit: type=1300 audit(1652997771.210:133): arch=40000028 ...
           comm="printfile.py" exe="/usr/bin/python3.10"
           subj=/home/root/printfile.py (complain) key=(null)
... audit: type=1400 audit(1652997771.210:134): apparmor="ALLOWED"
           operation="open" profile="/home/root/printfile.py"
           name="/usr/lib/libpython3.10.so.1.0" pid=1560 comm="printfile.py"
           requested_mask="r" denied_mask="r" fsuid=0 ouid=0
... audit: type=1300 audit(1652997771.210:134): arch=40000028 ...
           comm="printfile.py" exe="/usr/bin/python3.10"
           subj=/home/root/printfile.py (complain) key=(null)
... audit: type=1400 audit(1652997771.210:135): apparmor="ALLOWED"
           operation="file_mmap" profile="/home/root/printfile.py"
           name="/usr/lib/libpython3.10.so.1.0" pid=1560 comm="printfile.py"
           requested_mask="rm" denied_mask="rm" fsuid=0 ouid=0
... audit: type=1300 audit(1652997771.210:135): arch=40000028 ...
           comm="printfile.py" exe="/usr/bin/python3.10"
           subj=/home/root/printfile.py (complain) key=(null)
... audit: type=1400 audit(1652997771.210:136): apparmor="ALLOWED"
           operation="open" profile="/home/root/printfile.py"
           name="/lib/libc.so.6" pid=1560 comm="printfile.py"
           requested_mask="r" denied_mask="r" fsuid=0 ouid=0
```

Listing 11-19: The AppArmor complain messages for printfile.py

You can see that multiple access violations occurred while just calling *printfile.py* in its intended way. If you put the initial profile in enforce mode, the application won't work anymore. Therefore, you have to use the depicted output to extend the AppArmor profile for *printfile.py*. For example, you have to grant read access (r) to */etc/ld.so.cache*, execution rights (ux) for */usr/bin/python3.10*, and permissions for reading (r) and mapping (m) */usr/lib/libpython3.10.so.1.0*.

Listing 11-20 shows the final profile after four iterations of execution in complain mode, profile refinement, and reloading.

```
/home/root/printfile.py flags=(complain) {
    /home/root/testfile              r,
    /home/root/logfile               r,
    /etc/ld.so.cache                 r,
    /usr/bin/python3.10              ux,
    /usr/lib/libpython3.10.so.1.0    rm,
    /lib/libc.so.6                   rm,
    /lib/libm.so.6                   rm,
    /usr/lib/locale/locale-archive   r,
    /usr/lib/python3.10/             r,
    /usr/lib/python3.10/**           r,
    /home/root/printfile.py          r,
}
```

Listing 11-20: The AppArmor profile for printfile.py *after refinement*

After this manual characterization phase, the created profile can be loaded in enforce mode and tested for its behavior (Listing 11-21).

```
# aa-enforce /etc/apparmor.d/home.root.printfile.py
Setting /etc/apparmor.d/home.root.printfile.py to enforce mode.
# ./printfile.py testfile
--- --- ---
This is a test file!
--- --- ---
# ./printfile.py logfile
--- --- ---
All the logs...
--- --- ---
# ./printfile.py secrets
Traceback (most recent call last):
  File "/home/root/./printfile.py", line 7, in <module>
    with open(file_path, 'r') as f:
PermissionError: [Errno 13] Permission denied: 'secrets'
# ./printfile.py /etc/passwd
Traceback (most recent call last):
  File "/home/root/./printfile.py", line 7, in <module>
    with open(file_path, 'r') as f:
PermissionError: [Errno 13] Permission denied: '/etc/passwd'
```

Listing 11-21: Testing printfile.py *in enforce mode*

Printing the *testfile* and *logfile* files works as intended. However, if attackers try to read the *secrets* file in the same folder or even the */etc/passwd* file, AppArmor successfully protects from severe damage.

This simple case study showed the basic feasibility of application characterization and corresponding AppArmor profile creation. However, even this trivial example took several profiling iterations, and the resulting profile will need to be maintained continuously—for example, if you switch to another distribution or even a newer version of Python. Further, as you can imagine, more complex applications require significantly more characterization and testing efforts.

Summary

Access control is an enormously broad topic that could fill a whole book on its own. It encompasses the basic configurations of users, groups, directory structures, and access permissions (as discussed in this chapter for the Linux DAC system), the deactivation of hardware debugging features and tools not meant for end users, and the complex field of OS-enforced MAC policies that have to be fine-tuned to the individual behavior and resource-access demands of a specific application. And while I don't expect you to invest all your time designing perfect access-control settings, there's no way around this matter in secure device engineering.

In practice, we have to find practically feasible compromises. A complete whitelisting approach might be hard to implement and can lead to broken applications if misconfigured, for which security will be blamed. Blacklisting, on the other hand, won't be able to immediately catch new threats that appear in the field. A fine granularity of permissions can be managed over time only if you are willing to expend significant effort, but if your access-control concept is too simplistic, your adversaries will thank you for removing that annoying obstacle in the way.

Finally, I'd like to point out that access-control mechanisms always have a strong relation to system-integrity protection, as described in Chapter 8. Just imagine if you painstakingly defined a perfect set of access rules only to find out that an attacker can reset them all to 777 within minutes. That would hurt.

12

SYSTEM MONITORING

Monitoring often comes with a negative connotation because it suggests that data is collected for surveillance by something or somebody. However, many digital business models like predictive maintenance wouldn't work without monitoring and subsequent data analytics. In the same way, the continuous protection of devices requires data logging and analysis to detect and trace back malicious activities.

The creation of extensive logfiles in IT systems has been common for decades. However, when it comes to embedded systems, logs might not receive the attention they deserve. In the past, low storage capacities and missing internet connections were legitimate reasons for putting system monitoring in second place, but luckily, these days, those limitations have continued to decrease.

In this chapter, I explain the benefits of monitoring devices for security reasons. In addition, I discuss resource limitations on embedded systems and multiple aspects of logging processes and their management. To wrap everything up, the book's final case study looks at available log data on an STM32MP157F device and how to analyze it.

Monitoring for the Right Reasons

Many companies have been accused of being "data krakens" because they collect all the data they can lay their hands on, whether from web services, IT infrastructures, or end-user devices. For them, this collection leads to profitable business models, but this development obviously contradicts privacy efforts to protect humans from tracking, surveillance, and spying.

On the legal side, the European GDPR is an example of counteracting excessive data collection, but other legal requirements—such as UN Regulation 155 in the automotive sector, IEC 62443-4-2 for the industrial automation industry, and the Critical Infrastructure Protection (CIP) standard CIP-007-6 of the North American Electric Reliability Corporation (NERC)—explicitly require security monitoring of connected products, either by manufacturers or operators. In a nutshell, be aware that the two sides of the data collection and monitoring coin always have to be balanced carefully.

In some areas, monitoring has been common practice for a long time; for example, surveillance cameras and security staff keep an eye on the physical security threats of buildings and corporate sites. The banking sector has a long tradition of monitoring transactions and reacting to unusual activities. Last but not least, network traffic monitoring by firewalls and intrusion detection systems is part of every sane IT infrastructure. Collecting data and monitoring systems in the name of security is clearly often acceptable, but it always must stay within reasonable bounds.

System monitoring has various advantages for device security. Log data can be especially useful in two cases. First, every attack on your device runs through multiple phases including reconnaissance, delivery, exploitation, installation, command and control, and actions on objectives. Each phase might leave traces in the device's logfiles that enable you to detect the attack early, react accordingly, and thereby avert further damage. Second, log data can be an immensely valuable source during forensic processes after an incident happened. Imagine that your devices were attacked in the field, but you don't have any data to reconstruct and understand what happened. Being blind in such a situation not only leaves you clueless but also can be a significant risk for your business.

In general, device monitoring raises transparency throughout your device population in the field and gives you an overview of when, where, and how your products are used. In critical infrastructures, such monitoring might even be necessary to fulfill legal or certification requirements. Also, as mentioned in Chapter 9, knowing the state of firmware versions deployed on your devices in the field can be helpful in understanding the threat landscape of your customers.

Besides the pure security use cases, monitoring can even be a supporting tool for handling and analyzing customer complaints. Log data might, for example, prove that an end user performed manual configuration changes that led to unauthorized operation modes, which overstressed mechanical components and caused a machine to break.

Monitoring the Right Things

Embedded systems running Linux, communicating with a variety of services, and interacting with sensors and actuators have reached a complexity that doesn't allow for recording the whole device state at any given point in time. The only option is *selective monitoring* of system properties and events.

WARNING   *Logging system data is a double-edged sword. It might be of great use to your service engineers during troubleshooting, but if your log contains usernames, passwords, and other sensitive data, attackers might very much appreciate the information free of charge.*

User Interactions and Access Control

A good starting point is to monitor events that are related to user interaction and access control.

User Sessions

If humans log in to a device, they don't do it without intention, whether authorized or malicious. Knowing the user login history and being able to match it with real-world activities of a certain human might reveal that an account was misused. For example, the person corresponding to a virtual user could have been on vacation and therefore clearly not acting.

In addition, a high number of failed login attempts can indicate that a brute-force attack has been performed. Finally, the time and date information of user sessions might help in reconstructing an attack's timeline.

Access-Control Violations

As described in Chapter 11, users and processes should be restricted to the minimum permissions necessary to fulfill their tasks. Besides the positive effect of access restrictions at runtime, those measures can also yield valuable information about which user or process *tried* to access a forbidden resource, which might help detect attacks in an early phase.

Filesystem Activities

Temporary files that appear suddenly and permanent changes to configuration or system files can indicate malicious activities. They could be initiated by processes running on the device, possibly because they've been compromised by exploitation of an unknown vulnerability. But a human user also could be the origin of manipulation, which could hint at an insider attack. Monitoring at least a subset of critical files and their events can be valuable in such cases.

Removable Media

Sometimes just plugging a USB thumb drive or a memory card into a device can trigger an attack. If your product offers such features, it absolutely makes sense to log information about when such media was plugged in or removed and maybe even which identifiers it had.

Communication

Although monitoring all data running on all communication channels of a device is usually not possible because of the vast amount of data transmitted, certain metadata or specific sent or received information can provide valuable insights.

Network Communication

Communication data received from external sources as well as data your device sends can yield hints of malicious activities. For example, a high amount of traffic from certain IP addresses might represent targeted DoS attacks. Nonstandard packets of communication protocols can represent adversaries testing your device's reactions upon manipulated requests.

New connections from your device to unknown locations and IP addresses or an unexpected, increased amount of outbound network traffic also might indicate that the device is already compromised.

Low-Level Communication

In contrast to classic IT systems, an embedded system often has a variety of low-level interfaces like an I^2C bus, serial connections, or general-purpose input/output (GPIO) pins. Their communication usually carries sensor or control data, which might again be a source for detecting unexpected behavior like forcing actuators into a dangerous operation mode.

Logging the state and communication data of these interfaces might not be a standard feature, but depending on their criticality, implementing it might be worth considering.

Application Behavior

In contrast to looking at security monitoring from a user or communication interface perspective, considering an application-centric approach might make sense.

Service Activities

Some services provide interesting information about your device's state, especially those with remote connections. For example, an SSH daemon that allows remote sessions may provide a history of login attempts with corresponding IP addresses and usernames.

A web server also is able to log the HTTP requests it receives, which can reveal adversarial activities on application layer communication.

Custom Applications

Proprietary software components that are, for example, relevant for your business model might provide deep insight into the use of your device. Therefore, it should be quite natural to integrate monitoring facilities into important applications you develop on your own.

Third-Party Applications

Whenever you allow users to install applications developed by third parties on your device, you face common threats originating from untrustworthy software components. Besides strict access management for those programs, continuous monitoring of their behavior is a reasonable measure.

System Behavior

Last but not least, the overall "health status" of your device may reveal attacks or at least unexpected behavior you can analyze further.

System Utilization

Typical system utilization values, such as CPU load and memory consumption, are usually known by developers and maintenance staff. A device that shows unexpectedly high values can indicate additional software running on the device—for example, a crypto miner or backdoor service installed by attackers. But it might also just be a side effect of an attack targeting low-level or network interfaces.

Process and System Crashes

Do your device's processes crash from time to time? I hope not, but maybe they do only in rare cases that you didn't cover during testing. If single processes or even the whole system crashes multiple times, it might be due to an attacker probing your device for potential vulnerabilities. If it's detected and analyzed early enough, you might be able to take action and prevent further damage.

Errors and Warnings

Although error messages and warnings can be part of perfectly normal device behavior, they can also be evidence that an adversary is tampering with a device's services or configuration options during a reconnaissance phase.

Risk-Based Monitoring

Which monitoring measures are reasonable for your product should be decided on the basis of your device's threat and risk analysis, as described in Chapter 1. For example, if you discovered that high network loads are a risk for your device's real-time operations, monitoring network communication and system utilization is a good idea. If your device allows for running third-party Docker containers, monitoring the activities of those potentially dangerous software bundles should be on your list. And if your device has a web interface for configuration purposes, logging web server events becomes a necessity.

NOTE   *Many more sources of valuable information might exist for security monitoring that are specific to your device. Find them and use them to secure your device.*

Designing a Monitoring Scheme

While system monitoring is not new for IT systems, implementing it efficiently is always a challenge—especially when it comes to logging events and processes on embedded systems. Depending on the capabilities of a specific product and the requirements for its use, a trade-off between on-device and server-based processing must be found.

Figure 12-1 shows a generic data-flow architecture of log data, starting with its collection, local storage, and eventual on-device analysis. While constrained devices will keep this part rather lean, stronger devices might aggregate more data and already perform on-device analysis to maximize potential insights.

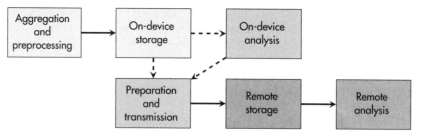

Figure 12-1: A generic logging architecture

Usually, networked devices transmit at least part of the collected information to a remote server, whether on the local network or on the internet. This not only allows for storing larger amounts of log data but also enables performance-intensive data analytics for single devices and across whole device populations. The latter especially leads to significantly increased quality of security monitoring.

Challenges for Embedded Systems

When it comes to (I)IoT scenarios with rather constrained devices and possibly pretty large populations, the specific design of the monitoring process faces several challenges.

Limited Resources

Embedded systems can be limited in several dimensions, which leaves developers with the difficulty of determining the amount of resources to use for monitoring. Some devices are battery powered, and collection (let alone transmission) of log data would be a further burden on battery life. For products based on small microcontrollers, log data collection isn't possible from a performance perspective because there's simply no time left for such tasks. Some systems have limited storage space and store only small amounts of log data, while others don't have the high-bandwidth network connection necessary for transferring monitoring data to central servers. Some devices have all these limitations.

For existing products, which are optimized to their single, dedicated task, it's often difficult or nearly impossible to integrate security monitoring as an add-on. But that shouldn't be an excuse to discard all monitoring features. If you identify the need for security monitoring early in the development life cycle, you have a chance to reserve resources for this absolutely relevant purpose.

Synchronized Time Sources

Correct timestamps are essential for correlating events within a device and with those of other devices and system components. For this purpose, time sources have to be synchronized, which can't be taken for granted on embedded systems.

Support for synchronization protocols, like NTP, likely has to be enabled on purpose, and integrators who use your product as well as operators of these systems have to provide a suitable infrastructure, like master clocks and time servers within their networks.

Secure Communication

Secure transmission of monitoring data from a device to a central collection server comes with several prerequisites. The device has to be able to authenticate the central server; otherwise, it could be tricked into sending valuable data to unauthorized parties.

The server also has to be able to verify the identity of the device providing data, because fake devices could significantly disturb the monitoring process by sending manipulated data. In addition, the data transmission itself should be protected in all aspects of secure communication, as described in Chapter 7.

Integrity-Protected Local Storage

If you decide to partly or even completely rely on device-side logging without external transmissions, you have to prepare for the question, "How do you actually guarantee that the log data wasn't altered at some point?" This question might even be posed by legal entities or in a court of law, for example, if your device is part of a nation's critical infrastructure.

System-integrity protection as described in Chapter 8 is a fundamental requirement for solid solutions regarding this challenge.

Confidentiality-Protected Local Storage

As mentioned in the previous section, log data might be useful not only for debugging your device but also for attackers during their reconnaissance phase. Therefore, you can definitely regard logfiles as assets that need confidentiality protection.

Measures like encrypted filesystems, as explained in Chapter 5, can be a solution. Another option is the implementation of a hybrid encryption scheme using the public key of a central log server to encrypt a random local symmetric key, which is, in turn, used to encrypt the locally generated log data. In that case, only the remote server in possession of the corresponding private key would be able to decrypt and analyze the log information.

Monitoring of the On-Device Logging Process

Continuous security monitoring can play a central role in the detection of attacks, timely reactions to incidents, and comprehensive forensic analysis after a compromise, which means the involved on-device logging processes are expected to function properly. However, it would be naive to assume that monitoring processes are robust by nature and immune to all sorts of influences. It's important to install measures that check whether the involved logging procedures are working correctly.

No matter whether the local log storage is only a few megabytes or some gigabytes, it is always finite. In some cases, it might be tempting to say that a certain memory can hold "more log events than a specific device could ever generate," but keep in mind that logging behavior can change with future firmware versions, devices in industrial scenarios might operate for decades, and new features and content could significantly reduce storage capacities. Monitoring the log storage capacity is, therefore, a mandatory task. Also, you have to make a decision about how to react if storage space is exhausted, or even before that happens. For example, if possible, logs can be compressed and archived to a remote location, or the oldest events can be overwritten by new ones coming in.

In addition to local storage-capacity issues, remote connections used to transmit log data also could be affected. You can easily imagine how the bandwidth of such communication could decrease abruptly or completely disconnect. In such cases, it's the device's responsibility to decide whether collected data is temporarily stored at a local destination until the connection is reestablished and the remote location is able to catch up again, or if monitoring data should be discarded at least partially or even completely.

Further, your logging applications could unpleasantly run into unknown bugs, or adversaries might attack your monitoring system on purpose. Both scenarios could result in crashes of critical system parts and leave you blind in terms of monitoring data. Even though your device can't recover from all possible situations, automatically restarting monitoring services after crashes and locally logging events regarding the eventual loss of monitoring capabilities can be worthwhile.

Central Log Analysis and Management

In many use cases, having a central storage location for monitoring data as well as the analysis and correlation of information from the whole device population is of great value. Among other advantages, this approach allows you to react to security-related events in the field within a short time frame. If an attacker is messing with critical configuration or system files, you might want to know that as soon as possible. This approach also enables you to include a long history of device log data into current analyses, and once the data has been transmitted, on-device manipulation or destruction of log information would become obvious.

However, implementing the second row of the logging architecture shown in Figure 12-1 is all but simple. One challenge in (I)IoT scenarios can be the scalability of the central monitoring system and the availability of corresponding analysis capacities. Of course, this depends on the size of your device populations. While a few thousand products might be manageable, scalability gains center stage when monitoring a six-digit number of devices or even more. This requires not only a vast amount of central storage capacities but also people and algorithms that sift through all the data to identify unexpected device behavior, emerging malicious activities, or indicators of compromise (IoCs).

Systems used for this purpose are often known as *security information and event management (SIEM)* because they collect event data relevant for security monitoring and provide a means to find the proverbial needle in the haystack. Examples of such analysis platforms, open source or commercial, include the Elastic Stack, Graylog, and Splunk, just to name a few. While big data analytics and artificial intelligence can provide strong support for this task, in many cases, judgment and eventual manual investigation by a human expert is necessary.

As explained in Chapter 1, every secure product life cycle has to establish some kind of incident- and vulnerability-response processes. Make sure that the teams operating the SIEM system have a strong connection to the product development and management teams, which will enable you to gain efficiency in your incident and vulnerability handling.

With all the advantages of central monitoring systems and processes, don't forget to critically assess which data you *really* need for your chosen monitoring approach. Piling up stacks of unnecessary data only makes your solution inefficient and could lead to conflicts with the European GDPR or similar laws, especially if your database contains personally identifiable information (PII).

NOTE *If you're not familiar with the legal restrictions of PII collection, thoroughly acquaint yourself with that topic. Even rather "technical" data like IP and MAC addresses might be traced back to natural persons and, therefore, require special treatment or should not be collected at all.*

Case Study: Logging Events on an STM32MP157F Device

This case study presents typical tools and configurations to extract monitoring data from a Linux-based embedded system like an STM32MP157F-DK2 board.

User-Session Monitoring with journald

Linux systems that run `systemd`, like my STM32MP157F-DK2 firmware does, come with the `journald` tool, which collects valuable information about basic system processes.

For example, Listing 12-1 shows a series of log entries extracted from `journalctl` by using `grep logind`.

```
# journalctl | grep logind
...
Apr 28 21:07:31 stm32mp1 systemd-logind[650]: New session c1 of user root.
Apr 28 21:13:51 stm32mp1 systemd-logind[650]: Session c1 logged out. ...
Apr 28 21:13:51 stm32mp1 systemd-logind[650]: Removed session c1.
Apr 28 22:54:57 stm32mp1 systemd-logind[650]: New session c2 of user root.
Apr 28 22:55:10 stm32mp1 systemd-logind[650]: Session c2 logged out. ...
Apr 28 22:55:10 stm32mp1 systemd-logind[650]: Removed session c2.
May 14 13:26:18 stm32mp1 systemd-logind[650]: New session c3 of user lservice.
May 14 13:39:24 stm32mp1 systemd-logind[650]: Removed session c3.
May 27 11:58:58 stm32mp1 systemd-logind[650]: New session c4 of user root.
```

Listing 12-1: Typical journald entries for user sessions

The logs clearly show that the root user had two sessions on April 28 and that the local service user lservice was logged in for around 13 minutes on May 14. If this doesn't correlate with an official inspection by a technician from your company, it might be an indication of unauthorized access.

The journald daemon can run in several modes, two of which are *volatile* and *persistent*. While the first option stores journal data only until the system is rebooted, the second one makes journald store its log data under */var/log/journal* in a persistent way, which can be helpful for forensics. You can set the corresponding Storage=persistent option in its configuration file */etc/systemd/journald.conf*.

Further configuration parameters like SystemMaxUse= and RuntimeMaxUse= as well as SystemKeepFree= and RuntimeKeepFree= determine the limits of journal file sizes for on-disk and in-memory storage, respectively, so critical situations caused by too much memory consumption of logfiles can be avoided.

Kernel Event Monitoring with auditd

The Linux kernel provides an audit framework that collects information about potentially security-relevant events happening within the kernel. It's the same framework that's used by MAC systems like SELinux or AppArmor to watch and restrict access to system resources, as described in Chapter 11.

The auditd user-space tool builds upon this framework and enables the persistent storage of security events in a device's nonvolatile memory.

Installation

If you successfully installed AppArmor or another popular MAC system on your device, the audit framework is probably already up and running. Otherwise, you can set CONFIG_AUDIT=y within your Linux kernel's configuration to enable it.

The meta-oe layer for Yocto contains the recipe to install the auditd tool from *meta-oe/recipes-security/audit*. It can be simply added to your image by setting IMAGE_INSTALL += "auditd". After booting your system with the newly installed software, you should see that your system now contains the */var/log/audit/audit.log* file, which is the default place to persistently store kernel audit data.

Customization

The audit framework is a powerful tool with deep access to system processes, so it's important to explicitly specify the kind of events you want to monitor. You can use auditctl to add watch rules to a running auditd service, as shown in Listing 12-2.

```
# auditctl -D
No rules
# auditctl -w /etc/passwd -p rwa -k users_credentials
# auditctl -l
-w /etc/passwd -p rwa -k users_credentials
```

Listing 12-2: Adding audit rules with auditctl

The -D parameter removes all currently active rules. The second command in Listing 12-2 installs a rule that monitors the */etc/passwd* file (-w /etc/passwd) for read (r) and write (w) access as well as file attribute changes (a). The -k option allows for adding an arbitrary key string that gives the rule a certain meaning and accelerates log searching at a later time.

However, the rules set by auditctl are available only until the system performs a reboot. To install watch rules persistently, you have to add them to the */etc/audit/audit.rules* file. As shown in Listing 12-3, the rules in this file are actually equal to the command line calls to auditctl, just without the tool name at the beginning.

```
## SSH daemon configuration
-w /etc/default/dropbear -p wa -k ssh_config
-w /etc/dropbear -p rwa -k ssh_config

## Users and credentials
-w /etc/passwd -p rwa -k users_credentials
-w /etc/shadow -p rwa -k users_credentials

## auditd configuration
-w /etc/audit/ -p wa -k auditd_config

## Audit management tools
-w /sbin/auditctl -p x -k audit_tools
-w /sbin/auditd -p x -k audit_tools
```

Listing 12-3: An example of persistent audit rules

File-access monitoring can be useful in a variety of scenarios. For example, if you enable SSH access to your device based on the popular dropbear daemon, it might be reasonable to watch for changes of the corresponding configuration file, which—if manipulated—could potentially open a backdoor to your device. Further, access to */etc/passwd* and */etc/shadow* are common indicators for malicious activities. Advanced attackers might also target the audit system itself, which makes the files containing audit rules and the audit tools valid targets to watch.

After enabling the rules, you can use the ausearch tool to filter audit data, as demonstrated in Listing 12-4 for the installed SSH configuration watch rules.

```
# ausearch -k ssh_config
time->Thu Apr 28 23:12:57 ...
type=PROCTITLE msg=audit(1651187577.140:366): proctitle=...
type=SYSCALL msg=audit(1651187577.140:366): arch=40000028 syscall=290 ...
... uid=0 gid=0 ... comm="auditctl" exe="/sbin/auditctl" ...
type=CONFIG_CHANGE ... op=add_rule key="ssh_config" ...
# touch /etc/default/dropbear
# ausearch -k ssh_config
...
time->Thu Apr 28 23:24:47 ...
type=PROCTITLE msg=audit(1651188287.600:379): proctitle=...
type=PATH msg=audit(1651188287.600:379): ... name="/etc/default/dropbear" ...
type=PATH msg=audit(1651188287.600:379): ... name="/etc/default/" ...
type=CWD msg=audit(1651188287.600:379): cwd="/home/root"
type=SYSCALL msg=audit(1651188287.600:379): arch=40000028 syscall=322 ...
... uid=0 gid=0 ... comm="touch" exe="/bin/touch.coreutils" ...
```

Listing 12-4: Using ausearch to find suspicious activities

The first call to ausearch with the ssh_config key reports that a new rule with this key was added by the auditctl tool. Afterward, I just touched (didn't even manipulate) the configuration file located at */etc/default/dropbear*. The second call to ausearch clearly states that the root user (uid=0 gid=0) used the touch tool to access the file */etc/default/dropbear* while being in the */home/root* directory only 12 minutes after the new rule was loaded. This example shows the beneficial strengths of having monitoring data available for critical system files.

Besides watching file access, auditd is also able to intercept syscalls. However, since such rules directly affect performance, you should use them only if you consider them absolutely necessary.

Service and Application Event Logging

While auditd provides powerful services to monitor kernel behavior and to log accesses to system resources, it doesn't capture an important part of your device: specific events generated by services and applications.

Logging Application Events with syslog

Within my STM32MP157F firmware, BusyBox implements a minimal version of `syslogd` that some applications use to store log information in the */var/log/messages* file. One example for such an application is the lightweight dropbear SSH daemon.

Listing 12-5 shows corresponding log messages after several SSH login attempts.

```
# grep /var/log/messages -e dropbear
Apr 29 09:06:38 stm32mp1 authpriv.info dropbear[819]:
  Child connection from ::ffff:192.168.13.17:37214
Apr 29 09:06:40 stm32mp1 authpriv.notice dropbear[819]:
  pam_unix(dropbear:auth): ... rhost=::ffff:192.168.13.17  user=rservice
Apr 29 09:06:42 stm32mp1 authpriv.warn dropbear[819]:
  pam_authenticate() failed, rc=7, Authentication failure
Apr 29 09:06:42 stm32mp1 authpriv.warn dropbear[819]:
❶ Bad PAM password attempt for 'rservice' from ::ffff:192.168.13.17:37214
Apr 29 09:06:51 stm32mp1 authpriv.notice dropbear[819]:
❷ PAM password auth succeeded for 'rservice' from ::ffff:192.168.13.17:37214
Apr 29 09:07:01 stm32mp1 authpriv.info dropbear[819]:
❸ Exit (rservice) from <::ffff:192.168.13.17:37214>: Disconnect received
Apr 29 09:07:11 stm32mp1 authpriv.info dropbear[825]:
  Child connection from ::ffff:192.168.13.17:48656
...
Apr 29 09:07:16 stm32mp1 authpriv.warn dropbear[825]:
  Bad PAM password attempt for 'root' from ::ffff:192.168.13.17:48656
...
Apr 29 09:07:20 stm32mp1 authpriv.warn dropbear[825]:
  Bad PAM password attempt for 'root' from ::ffff:192.168.13.17:48656
...
Apr 29 09:07:23 stm32mp1 authpriv.warn dropbear[825]:
  Bad PAM password attempt for 'root' from ::ffff:192.168.13.17:48656
Apr 29 09:07:23 stm32mp1 authpriv.info dropbear[825]:
❹ Exit before auth from ...: (user 'root', 3 fails): Exited normally
```

Listing 12-5: SSH login attempts logged by `syslogd`

The log data first shows a `Bad PAM password attempt` ❶ for the user rservice, shortly followed by a successful `PAM password auth` ❷ for the same user. The established session is closed only 10 seconds later ❸. Further, three failed login attempts for the root user can be seen that finally make the SSH daemon quit the login process ❹. Such log data can be extremely useful for detecting brute-force attacks on SSH accounts or login attempts for unusual users and from unexpected IP addresses.

Using Application-Specific Logfiles

Some applications do not rely on `syslogd`'s services by default, but rather create and manage their own logfiles. One example is the `apache2` web server running on my STM32MP157F-DK2 board. Its logfiles *access_log* and *error_log* can be found under */var/log/apache2/*. Listing 12-6 shows sample HTTP requests from the IP address 192.168.13.17.

```
# cat /var/log/apache2/access_log
...
192.168.13.17 - - [29/Apr/...09:35:46 +0000] "GET / HTTP/1.1" 200 45
192.168.13.17 - - [29/Apr/...09:35:58 +0000] "GET /admin/ HTTP/1.1" 404 196
192.168.13.17 - - [29/Apr/...09:36:27 +0000] "GET /config/ HTTP/1.1" 404 196
192.168.13.17 - - [29/Apr/...09:37:29 +0000] "GET /cgi-bin/ HTTP/1.1" 404 196
192.168.13.17 - - [29/Apr/...09:38:33 +0000] "GET / HTTP/1.1" 200 45
...
```

Listing 12-6: Sample access log entries from apache2

This information provides not only the history of successfully delivered web pages by the web server but also requests that might reveal adversarial activities typical for the reconnaissance phase. Here, an attacker checked the availability of the */admin/*, */config/*, and */cgi-bin/* subdirectories. Again, early detection can prevent later attacks and damages.

Logging to a Remote Server

All the previously mentioned tools operate locally on a device, which might be sufficient for device-specific forensic purposes whenever you have physical or remote access to it. However, as suggested earlier in this chapter, the central collection of log data can be beneficial in many ways. Although the setup of a central monitoring infrastructure goes beyond the device-centered focus of this book, I would like to point out that all the data collected by these tools can be transmitted to remote locations.

For example, the `journald` daemon can be extended by a service called `systemd-journal-remote` for logging data to a remote server. The `audisp` tool and its `audisp-remote` plug-in can enable central log aggregation for data collected by the Linux audit framework and `auditd`. Alternatively, specific tools like `auditbeat` can be used to send audit data to an Elastic Stack, for example. Further, `rsyslog` and `syslog-ng` are modern `syslog` implementations that allow for logging to remote locations. Finally, some of these tools are even interoperable, which means that `journald`, for example, can be configured to forward log data to a `syslog` daemon, which in turn can take care of remote transmission.

Summary

It's simple to request that a device should aggregate and transmit system data and event information to a central server. However, when you start implementing such measures, you'll encounter several obstacles to overcome, from legal issues to device constraints to the human resources necessary for continuously operating security-monitoring services.

In this chapter, I discussed typical information that can be useful for security monitoring of embedded systems, from user sessions and their interactions to network traffic metadata to system crashes and error messages. Clearly, the more you want to monitor, the more on-device and server resources you need. A risk-based approach is absolutely reasonable to find a compromise between full device transparency and minimal resource usage for your specific product.

System monitoring is an essential layer within your defense-in-depth strategy because even if all the protection measures you implement fail, monitoring might enable you to detect ongoing attacks and anomalies. Monitoring can make the difference between getting away with a black eye and ruining your product's and your company's reputation.

AFTERWORD

When I decided to write this book, I set out to provide students as well as practitioners with a useful, practical overview of embedded system security that would help them navigate the jungle of possible threats, protection measures, security marketing, and complete despair. Well, here we are. If you belong to one of those groups and have made it to this point, I'm convinced you've discovered new territory, probably learned something useful, and maybe even identified your next personal challenge.

If you've already transferred the topics of this book into your day-to-day job and brought them to life in the specific embedded system on your desk, you can be proud of yourself. It was probably all but trivial and required tireless effort. However, don't celebrate just yet. This is only the beginning of your security journey. It's not the end of the story. Industries like pay-TV, automotive, and gaming consoles have already learned that if there is something large enough to gain, attackers will do whatever it takes to find it.

During the last two decades, the topic of *side-channel analysis* slowly found its way out of the academic arena and into select industries. These attacks exploit physical characteristics like runtime, power consumption, or electromagnetic emission of crypto algorithms and other protection measures to extract information about secrets and intermediate values processed within a microchip. Although this approach requires specialized knowledge and suitable hardware and software, it has already been practically applied to pay-TV systems, electronic locks, and automotive components, just to name a few.

However, if you have to face such powerful attackers, you're not lost. You have a set of countermeasures and protected implementations to choose from.

Stefan Mangard, Elisabeth Oswald, and Thomas Popp wrote *Power Analysis Attacks: Revealing the Secrets of Smart Cards* (Springer, 2007) as one of the first books in the field, if you're interested in the foundations of this topic. Additionally, *The Hardware Hacking Handbook* (No Starch Press, 2021) by Jasper van Woudenberg and Colin O'Flynn (this book's technical reviewer) contains a variety of practical examples for good and bad implementations, and provides tips to enhance your personal side-channel analysis skills.

Another powerful class of threats are *fault injection* attacks that use voltage or clock glitches, electromagnetic pulses, or even laser beams to intentionally force microchips to jump over instructions or process corrupted data. Does it sound like science fiction? Such attacks obviously require adversaries with sophisticated knowledge and professional equipment, but they have already been performed on several gaming consoles in practical settings—for example, to circumvent firmware authenticity verification during a secure boot process. Afterward, attackers were able to boot and execute their custom software on those devices. Again, a practical introduction to the topic including real-world examples can be found in *The Hardware Hacking Handbook*.

In addition to advanced attacks on the hardware level, rising complexity on the software level leads to an increased attack surface. Therefore, *secure software segmentation* of applications with varying criticality is another follow-up security topic for complex software architectures on devices. For example, some products already implement virtualization or container technologies to separate user-defined software from a manufacturer's system applications. And suddenly, threats like applications breaking out of their restricted environments, which we know from cloud systems, become absolutely relevant for embedded systems. In addition, devices aiming for rather high security might move critical software applications to dedicated, secure execution environments, such as ARM TrustZone. But this also requires hardware support, a specific firmware architecture, and significant implementation expertise, all of which contribute to system complexity and facilitate further attack vectors. In short, you won't ever grow bored.

Despite all that, always remember one point: engineering secure devices doesn't require magical powers. All you need are engaged, motivated, and clever people who work together as a team. Go for it!

INDEX

attacks
backdoor, 227
brute-force, 28, 93, 235
code lifting, 87, 92
Compression Ratio Info-Leak
Made Easy, 127
crafted updates, 161
crypto minor, 227
data breaches, 200
denial-of-service, 11, 181, 183,
186, 190
downgrade, 126
eavesdropping, 90
elevation of privilege, 203
firmware modification, 178
flooding, 183
invisible manipulation, 14
jamming, 182
log manipulation, 230
malicious software, 143
man-in-the-middle, 44
mix-and-match, 154
phases, 224
physical access, 13, 200
physical transfer, 105
privilege escalation, 98
public-key replacement, 145
resource exhaustion, 186
supply chain, 143
SYN flooding, 194, 195
theft of signing key, 148
unknown methodologies, 160
update misuse, 179
attribute-based access control
(ABAC), 201
Aumasson, Jean-Philippe, 48
authenticated boot, 144
authenticated encryption (AE), 37–38,
123, 155
encrypt-and-MAC, 37
encrypt-then-MAC, 38
MAC-then-encrypt, 38
authenticated encryption with
associated data (AEAD)
AES-GCM, 38, 71
ChaCha20-Poly1305, 40, 71, 78,
126, 136
RFC 8439, 40

authentication, 103, 106
challenge-response, 52, 104
chip, 105
protocol, 104
authenticator, 104
implicit, 106

B

banana principle, 160
banking, 224
Bernstein, Daniel J., 35, 40, 47, 82
Biden, Joe, xxiii
binary large object (BLOB), 91
biometric data, 86
blacklisting, 212
BLAKE2s, 59
block cipher modes of operation
Cipher Block Chaining (CBC),
33–34, 37, 95
Counter (CTR), 34, 56
Electronic Codebook (ECB), 32–33
Galois Counter mode (GCM),
38–39
Offset Codebook (OCB), 40
XEX-Based Tweaked-Codebook
Mode with Ciphertext
Stealing (XTS), 95
block ciphers. *See also* Advanced
Encryption Standard
Data Encryption Algorithm, 29
Data Encryption Standard, 29
3DES, 29, 127
Bluetooth, 70, 103, 112
bootloader, 142, 164, 167
multistage, 168
boot process, 57, 142
authenticated, 144
chain, 143
encrypted, 144
high-assurance, 144
measured, 144
secure, 145. *See also* secure boot
trusted, 144
unlock feature, 149
verified, 144
BSI (German Federal Office for
Information Security),
58, 67

pseudorandom number generator
(continued)
    reseeding, 57
    seeding, 56
PSK (pre-shared key), 125
PSS. *See* Probabilistic Signature Scheme
public-key infrastructure (PKI),
    107, 128
Python, 58, 62, 129, 218
    `cryptography`, 113, 118
    `os`, 62
    `os.urandom()`, 62
    `random`, 62
    `secrets`, 62
    `secrets.randbelow()`, 66
    `secrets.token_bytes()`, 62
    SSLyze, 132
    `subprocess`, 113

R

Radare2, 87
randomness
    bias, 53, 63–65
    case study, 63–67
    entropy, 52
    entropy source, 54
    independence, 53
    patterns, 53, 63, 67
    pseudo, 51
    source, 128
    true, 51, 53–56
    uniform distribution, 53, 63–64, 66
random number generator (RNG),
    51, 128
    case study, 58–62
    hybrid, 57
    pseudo, 56. *See also* pseudorandom
        number generator
    true, 53, 55
ransomware, 11
RAUC, 169
real time, 9, 181
    firm, 185
    hard, 185
    soft, 185
real-time core, 188, 192, 196
real-time operating system (RTOS), 98,
    156, 164, 189

reconnaissance, 236
redundancy, 136
remote access, 121
remote processor messaging
    (RPMsg), 197
removable media, 225
resource allocation
    dynamic, 186
    fixed, 186
reverse engineering, 14, 87, 91, 143,
    156, 200
RFC 2104, 36
RFC 2898, 93
RFC 3447, 43
RFC 4122, 103
RFC 4493, 37
RFC 5246, 126
RFC 5280, 107
RFC 6960, 107
RFC 7914, 93
RFC 8439, 40
RFC 8446, 124
Rijndael, 30
ring oscillator (RO), 54–55
    jitter, 54
ring topology, 136
Ripple20, xxii, 160
Rivest-Shamir-Adleman (RSA), 41–48,
    71, 81, 113, 126, 145,
    152, 172
    case study, key generation, 117–118
RNG. *See* random number generator
RO. *See* ring oscillator
robustness
    case study, 192–197
    digital, 181
    physical, 181
Rogaway, Phil, 40
role-based access control (RBAC), 201
ROM (read-only memory), 142, 146, 150
root certificate, 107
root filesystem, 164
root hash, 156
RSA. *See* Rivest-Shamir-Adleman
RSAES-OAEP, 43
RSA-OAEP, 43
RSASSA-PSS (RSA Signature Scheme
    with Appendix), 126

US FD&C Act, 160
UUID (universally unique identifier), 60, 103, 171
    RFC 4122, 103

V

van Woudenberg, Jasper, 83, 240
VeraCrypt, 88
verified boot, 144
virtual local area network (VLAN), 192
virtual private network (VPN), 137
Voice over IP (VoIP), 128
vulnerability management, 200, 231
    monitoring, 23, 169
    reporting, 22

W

warnings, 227
web server, 110, 128, 202, 210, 226, 236
white-box cryptography, 92
whitelisting, 211
Wi-Fi, 8, 70, 103, 112, 182
Wireshark, 132
wolfSSL, 71

X

xattr (extended file attributes), 207
XTS (XEX-Based Tweaked-Codebook Mode with Ciphertext Stealing), 95

Y

yescrypt, 93
Yocto Project
    bitbake, 195
    debug-tweaks, 207
    deploy, 174
    extrausers, 207
    meta-oe, 232
    meta-security, 215
    meta-st-x-linux-rt, 194
    meta-swupdate, 171, 173
    mosquitto recipe, 129
    OpenSTLinux, xxvi, 215
    st-image-core, 174, 193, 207
    useradd, 207

Z

zero round-trip time (0-RTT), 126

The fonts used in *Engineering Secure Devices* are New Baskerville, Futura, The Sans Mono Condensed, and Dogma. The book was typeset with LaTeX 2_ε package nostarch by Boris Veytsman with many additions by Alex Freed and other members of the No Starch Press team *(2023/06/10 v2.2 Typesetting books for No Starch Press).*

RESOURCES

Visit *https://nostarch.com/engineering-secure-devices* for errata and more information.

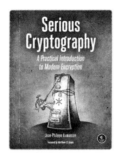

Never before has the world relied so heavily on the Internet to stay connected and informed. That makes the Electronic Frontier Foundation's mission—to ensure that technology supports freedom, justice, and innovation for all people—more urgent than ever.

For over 30 years, EFF has fought for tech users through activism, in the courts, and by developing software to overcome obstacles to your privacy, security, and free expression. This dedication empowers all of us through darkness. With your help we can navigate toward a brighter digital future.